Blindness Through the Looking Glass

# CORPOREALITIES: Discourses of Disability

Series editors: David T. Mitchell and Sharon L. Snyder

A complete list of titles in the series can be found at www.press.umich.edu

# Blindness Through the Looking Glass

*The Performance of Blindness, Gender, and the Sensory Body*

Gili Hammer

Foreword by Georgina Kleege

*University of Michigan Press*
Ann Arbor

Published in the United States of America by the
University of Michigan Press
Manufactured in the United States of America
Printed on acid-free paper
First published September 2019

A CIP catalog record for this book is available from the British Library.

*Library of Congress Cataloging-in-Publication data has been applied for.*

ISBN 978-0-472-07428-0 (hardcover : alk. paper)
ISBN 978-0-472-05428-2 (paper : alk. paper)
ISBN 978-0-472-12608-8 (e-book)

Cover illustration: Simonne De Sousa, *FENI*, 2017. Source: Henry + Lydia, Etsy.

Cover description: Against a bright coral-colored background appears a simple line drawing of
a woman's head and neck, drawn in a single continuous line in black ink. To the left and below
the figure are the book's title, subtitle, author's name, and the words "Foreword by Georgina
Kleege."

*For Bam (Avraham), Avi, and Yotam*

# Contents

⸙

Section III: Blindness and the Sensory Body

Digital materials related to this title can be found on the Fulcrum platform via the following citable URL: https://doi.org/10.3998/mpub.9271356

# Foreword

GEORGINA KLEEGE

⸺◦∞◦⸺

About once a month someone asks me, "Do you know what you look like?" Because I use a white cane, the questioner probably assumes that I can see absolutely nothing. The truth is, when I stand before a mirror I can perceive my general silhouette along with the colors of my skin, hair, and clothing. Moreover, I know the details of my appearance: that I am tall, that I have white hair that friends generously refer to as silver, that my facial features are somewhat larger than average. I also have more personal knowledge: while I used to look more like my father, I now look more like my mother. But in point of fact, I do not really know what I look like; that is to say, I don't know the impact my appearance has on sighted people. What I know about my appearance comes from what others tell me, which is enough for me, but can be dismissed as mere hearsay. But whatever I may think about the way I look, I know that appearance has consequences.

I have not surveyed my blind friends and acquaintances, but I suspect that this is a question more frequently posed to blind women than to blind men. Women, blind or sighted, are assumed to be more preoccupied with appearance, and whether they attend to it or not, the culture assigns meaning to the way they look. Blind schools and rehabilitation programs offer training in grooming for males and females, but the classes specifically for girls and women extend beyond self-care, into self-enhancement and adornment. Practical tips about nail-trimming and sock-matching are helpful to anyone with impaired vision, but the additional training in makeup, hairstyling, and fashion trends for blind women sends the message that those who ignore these details risk something.

As the blind women in this study attest, their appearance has consequences. Clothing, makeup, and hairstyles send messages to potential romantic and sexual partners, as well as to strangers who might interpret some detail as an invitation to exploitation or abuse. A blind woman's appearance also has an impact on her employability. If a blind woman knows the dress code for a job interview, she might be able to quell the fears and prejudice of a potential employer. A blind woman's appearance can even send messages about her fitness as a parent. If a blind woman doesn't know how to put together a matching outfit, how can she tell if her child's skinned knee is infected?

The conclusions this study draws do not include the fatuous surprise that blind women can learn beauty standards. Living as we do in visual culture, it's hard to imagine how we can avoid learning these values. Media proclamations about the latest hemlines and hairstyles, or the particular set of physical attributes that make one movie star or fashion model more beautiful than another, invade consciousness whether one can see or not. Maternal admonitions to change into something more presentable are contradicted by the judgments of peers: "That makes you look like your mother." Sales clerks, hair stylists, and aestheticians are all too happy to give advice and instructions in order to make a sale. In addition to making all of this obvious, *Blindness Through the Looking Glass* shows how blind women move within and around these strictures, at once keenly aware of the consequences of their choices and yet also defiant in their non-compliance.

What stands out in this book are the voices of the blind women who participated. Although assigned pseudonyms, they are not anonymized into mere statistics. They voice their opinions and qualms and ask their own questions, including questions about the researcher's own appearance. More strikingly, they pose challenges to her theories and research methods. It is clear that they participated in this study not merely by being interview subjects, but by reshaping the researcher's premises, and negating the possibility of foregone conclusions.

They even ask the question most often levied at a study of this kind, "How can you, a sighted woman, undertake to study the lives of blind women?" This question crossed my mind, and probably my lips, when I first met Gili Hammer as she began this project. Over the years I have been approached by numerous sighted researchers in psychology, sociology, philosophy, and education who start from the premise that blind people are alien and exotic creatures in desperate need of help. Gili's attitude was not only more sensitive and respectful but more willing to benefit from the experience and expertise of her research participants. It was clear from our first meeting that she was not using the blind women in her study to prove her own theories, but rather to offer a fresh perspective on what she and other sighted people might take for granted about gender norms and aesthetic values. I was also impressed by her courage to put her own body on the line as she volunteered to pedal through the desert with a blind and sighted tandem bike club, and to put herself in the hands of a blind student of medical massage.

Ultimately, this book is less about blind women in contrast to their sighted peers and more about how human beings know the world and themselves through their senses. It opens up the possibility of similar research in other national contexts, and offers creative ways to perform ethnography where the line between researcher and subject is less starkly drawn. While the women who speak from these pages express the need for social change that will improve their lives, they also lay claim to pleasure and joy. And this is what will stay with me.

# Acknowledgments

Writing and publishing a scholarly book is an adventure, and I was fortunate to have the highest level of support from a variety of sources. I am thankful for Georgina Kleege's, Tamar Elor's, and Aziza Khazzoom's endless encouragement and guidance, and to Janet Christensen's insightful and invaluable friendship, advice, and editorial work. I am grateful to Hodel Ophir, Ben Belek, Nadeem Karabi, Marcy Brink-Danan, and Limor Meoded-Danon for their insightful comments on earlier drafts. I am also grateful to the anonymous reviewers of the book's manuscript for their very important feedback and to Petra Kuppers, Catherine Kudlick, Nachman Ben-Yehuda, Vered Vinitzky-Seroussi, Carola Hilfrich, Elizabeth Able, Katharine Young, Marsha Saxton, Ruth Behar, Rosemarie Garland-Thomson, Michael Schillmeier, Minoo Moallem, Tali Sarnetzky, Adi Finkelstein, Colin Ong-Dean, David Howes, Noga Buber Ben-David, Terry Tracy, Raya Morag, Sigal Gooldin, Nili Broyer, Nurit Stadler, and Nissim Mizrahi for offering their scholarship on earlier portions of this project. LeAnn Fields and the editors of the *Corporealities: Discourses of Disability* series from the University of Michigan Press provided invaluable support, and I am thankful for their help in bringing this book to the academic home I most desired.

I am also grateful for the fellowships I received that supported this project, from NA'AMAT Movement of Working Women and Volunteers, the United States–Israel Educational Foundation Fulbright Doctoral Student Grant, the Faculty of Social Science, the Shaine Centre for Research in Social Sciences, the Levi Eshkol Economic and Political Research in Israel, and Lafer Center for Women and Gender Studies, all at the Hebrew University of Jerusalem, Israel.

This book was possible due to my family's endless support and belief in me, especially Avi, my husband, and Yotam, my son, who was born during the process of revising this book. Their love, friendship, and confidence in me allowed me to combine research, writing, teaching, and parenthood, and to believe in my ideas. Finally, my deep gratitude is owed to the research participants for raising my awareness of my sensory body, providing me new methods of experiencing and researching social life, and making this research possible.

Revised portions of this book appeared in *Gender & Society*, *Ethnography*, *Disability Studies Quarterly*, and *Signs: Journal of Women in Culture and Society*.

*One*

# Introduction

⸺oᗒᗕo⸺

This book is about how blindness, as well as sightedness, is constructed as social, cultural, and embodied experiences. While cultural association of sight with knowing is widespread and profound, with sight imprinting visual standards of concepts such as beauty and femininity onto our collective consciousness, this book challenges seeing as the dominant mode though which we understand gender, social performance, and visual culture. Offering an ethnographic investigation of blindness and sight, putting them both "on display," I discuss blind people's auditory, tactile, and olfactory experiences, as well as vision and sight, and explore the ways blind and sighted individuals perform blindness and "sightedness" in their everyday lives and in public spaces. As a sighted woman living in a visual culture, I address both blindness and sight as embodied experiences and social categories from which to investigate the relations between gender norms of beauty, femininity, and appearance, and between visuality and sight. In other words, I address blindness and sight as points of departure allowing: rethinking the ways gender and femininity are performed and experienced in everyday life (for example, by women who do not rely on sight as their dominant mode of perception); identifying the multiple senses involved in the formation of gender identity and within social interactions; and revealing alternative, nonvisual ways to understand, interpret, and implement concepts such as beauty, appearance, and femininity within a cultural context identified as "hyper visual."[1]

With these premises in mind, I came to research blind women, choosing this research population as offering an opportunity to deconstruct the long-standing cultural bond between femininity and sight. This led to nearly a decade of researching blindness and sight, a journey of defamiliarizing myself with the "natural" meaning of sight, and with what is called in disability studies my (temporary) "abled-bodied" identity. Since blind women are indeed familiar with the meaning of cultural concepts such as "beauty," "sexy," or "good-looking," my study did not focus on the "if" question of whether blind women understand what beauty and femininity are but on the "how" and "why" questions, exploring the creative and conscious choices they make when responding to visual norms, offering an ethnographic analysis of the ways blind women experience, interpret, respond to, and sometimes resist normative images of gender, blindness, and disability. Moreover, since both blindness and sight are grounded in a world of vision and visual images (not a sighted world, but a world with sighted and blind people in it), the most interesting questions to ask when studying blindness do not focus on whether blind women are under the same power regime as sighted women, but *how* the gaze functions when sight does not serve as the dominant mode of perception. What is the relation between visuality and women's agency? And how do the sensory apparatuses other than sight affect social relations and interactions?

These are the questions this book explores, with three objectives. First, by chronicling the gender performances of a group typically left on the margins of academic discourse and commonly excluded from discussions of beauty and femininity, this book examines the everyday gender performance of blind women. While blindness has served as a central metaphor defining the boundaries of cultural order within human thought, everyday narratives of flesh and blood blind people are rare. Moreover, "ableist" assumptions about blindness have led social sciences to take sight for granted when examining everyday social performance and gender construction, and in fact have tended to focus almost exclusively on the way women see and are seen when investigating the formation of gender. The first-person narratives brought forward in this book attempt to remedy this lacuna, arguing for the significance of blind women's experiences in offering an alternative conceptualization of concepts such as gender, visual culture, and the sensorium.

The second objective of this book is to employ blindness as a means *to investigate sight*, to prompt considerations of what it means to be a sighted person and how a "sighted" identity is socially constructed and shaped. Blind women's gender performance allows revealing hidden elements relevant not only to blind women's gender formation but also to sighted women's femininity, such as the role of the sensory body and sensory pleasure, and the performative and embodied aspects of visuality. In addition, sighted people's encounters with blindness examined here are helpful in better understanding the processes of seeing and the ways individuals perform what Michalko (1998) termed "sightedness" in their everyday lives, the means through which they come to understand themselves as "sighted." *Blindness Through the Looking Glass*, therefore, asks to investigate the ways both blindness and sight are put on display in society. Inspired by Herzfeld's (1987) *Anthropology Through the Looking-Glass,* in which he used his ethnography in Greece as a mirror on the anthropological endeavor itself, I employ blindness and disability studies to reflect on ableism and, in this case, on sightedness when considering the notions of gender, visual culture, and the sensory body.

The third objective of this book is to investigate *the nature of the relationship* between blindness and sight, refuting the simplistic division of sight and blindness as separate worlds of meanings. To do so, this book examines the ways both blindness and sight are represented and experienced within social relations, promoting an interpretation of blindness and sight as intertwined, and a more nuanced understanding of the relationship between sight and the other senses. My research with blind and sighted people involved in the field of blindness revealed that blindness and sightedness are not fixed, essentialist categories with a biologically given basis, but that they are socially constructed. In the analysis, this book provides ethnographic examples of *how* this social construction happens and of the ways blindness and sightedness are performed into existence and in a particularly sensory and gendered way.

These objectives are explored in this book through ethnographic research conducted with blind people in Israel. The study included in-depth interviews with forty women, mainly blind from birth or from a young age, focusing on their everyday choices and experiences of gender and femininity. In addition, the research included three years of ethnographic observations in spaces inhabited by blind people or where blindness is presented to the sighted public, such as a "beauty care" class for blind girls, a "life-skills" class for blind adults, a tandem cycling group pairing sighted and blind cyclists, and a dark museum experience in which sighted visitors are led by blind guides. While my research methodology will be elaborated in detail in chapter 2, it is important to note that an ethnographic study offered me the opportunity to investigate the formation of blind women's gender identity and blindness and sight as cultural concepts, from varied subject positions of blind and sighted people in the field, and allowed developing what I call the method of "sensory knowledge."

Although the research was done in Israel, its findings have a dual impact and can be generalized more broadly to women's experiences in visual cultures. On one hand, the discussion contributes to understanding particular ways in which bodily difference in general, and blindness in particular, is accommodated and maintained in the Israeli context, situating blindness within "Israeli disability politics" (Mor 2006). In this, the book exposes specific inclusion and exclusion mechanisms impacting blind women in Israel, such as the militaristic culture, the pro-natal ideology, and the religious environment,[2] contributing to understanding what Roginsky (2004) in her research on nationalism in Israeli folk dance identified as the "imperfect body" (375) concept in Israeli society.

On the other hand, the findings capture the formation of cultural categories such as gender, sexuality, disability, sight, and blindness within modern-Western contexts more broadly. Contributing to understanding an experience identified by scholars of gender and visual culture as common among women in general—that of serving as a spectacle—the discussion tells a larger story about women's visuality. Research findings show that given the global flow of information the women in this study are exposed to, they are embedded in upper-middle class American discourses of femininity and into Western beauty ideals.

It is important to note, however, that the main objective of this book is not to discuss disability in Israel but rather the performance and formation of blindness and sightedness through the lens of gender, visual culture, and the senses. Consequently, the discussion avoids suggesting that the findings and the participants' experiences can be generalizable to blind women in all cultures, as demonstrated when addressing in specific parts of the book the intersection of femininity and blindness with ethnicity and nationalism in the Israeli context.

In terms of language and terminology, in this book, I refer to the interviewees as blind women rather than visually impaired or women with blindness. While aware of disability studies scholars' important call for the use of people-first language such as the phrase "people with disabilities" rather than "disabled" in order to recognize disability as only one component of identity (Linton 1998, 2006), I have chosen the term "blind women" for two reasons. One is that it is helpful in distinguishing the majority of the interviewees from visually impaired women, or from those who became blind later in life; and the other is that it acknowledges the way most research participants identified themselves. In some cases, women I interviewed even objected to the use of "women with blindness." As Orly (pseudonymous, as are all names in this book), a thirty-year-old congenitally blind woman, explained, "I like the direct term, 'blind.' Because all those upgrading versions . . . I don't like them." "I don't *have* blindness." She elaborated:

> I don't possess it, I don't have the property of blindness, and I'm not visually impaired, because I'm a totally blind person. So let's name it

[ . . . ] if I had wanted to hide my blindness, I wouldn't have gone out, I wouldn't be working, wouldn't have married, given birth or had children, and I would be hiding myself with my blindness indoors. This is who I am and that's it.

Thus, while keeping the sentiments of women such as Orly in mind, I do not ignore the connotations the word "blind" carries but carefully consider the terminological aspects of language and the everyday use of visual terms, focusing on the meeting between its symbolism and the experiences of blind women, who throughout the book describe strategies they employ to respond to, negotiate, and challenge the stigmatizing connotations of the term. When referring to interlocutors I met in research observations, I use the term they chose in identifying themselves, whether sighted, blind, or visually impaired.

In this book, I also pay careful attention to the use of visual terms and phrases in general, as this research has given me a much greater awareness of the extreme visual orientation of our daily and academic language, both of them saturated with terms such as "perspective," "observation," "insight," and "point of view."[3] Yet, in part inspired by blind writers who have claimed their right to use visual language,[4] I have come to realize that avoiding visual terms is impossible and unnecessary. Nevertheless, I remain constantly aware of the visual structure of the language I use. I have sometimes tried to challenge it by using alternative phrases and terms such as "standpoint" instead of "viewpoint" and "refer to" instead of "see" when citing references, while in other instances I deliberately employ visual terms such as "shedding light" in order to provoke a visual image or to draw attention to our visual-oriented culture. When translating the empirical materials from Hebrew into English, in addition to my effort to maintain the colloquialisms of daily language, I was also aware of my use of visual language, especially when in some cases the English translation forced the use of more visual terms when translating words that do not carry visual etiology in Hebrew, such as the word "insight" (*tovana*).

It is also important to note that in this book I do not make a comparative argument regarding blind women's experience of gender, visual culture, and the senses, versus the experiences of blind men or sighted women.[5] I do, however, offer insights into the complicated position of blind women as subjects of the gaze, for example, and the unique contradictions they experience as blind women living in a visual culture. Following the footsteps of other sociological studies on blindness, I address blind women's experiences as allowing defamiliarizing topics such as gender socialization, the role of the senses within gender performance, and the concept of the male gaze, all of which may indeed be relevant for the study of sighted women and blind men. As Friedman (2013) notes in her study of the ways blind people perceive sexual attribution, "[Blind people's] nonvisual modes of perceiving bodies bring to light aspects of the process of visual sex attribution that we may otherwise take for granted as sighted people" (7).

## Theoretical Framework: "Blindness as Insight"

Blindness has played a unique role within the history of human thought, inspiring philosophical debates, theories of perception, religious traditions, cultural mythologies, literary representations, and folklore around the world.[6] As Rodas (2009) described:

> Blindness has served as our metaphor for fairness, for ignorance, for trust, for love, for vulnerability, for insensibility [ . . . ] Our idea of blindness is structured around a universe of blind heroes and villains, poets and seers—Oedipus, the Oracle at Delphi, Samson, Lear, Rochester, Helen Keller, Ray Charles, Stevie Wonder. (117)[7]

The omnipresence of blindness as a motif in our cultural imagination is unique, functioning as a "special disability" (Wheatley 2010, 23) inflicted as a punishment from the gods, or bestowing a reward in the form of gifts, such as an ability to predict the future or a musical talent. From an anthropological perspective, this metaphorical faculty of blindness rests upon a deep human anxiety about the role of sight in identifying what counts as "human," as evidenced by the association of seeing with knowing, and alternatively, blindness with darkness, ignorance, and castration.[8]

This cultural fascination with blindness has also affected emerging writings, with the publication of books recognizing blindness as a rich site of research that allows challenging visuality as the dominant mode though which gender, race, social otherness, visual culture, and disability are conceptualized.[9] Blindness' unique capacity to function as an "analytical insight" (Bolt 2014, 1) revealing sociocultural structures commonly treated as "self-evident" (Friedman 2013, 7) has informed, for example, Bolt's (2014) discussion of "ocularnormativism" within twentieth-century works of literature, a concept he defines as "the mass or institutionalized endorsement of visual necessity" (4), Friedman's (2013) analysis of systems of gender and sex attribution, Omansky's (2011) research of blindness as a borderland identity, Obasogie's (2013) investigation of how race is understood, and Wheatley's (2010) investigation of disability identity construction in different historical contexts.

In this book, I join this line of thought, emphasizing the socially constructed nature of blindness and considering the ways blindness allows exposing visual, gendered, and sensory elements within our social lives. In this, I also follow the footsteps of former studies, such as the seminal work of Scott (1969), who offered one of the first studies of blindness from a social standpoint, in which he provocatively argued for the ways "the disability of blindness is a learned social role" (14), investigating the socialization blind people experienced in institutions and blindness agencies in America. In his book, Scott coined the famous line to which I will return later in this book: "Blind men are not born, they are made" (121). Another source of scholarly work that has paved the sociological research of blindness is Deshen's 1992 work, which articulated the method of "disability anthropology" while addressing issues such as employment, religion, accessibility, and politics in a community of blind people in Tel-Aviv.[10] My investigation of the construction of blindness in everyday life also follows memoir and autobiographical writings on blindness, including works such as Kleege's (1999), Michalko's (1998), Hine's (1997), Kuusisto's (1998), and Hull's (1992), which recognize blindness as a rich experience of the world and a whole mode of being.

Addressing blindness as an opportunity to rethink the ways we perceive gender, visual culture, and the sensory body, I integrate these scholarships, together with feminist disability studies, anthropology of the senses, and research in visual culture, into a multifaceted discussion. In this, I join critical disability studies' emphasis on what Friedman (2013) terms "a continuum between able and disabled bodies, recognizing variations in sensory perception as normal and fundamental to human experience, rather than 'impairments'" (11). However, unlike past investigations, when examining the capacity of blindness in fostering a critical consciousness regarding the ways gender, femininity, and the senses are constructed, I focus on the *meeting* between the symbolism of blindness and the daily experiences of blind and sighted people. Asking about the individual's negotiation of both blindness and sightedness, as well as about the dynamics taking place when people with a variety of visual skills come together, I foster a unique conversation between representations of blindness and blind women's daily experiences, and with sighted people's understanding of these categories. Taking into account both the symbolism of blindness *and* daily experiences of blind (and sighted) people, I investigate the ways both blindness and sight are negotiated by members of society, challenging the passivity with which blind people have been commonly depicted in academic research and popular culture, and instead emphasizing the performative, embodied characteristics of vision and sight. In addition, rather than forming a distinction between representations and experiences, my ethnography taught me that they inform one another. Experiences of both blind and sighted people are influenced by representations and ideologies of blindness and sight. Sighted people commonly understand their sightedness as natural and neutral, and refer to sight as their leading sense and as an objective sensory mode representing reason. Blind people are also influenced by ideologies of blindness and, as demonstrated in this book, participate in the social phenomenon of the gaze. The discussion therefore takes both representations and experiences into account, investigating the ways they influence one another.

This book's ethnographic emphasis on the performativity of blindness and sight also fills a gap within sociological and philosophical theories, which have commonly ignored the everyday experience of these categories. Scholars of modern power relations have embraced Foucault's (1977) Panopticon, sketching modern subjects as symbolically blind and, therefore, without the ability to see their "guards." As a result, sociological theories have addressed modern power relations as consisting of an invisible gaze exercised by an all-seeing guard over a prisoner who is "subjected to a field of visibility" (Foucault 1977, 198) and who knows it but is unable to see the guard. This symbolic blindness has greatly influenced, for example, scholarly conceptualization of women's bodies, recognizing women's bodily, aesthetic, and kinesthetic practices as governed by an invisible, constant gaze accompanying their every move.[11] However, the actual experience of blindness or of blind women, as well as the ways concepts and identities such as blindness and sight are constructed, have been largely ignored. In contrast, this book closely examines blind and sighted people's everyday experiences in order to delineate the ways sighted and blind people are in fact not blind to the gaze, asking about the ways women *actively* respond to a permanent state of visibility and the ways in which sight and the visual mediate the construction of gender identity, the sensory self, and visual concepts such as gaze, staring, and display.

## Book Structure

This book offers an investigation of blindness through three intertwined analytical sections: *gender, visual culture, and the sensory body*. During the process of data analysis, the effects of blindness on femininity, the visual experience, and the senses stood out as central themes, presenting the possibility of examining blind women's use of their bodies, the experiences of seeing and being seen, and the relations between sight and the other senses. Each of these subjects is discussed in a separate section in this book, each consisting of two to three chapters that move between different research sites. These three sections offer a dual analysis that, on the one hand, allows investigating blindness through gendered, visual, and sensory prisms, while on the other, rethinks gender socialization and performance, dynamics of staring and the gaze, and sensory self-formation through the prism of blindness. Each section consists of an introduction of the main arguments, situating the discussion within a relevant theoretical framework, and a conclusion that ties together the chapters, explicating the overall narrative of the section as a whole.

Preceding the analytical examination, the book begins with a description of the research methods and sources in chapter 2. In this chapter, I not only present the methodology employed in this study but also discuss my own positionality as a sighted woman researcher. Further, the chapter discusses the method of "sensory knowledge" this research engendered during the process of data collection and analysis—knowledge drawn from examining the sensory experience of bodies and objects in space, offering special attention to visual, tactile, sonic, and olfactory skills. In this regard, this chapter discusses the ways blindness offers a new perspective on central concepts within qualitative research, such as the researcher's gaze and research observation, and articulates the ethnographic inquiry as a sensory endeavor.

The thematic sections of the book begin with a section on blindness and gender, focusing on gender, femininity, and sexuality among blind women. Based mainly on blind women's narratives regarding their feminine performance, in this section I ask to rethink the prevalence of the linkage between femininity and the visual, arguing for the ways blind women indeed participate in visual culture, as well as demonstrating *how* visual culture affects them as women. This section consists of three chapters (3, 4, and 5) that address the intersection of blindness and gender from different perspectives. Chapter 3, "Socialization toward Visual Norms," answers the "how question" of the ways blind women become aware of visual norms of gender performance, describing the ways they receive visual information regarding appearance and femininity. Chapter 4, "Practices of Appearance Management," discusses the "what and why questions" of blind women's feminine appearance, addressing the ways blind women employ visual knowledge and conduct "appearance management." Contributing to feminist discussion of "appearance work," I offer in this chapter a micro analysis of the ways blind women perform appearance in their everyday life, describing appearance management's dual role as a tool of stigma resistance as well as a disciplinary mechanism of the feminine and disabled body. Chapter 5, "Dating and Intimate Relations," focuses on an additional important site of gender identity: dating and romantic relations, illustrating the ways blindness simultaneously functions to preserve and challenge stereotypical gender roles within this realm. This section as a whole identifies the role blind women take as active agents managing their gender identity with an awareness of the value of sighted norms, providing new perspectives on visual gender norms and feminine practices applicable to social study of the gendered body in general.

The second section of the book focuses on blindness and visual culture and, more specifically, on what blindness teaches us about the dynamics of the gaze, staring, and display. In this section, I analyze the different types of gazes blind women experience in their everyday life and the staring mechanisms society directs at blindness as a cultural category in a museum exhibit, bringing together theories of visual culture with scholarship of blindness and disability studies. This section consists of two chapters (6 and 7) that offer different answers to the questions of how we see and what we see when we look at blindness, and what the conditions and consequences are of the (blind) other looking back. Chapter 6, "Blind Women's Negotiation of Staring and the Gaze," discusses the display of blind women on the street, examining blind women's experiences of staring as subjects of the "gaze." Blind women's narratives on this matter illuminate the relations between different gazes directed at them (including the male gaze and the normalizing gaze), as well as the active role of the staree who may choose to be involved in intersubjective visual communication with the starer. Chapter 7, "Visual Dynamics at the Dark Museum Exhibit," discusses the display of blindness and, I argue, of sight in a dark museum exhibit where sighted people are led by blind guides. Based on interviews and observations I conducted in the exhibit, I discuss this case study as an opportunity to learn of the orientalist gaze directed at blindness. The two chapters of this section allow investigating different forms of looking at the other, indicating the contradictory dynamics of gazing that take place in visual culture and conceptualizing the gaze more broadly as a mechanism conducted through senses other than sight.

The third analytical section of this book turns to discuss *blindness and the sensory body*, offering insights into the ways a sensory skill is experienced and expressed. Arguing that blindness can be interpreted as a "sensory culture" that accentuates the role of the sensory body within gender performance and social relations, in this section I locate my analysis of blindness within the scholarship of the anthropology of the senses and alongside other studies that pay special attention to the senses in the fields of dance, sports, and the arts. Nevertheless, I do not ask to emphasize how blind people are different or have unique, exotic sensory abilities but rather ask to build on blind women's narratives and on my observations to demonstrate the centrality of the sensory body within gender performance and social relations in general, bringing forward sensory realities shared by all people, yet accentuated by blindness. This section consists of two chapters (8 and 9). In chapter 8, "Blind Women's Sensory Capital," I examine the term "sensory capital" within blind women's gender performance, emphasizing the somatic meanings of appearance management and the role of the senses within women's experiences of discipline, pleasure, and empowerment. In chapter 9, "Intersensory Experiences and 'Dialogical Performances' of Blindness and Sight," I examine the intersection of blindness and the sensory body through the social meeting with blindness that happens in a tandem cycling group of blind and sighted participants. In this ethnographic example, dialogical encounters between people with different visual abilities take place based on intersensory experiences they share, experiences that enrich blind and sighted people's use of their senses, and understanding of their sensory selves.

Chapter 10 offers a concluding discussion of the arguments in the book, focusing on the potential of blindness to serve as what I call "a critical consciousness" revealing hidden and taken-for-granted elements within the research and daily experience of gender, visual culture, and the senses. This final discussion identifies the ways blindness functions as a realm of contradictions that, on one hand, restricts blind people to the world of the sighted and to visual norms and, on the other, broadens blind women's range of choices within social and gendered relations. As such, blindness challenges cultural binaries, serving as an existence of contradictions, an "inconvenient" one in Borges' (1984) words.

The book closes with an epilogue offering a personal narrative of my experiences as a sighted woman negotiating my visuality. In this, I also address the ways this work has informed my current research and analytical thinking, as well as the changes that have taken place in the field since I began this work.

---

In his book, *The Mystery of the Eye and the Shadow of Blindness*, Michalko (1998) introduced blindness as "an occasion to think about life, our choices, our decisions, how we choose to understand each other, and the way in which we choose to live collectively in the human community" (4). Blindness has indeed influenced the way I understand concepts such as gender and the sensorium, and experiences such as seeing and being seen.

Michalko's introduction also reminds me of the critical awareness inspired in me by my first research observation, which took place in May of 2007. I visited a folk dance class at a municipal center for the blind, where, led by a twenty-five-year-old sighted male guide, blind and visually impaired participants practiced folk dancing in a large and pleasant room. From the side of the room, I watched them as they held hands in a circle—which proved useful in keeping them moving in the same direction and steps. The guide used primarily verbal instructions, standing at the center of the group, sometimes gently touching the dancers. While explaining the steps, he used codenames such as "swing," "water-water," "cha-cha-cha," and "bend and march on the left," giving attention to the more complicated moves by repeating them and associating them with feelings and sensations, saying, for example, "let's be more jumpy in this move." Watching them, what caught my attention was the participants' control of their bodies and how quickly they understood and memorized the dance steps. Immediately after leaving the dance class, I walked outside the center and entered the busy urban intersection outside it. I felt disoriented, leaving a completely different world where announcements on billboards are written in Braille, and where blind and visually impaired people move freely, without the need for their white canes or guide dogs. As in Kuusisto's (1998) *Planet of the Blind*, blindness was not treated in the center for the blind as a problem that needed to be cured or fixed but as a physical and human condition that holds specific abilities and sensitivities. While standing at my bus stop, surrounded by the noise and stench of the city, with people smoking right next to me, practically on me, a girl bumped into me with her bicycle and the thought came to me that I preferred the bubble-like world at the center. "Outside, the people around me are supposedly sighted," I wrote in my journal, "but the truth is, they can't see a thing."

This preliminary ethnographic moment after leaving the dance class guided my initial acquaintance with blindness and was the beginning of my critical reflection on my own social affiliation and the privileging of the eye within the research process. This critical awareness continued throughout the course of this study, with research participants asking me, "Are you blind?" when I approached them for an interview and when considering my cultural biography as a sighted woman. My surprise at the fact that sight was not needed in the dance class and my feeling that the sighted people outside the center did not see one another, made me wonder about the ways culture defines blindness and sight and about the gap between the social imagery of blindness and the "blindness" I encountered that day, both of the blind people at the center and that of the sighted ones outside.

As this research evolved, blindness and sight became categories of mutual relations rather than binary opposites, and I learned to critically examine clichés romanticizing blind people as "seeing" better than sighted ones or of sighted people as "blind." With time, I also went through a process of "re-familiarization" with sight, learning to see differently. Sight has become thicker, consisting of ranges and nuances, including colors, shapes, lights, sensations, depth, and movements, reminding me of what Kleege (1999) wrote in her book *Sight Unseen*, regarding the ways she "had to write this book to learn what it means to be blind" (3). In my case, I had to conduct this research not only to better understand the life experiences of a blind woman but to learn what it means to be a sighted one.

In this book, I ask to employ the critical awareness I took with me from my first observation, an awareness that inspired this work, while engaging the metaphor of dance to ask, as a wise reader of this book suggested, about the dance that blind and sighted people do in a world that they share but have different power and claiming relations to. How do blindness and sight dance with each other? Who is leading, and how? I invite the reader to think about these questions and to join me on a journey that asks about the varied ways in which the visual is present within both the lives of blind and sighted people, and the ways blindness and sight inform each other, challenging binary boundaries around the senses and social identities and allowing for in-between spaces of visibility and invisibility to coexist.

*Two*

# An Ethnography of Blindness (and Sight)

## *The Method of Sensory Knowledge*

It is important [ . . . ] to redefine our orientation to sight, for anthropologists must learn to assess critically their own gazes. (Stoller 1989, 9)

The research of blindness and blind women by a sighted woman researcher requires a methodological consideration of questions regarding my position in the field, the way I approached the terms *blindness* and *sight* in the course of the study, as well as broader notions of what knowledge is and who holds it, and the interplay of power relations in such a study. In this chapter, I discuss these methodological considerations and offer details regarding the empirical ethnographic work the research is based on. In the first section of the chapter, I map the methodological considerations of the research, detailing the structure of the interview and the observation sites. Secondly, I reflect on the ways my role as a sighted researcher affected researcher-researched power relations and the ways I have come to understand my sightedness and the interlocutors' blindness. And thirdly, I discuss the role of my sensory body within the research process and the concept I call "sensory knowledge."

I use this chapter as an opportunity, therefore, not only to lay out the research methods but also to discuss the ways this research compelled me to contemplate more deeply qualitative methods in general and the researcher's gaze in particular. The methodological discussion paves the road for the analysis of gender, visual culture, and the senses that the rest of the book rests upon. It reveals the inadequacy of constructing blindness and sight as binaries, and that recognition of embodied ways of knowing is important not only within the research of blindness and disability but in every study involving the body (of the researcher and research participants) within fields such as anthropology, sociology, and women's studies.

Many of the methodological reflections I discuss here were shaped by a question I encountered again and again during the course of my work, raised by research participants, audiences in conference presentations, and colleagues, concerning my position as a sighted woman researcher—specifically why a sighted researcher would be interested in blindness. The first time I encountered this concern was in 2007 when I nervously sat down to make my first phone call to a potential participant in my research, a woman whose contact information I had received from a service center for blind people in the city where I lived. The woman I talked to was Haya, a fifty-seven-year-old congenitally blind woman, a mother of three daughters and grandmother of three, who plays the piano and works in the center for the blind as a music teacher. After reciting my introduction, explaining my research topic and the interview structure in the most welcoming, yet confident, voice I could produce, I heard a long pause. I held my breath. A few seconds passed before Haya asked, "Are you blind?"

My lack of preparation for Haya's question led me to recognize the deficit in the attention given to ability and disability within ethnographic theory outside disability studies, especially in comparison to writings on researchers' positionality regarding gender (Abu-Lughod 1995), ethnicity (El-Or 2010), religion (Luhrmann 2012), and class (Krumer-Nevo 2006). However, as I continued in my research, the frequency of this question concerned me; why, I wondered, am I being asked this so often, while my colleagues and fellow conference presenters seem to encounter questions about their position in the field or their motives for choosing their research topic much less frequently? What is it about blindness and my sightedness that raises this query among readers and listeners?

One possible answer is a justified concern in regard to ability-disability power relations, based on the history of past studies on blindness and disability that have too often been carried out and written from a sighted, ableist position, which silences blind people's own voices (Omansky 2011, 8).[1] Ableist depictions of blindness have treated blindness as a "problem" in need of a solution in education, public policy, and health. As Omansky (2004) explains:

> Research on blind people has been dominated by literature written from the perspectives of medicine, rehabilitation and psychology, fo-

cusing on disease and its effects, psychological aspects of blindness (grief and loss), adaptation and coping strategies, and employment. Blindness is positioned absolutely on the individual, as if it occurs in a social vacuum. This approach assumes that blindness is solely a medical event, and not a social process. (128)

This ableist approach to the research of blindness Omansky narrates reflects not only the theoretical approach of studies on blindness that address it as a medical-individual *problem* but also the researcher's lack of methodological reflexivity. Such studies typically lack a reflexive analysis of the researcher's authority, the sources and uses of the research knowledge and methods used, the researcher's positions in the field, and his or her interaction with the informant's subject positions. For example, did participants give consent? How was it obtained? Was the research done in an institute, where disabled people historically have been segregated from society?

This type of ableist and positivistic approach to the research of blindness was addressed by White (2003), describing how the literature on blindness and sexuality has been written predominantly from a sighted position, lacking blind people's perspectives about their own sexuality. And Bolt (2014) also asserts: "Those of us who have visual impairments are often in danger of being left out of our own conversation" (9).

Scholars who criticize this approach emphasize the need for empowering and emancipatory research paradigms within disability studies (Davis 2000; Petersen 2011) and the research of blindness (Omansky 2004). In addition, such studies, which this book continues, address blindness as both an impairment *and* a social construction. As Scott (1969) famously wrote in his pioneering research on the social construction of blindness and the role of "blindness agencies" in the socialization of blind people: "Blind men are not born, they are made" (121). Deshen (1992), who studied blind people in Israel, expressed a similar method, rejecting the essentialist approach and exploring the social construction of blindness through fieldwork and close acquaintance with research participants. In my work, I embrace the methodological foundations these studies have formed. Inspired by the literature of blindness from a disability studies' perspective (e.g., Michalko 1998; Kleege 1999; Kudlick 2005; French 1999) in my research and methods, I address the cultural construction of blindness as well as the everyday experiences of the people I met, while also giving attention to my own position in the field as a sighted woman.

In addition to the ableist history of the research on blindness, another phenomenon that may explain the reason the question about my sighted position came up again and again may be the ways we understand and define *what knowledge is* and *who* holds it. Since blindness is often stigmatized to be associated with ignorance, lack of agency, and disempowerment (Bolt 2005; Wagner-Lampl and Oliver 1994), some people identified my research population accordingly and assumed imbalanced power relations in my research procedures and therefore the potential of replicating the participants' social location as spectacles under my gaze. Such assumptions, however, are themselves ableist and expose the presence of stereotypical notions about blindness and sight, even in academia. As I demonstrate in this chapter, the fact was that the day-to-day methodological reality in the field was much more complex than any simple binary, as research participants commonly challenged researcher-researched power relations and consistently proved the flawed reasoning in the association of knowledge solely with seeing and sight.

The questions I received about being sighted, then, reveal some of the very assumptions about vision, knowledge, and agency this book challenges. However, the questions also allowed me to integrate an important reflexive awareness regarding disability, ability, and the senses into my project. Surprisingly, such methodological awareness has rarely been examined within sociological and anthropological qualitative studies (an exception is Beth Omansky's [2011] work on the "borderlands" of legal blindness, integrating her position as a blind researcher into her analysis). And despite the central role of a reflexive orientation within both ethnographic writing and disability studies (e.g., Oliver 1996; Shuttleworth 2001)[2] and the critique of visual primacy in ethnographic methods (see Classen and Howes 1996),[3] critical methodological questions regarding the role of blindness and sight within the ethnography of blindness have rarely been addressed. Discussions have typically referred to the gaze literally, taking for granted both the researcher's and participants' ability to see, and interpreting sight as a disciplinary act of power inflicted upon the observed.

In this chapter, I reflect on these methodological implications, especially regarding power relations, the researcher's gaze, and the role of my sensory body in the field. Rather than understanding sight as always-already power, in this chapter and in the book as a whole, I ask to deconstruct the visual notion of power relations, simultaneously considering the richness and complexity of visual dynamics (as I will also elaborate in chapter 4 on blindness and visual culture), as well as the role of senses other than sight within researcher-researched relations. By analyzing the role of my sensory body in the field, I shift the focus of the discussion from the eye and the gaze to the

1

8 · *Blindness Through the Looking Glass*

sensory experiences that blindness raises, critically examining the concept of "observation": its theoretical legacy and the empirical framework it obliges researchers to work in. In addition, my methodological discussion regarding my position as a sighted researcher broadens the reflexive meaning that can be attributed to both blindness and sight as legitimate sources for inquiry through examining the ethnographer's gendered and sensory body. Finally, following the footsteps of anthropologists of the body and the senses' reflexivity of their embodied position in the field (e.g., Grasseni 2008; Stoller 1989; Wulff 2008), I use this chapter to urge contemporary ethnographers to be more explicit about the ways we know what we know and how that is central to our ethnographic data collection and interpretation, addressing the reflexive call for researchers to "transform ourselves from . . . spectators into seers" (Stoller 1984, 94).

## Methodological Settings

> Since, in Fanon's understanding, a first person experience of the body can supplement—and in the case of racial stereotyping, contradict—the body image that others have forged and imposed on the subject, it is absolutely critical that such a first person experience be reclaimed. (Noland 2009, 201)

The emphasis on first-person experience expressed in the above quote guided this work, which is based on qualitative, ethnographic research conducted between 2007 and 2010 in Israel, as well as on my ongoing engagement in the fields of blindness and disability in Israel and the United States since 2006. Qualitative ethnographic research allowed me to focus on blind women's daily experiences, and on the ways blind and sighted people respond to representations of blindness and sight and experience these categories in their everyday lives. As Noland (2009) states in the above quote, when discussing the concept of agency in the work of Fanon, first-person experiences are powerful not only in expanding and adding to stereotypes imposed on a subject but also in challenging and contradicting them.

Considering the symbolic role of blindness within human thought and the stigmatizing association of blind women with dependency, subservience, and helplessness,[4] the task of challenging stereotypes imposed on a subject is highly relevant for discussing blindness and gender, which, similarly to racial stereotypes, are imposed on a subject's body image. Focusing on first-person experiences allowed me to bring forward narratives largely absent from ethnographic research and employ them in my analysis to reclaim identity and rethink the ways blindness and gender have been commonly theorized.

With these goals in mind, I based this work on two main methods: in-depth interviews with blind women and ethnographic observations in sites offering services to blind and visually impaired people or presenting aspects of blindness to the general public. I also conducted informal conversations with research participants, blind and sighted, and content analysis of media materials written by and about blind people in Israel and the United States, including, for example, government reports on legally blind people in Israel;[5] newspaper articles addressing blindness in legislation, policymaking, and education;[6] programs from conferences on blindness and disability;[7] and blog posts by blind writers.[8]

Forty women participated in the in-depth interviews, most of them congenitally blind, yet from varied backgrounds in terms of age, marital status, ethnicity, geographic location, and profession. The women in this research were between nineteen and sixty-six years of age. Nineteen of the interviewees are single, fifteen are married or in a long-term relationship, four are divorced, and two are widowed. Thirteen of the participants are mothers, and three of them are single mothers. The interviewees include thirty-eight Jewish and two Arab Muslim women, who identified as orthodox (five), traditionalist (eight), and secular (twenty-seven). Most of the participants can be identified as lower-middle class, while four women described themselves as coming from poor neighborhoods and growing up in poverty. All of the participants graduated from high school, and thirty-five of them completed higher education studies. The participants' geographic locations varied and included peripheral towns, central cities, and collective villages throughout Israel. The participants represent a variety of professions, including the arts (musicians, singers), social welfare (social workers, rehabilitation instructors), education (youth counselors, group leaders, coaches, teachers, students), health and medicine (medical masseurs, physiotherapists), language (translators), and communications and media.

My choice to conduct interviews mainly with congenitally blind women stems from my interest in examining the everyday experiences of gender and femininity among women who have been exposed to gender and sexual images differently than sighted women have. Indeed, all of the women I interviewed retain limited or no memory of colors, visual images, or people's appearance, as thirty-one of them have been blind from birth or from a young age, either as a result of medical malpractice, an accident, or genetics, and nine are congenitally visually impaired with a very limited field of vision or became blind during adolescence or adult life. While the most relevant social affiliations of the interviewees are blindness and gender, the discussion in the following chapters also takes into consideration the ways systems of gender and disability interact with additional social backgrounds such as age, economic class, and religion. I address these notions, for example, in chapter 3, when considering how social affiliations such as religion, age, and class affect women's appearance management practices.

Interviewees were approached through word of mouth in the "snowball" method, and prior to our first meeting, I had at least one phone conversation with each of them, during which I informed them of the interview structure, the confidentiality of the study, and the general topic—which I defined as blind women's concepts of gender and femininity and social attitudes toward blindness and blind people. During the semi-structured interviews, I began by asking participants questions about their life story and eventually moved to more specific questions about gender, femininity, and sexuality in their everyday lives. I encouraged the interviewees to choose the location for our interview; as a result, twenty-four interviews were conducted in the participant's home, six took place in the participant's workplace, and ten in public spaces such as a coffee shop, a shopping center, a university, or a center for the blind (I conducted more than one interview with six of the women during the project). These settings allowed me to take in various aspects of blind women's personal and public lives. Interviews in the home at times included food, family, and the opportunity to see personal items relevant to our discussion, such as clothes and items of feminine grooming, educational and professional diplomas, Braille books, computer software, musical instruments, and a color-identifying device, while interviews outside the home occasionally included a walk, a bus ride, or a stroll through the grounds of a university, allowing me to experience public spaces with a woman using a guide dog or a white cane, and therefore observe the reactions toward us and to share physical intimacy with the interviewee as she held my arm in unfamiliar environments. The interviews were transcribed verbatim, then translated from Hebrew into English, with an effort to maintain the colloquialisms of daily language. Twenty-six women received full transcripts of their interviews upon request, and the participants were also invited to read and respond to my written work, as well as to attend conferences where I presented segments of the research.

The lack of lesbian and transsexual women in my research (one woman identified as a lesbian) is not unusual, and is related to the difficulties of people with multi-marginality in society and to the heterosexual discourse

(Kafer 2003) in disability studies (see McRuer 2003). In addition, in the social conditions of Israel, the difficulties of people with multi-marginality are ever-present, and some of the people I interviewed mentioned negative experiences of exclusion and hostility when they chose to participate both within the disability/blind community and the gay and lesbian movement. The dominance of Jewish women within the sample can be attributed to the nationality-based segregation within Israeli society, which makes it difficult for a Jewish sighted researcher to develop relationships with Arab blind women. Finally, a word about ethnicity is in place. The interviewees have various ethnic origins: twenty-seven were born in Israel, three in countries of the Islamic world, seven in Europe, two in Africa, and one in South America. A third of the women can be identified as Mizrahi Jews, as they or their parents came from Islamic countries, and the others as Ashkenazi Jews, as they or their parents came from Europe. The reason I address women's ethnicity rather than race stems from identity politics in the Israeli context, which can be identified as an "ethnically divided society" (Smooha 1997), where ethnicity more than race serves as a dominant affiliation mediating issues of inequality, oppression, education, and political discourse (Hever, Shenhav and Motzafi-Haller 2002; Tabib-Calif and Lomsky-Feder 2014).[9]

Of the forty women participating in this study, two, Talia and Neriya, became central informants, and I have continued to be in touch with them since the research was completed. Each of them has informed this study uniquely, offering insights into the lives of blind women on different topics related to their distinct social backgrounds.

My acquaintance with Neriya, a blind woman in her mid-forties when we met in November 2008, yielded understandings mainly on the themes of femininity, motherhood, and activism. At that time, I was a twenty-eight-year-old graduate student, beginning my research with blind women. Our age difference and Neriya's many years of experience as a professional working with blind women, and as a mother herself, offered me insights I could only gain by carefully listening to the experiences she agreed to share with me. Neriya opened a window not only into her life as a blind woman and mother but also into her realm of social activism and rehabilitation work. I learned from Neriya's professional activities and from her leadership in projects serving blind mothers about gender, activism, and social change; from her negotiation of attitudes toward blindness and disability as a mother about the intersection of blindness and parenthood, gender, sexuality, and femininity; and from her story of the slow deterioration of her sight from childhood about the distinctions between visual impairment and blindness, and about congenital blindness as opposed to blindness that occurs later in life. Even though Neriya did not officially belong to my research population, as she had become blind only in her thirties, I had decided to meet her after hearing her name mentioned numerous times by people in the field. Eventually, she became a key informant, and we had multiple meetings, some so that she could rethink her previous answers to my questions and others so that I could observe or participate in projects she was involved in, such as the opening of the playroom she founded in Israel, the first specifically for blind mothers and their children, or a discussion on blind women held at the Committee on the Status of Women and Gender Equality at the Israeli Knesset. Our meetings took place both before and after my studies abroad. In November 2013, we met in my neighborhood in Jerusalem, where we had coffee together. She told me about her new projects and studies, and I told her about my post-doctoral plans and invited her to be a guest lecturer in one of my classes. We finally actualized the invitation in the fall of 2015 when Neriya gave a memorable guest lecture in a course I was teaching about disability and bodily difference, modeling a teaching style that challenges typical ableist-visual classroom dynamics.[10]

Through my friendship with Talia, who has been blind from the age of three and is closer to my age (she was thirty-one and single when we met in September 2007), I gained an understanding of the ways blind women negotiate dating, their sexuality, and others' gazes; and through her prose, love of cinema, and unique sense of humor, I became more aware of blind women's involvement in visual culture. Most of all though, I learned from Talia important lessons about blind women's sophisticated maneuvering within visuality. An indication of her general attitude, for instance, can be found in the subtitle of her blog, where she describes herself as "sometimes blindly optimistic, always optimistically blind." During our first interview, we discovered our mutual interests, and our friendship grew stronger after our second interview, eight months later, in my apartment. In the ensuing years while we lived in the same city, we shared activities such as shopping for clothes and taking a makeup course, and our conversations ranged from Braille, blindness, and body image, to our studies and our relationships with family and friends. Talia was the first person from the field to read my work and was one of the few people outside my PhD committee who read my doctoral dissertation cover to cover, responding with her thoughts on which chapter she "liked best." A little bit older than I and having no siblings of her own, she adopted me as her "little sister"—a nickname I happily embraced, being the eldest in my family and having always wanted a big sister.

Neriya and Talia, as well as other research participants, have offered me not only friendship but also insights into the intersection of gender and disability with a variety of other social affiliations and phases of a blind woman's life, such as marital status, job, education, and place of residence. I focus on Neriya's and Talia's narratives in chapter 4, addressing the ways they negotiate staring and the gaze.

Alongside the interviews, my work consisted of three years of ethnographic observations conducted from numerous positions in the field and varied in context and duration. In the short-term observations, my role was typically as an outsider observer of events created, initiated, or performed for or by blind and visually impaired people. I observed, for example, a dance class at a municipal center for blind participants, a "beauty class" in an educational institute, a demonstration in support of the central library for the blind, educational activities led by the Israel Guide Dog Center for the Blind, and a museum exhibit where visitors are led through a dark space by blind and visually impaired guides. Concurrently, I conducted long-term participant observations in sites offering services to blind and visually impaired people, including three months in a "radio-drama" class in which blind and visually impaired people write and perform radio scripts, six months in a "life-skills" class for blind and visually impaired adults in a rehabilitation program, a year as a member of a tandem cycling group that pairs blind and sighted cyclists, and ten months of observations in a medical massage training course in a national center for physical education and sports. Not all of these research sites are included in this book, as some are discussed elsewhere (Hammer 2013, 2017). In chapter 3, I address the beauty care class and the life-skills class when discussing gender socialization processes; in chapter 4, I offer an analysis of the dark museum exhibit when discussing the gaze directed at blindness in this setting; and in chapter 5, I explore the interactions among participants in the tandem cycling group when discussing blindness and the sensory body. In each of these chapters, I offer further details about the research methodology employed within specific observations, including the participants' demographics and my role in the field.

Conducting research observations alongside the interviews allowed investigating sight and blindness more generally, both as cultural categories and lived experiences, capturing both the ways blind people experience their everyday lives, as well as the ways the wider society "sees" blindness, as expressed by rehabilitation instructors, educational guides, and program coordinators. Although not all of these observations are included in this book, experiencing such a wide range of activities in education, rehabilitation, culture, art, and recreation offered an extensive understanding of the ways blindness is treated by society and experienced by blind and sighted people.

The analyses of the materials followed the classic method of discourse analysis and a "grounded-theory" qualitative coding method (Charmaz 2006), in which the analytical themes are inductively derived from the study itself (Strauss and Corbin 1990). Most of the concepts that appear in this book, such as appearance management, staring, and sensory capital, were not mentioned as specific topics before or during the interview or research observation; rather, they came forward as central during the process of analysis. Thus, the themes themselves presented the possibility of examining blind women's use of their bodies and the performance of blindness and sight within the theoretical frameworks of visual culture, the anthropology of the senses, and gender performance.

## I. Self-Positionality and the Researcher's Gaze

It is necessary to understand from the outset that positioning "insiders" and "outsiders" as binary would be misleading [ . . . ] such a false separation fails to acknowledge that research is an interactive process [ . . . ] No two people share *all* identities with anyone else; for that reason, no researcher can be either a complete "insider" or "outsider." (Omansky 2011, 26)

In this study, I quickly learned that when conducting research on blindness and with blind participants, being sighted is not taken for granted. One of the experiences that offered me this understanding occurred in November 2008, while I began my observations in a "life-skills" class, a course in a rehabilitation program in which blind and visually impaired adults practice domestic activities such as cooking, along with tasks in the public sphere such as going to the bank, post office, and grocery store. On my first visit, the class began with each person stating his or her name, and, in the case of a new student, his/her age, profession, and type of blindness or visual impairment. When it was my turn, Hanna, the (sighted) instructor, presented me as "the sighted anthropologist," establishing and verbalizing my sighted identity before offering me the opportunity to introduce myself, the study, and my intended role in the class.

These types of encounters pointed out my "sightedness" (Michalko 1998) and "temporary able-bodiedness" (Whyte and Ingstad 1995) as important components of the theoretical and methodological lens of this research, allowing the rethinking of the methodological and theoretical meanings of vision and blindness. Therefore, rather than asking to inhabit the phenomenological world of those who have been blind, or imagining how blindness feels, my sighted position served to engage in embodied research with other people of varied corporeal experiences, capturing what Pink (2009) identified in her book *Doing Sensory Ethnography* as "the multisensoriality of experience, perception, knowing and practice" (1). Unlike many ethnographic works on the body in which the ethnographer is either an "observant participant" or focuses on a specific group or bodily practice, such as dance, cycling, boxing, or martial arts,[11] my research could not involve my role as an observant participant, as I did not pretend to "go blind," nor did my study focus on a specific bodily practice but rather examined the everyday life of our sensory body. Alternately, my research goals were to offer a meaningful analysis of the sensory and embodied everyday realities shared by sighted, blind, and visually impaired people, and of the sensory realities blindness evokes as narrated *by research participants.*

While my sighted position did not force an ableist approach on the study, it did raise complexities resulting from the potential of emphasizing imbalanced power relations and the researcher's gaze. My experience, however, was that interviewees consistently challenged my position of authority as a sighted researcher. Inquiring about my method and position in the field, and addressing my own appearance and behavior, participants revealed that knowledge in the field is not produced from a one-sided hierarchical relationship in which I am the one holding (visual) knowledge about "them."

As frequently happens within ethnographic research when the subject of study takes an active role in navigating the terms and settings of the empirical process (e.g., Abu-Lughod 1998; El-Or 2010; Krumer-Nevo 2006), interviewees often made *me* the subject of study, putting themselves in the place of the researcher by expressing comments and queries about my methodology and position in the field. For example, women expressed different concerns about my research. This happened, for instance, in my interview with Aviva, a twenty-seven-year-old woman, blind from age six. I met Aviva, who emigrated from Ethiopia as a child, in a center for the blind located near her office, where she works as a social worker. Aviva identifies herself as interested in questions of gender, beauty, and appearance and is aware of the social meaning attributed to her skin color and the way she is perceived by society as a blind woman. Examples from Aviva's experiences managing her appearance and negotiating staring will appear in the following chapters. What was meaningful from a methodological perspective is that her critical awareness was also directed at me as a researcher, and she posed several inquiries before allowing the interview to begin, raising concerns about the theory with which I "come to the field," my general knowledge about blind women, the number of women with whom I had already met, the interview structure and nature of the questions, and my privacy policy. This also happened with Neta, a thirty-six-year-old congenitally blind woman. Like Aviva, Neta, as I will demonstrate in the next chapter, actively negotiates stereotypes related to gender, blindness, femininity, and beauty, including the beauty standards and the way society treats her both as blind and a plus-size woman. Working as a musician and singer, she is used to being on stage and directed her gaze to me as well. In our interview, which took place in her apartment, she specifically critiqued some of my interview questions. After asking her about the ways she manages and performs her femininity in her everyday life, she sighed, saying: "It's really general what you're asking. It's hard for me to answer." At the end of the interview, Neta continued:

> Look, I can tell you that your questions are very, very good, but, again, they're very general. I think it's . . . I mean, I don't know if you want to get to something more specific; there're many questions, it's hard to answer. . . . I think you need questions a little bit narrower. . . . It needs to be broken down into more concrete things, less abstract. But this is only my personal opinion. Do whatever you'd like.

Ayelet, a thirty-three-year-old congenitally blind woman, who during the interview critically reflected upon her blindness, education, class, and gender, also raised concerns about my work; this time, at the end of the interview. I met Ayelet in a public garden in her neighborhood, where we sat on a bench in the open air. At the end of the interview, after I asked my last formal question, Ayelet wanted to ask her own questions, taking her turn as the interviewer. "OK, you said that was your last question, so . . . what are you taking from all this? Not only from my interview, from all of us?" In response, I elaborated on the "life-story" format of the interview, and the "grounded theory" I employ in analyzing my research materials from the field. Ayelet asked, unsatisfied: "And what do you mean by a 'field,' a 'research field'? What is this 'field'?" I explained the varied meanings of a "research field" in contemporary anthropology, which, I told her, in the past might have included a remote tribe, but today is more likely to relate to a specific social, religious, or ethnic group. Ayelet replied angrily: "But that's really scary, it's like, what am I, a tribe you research? You understand?" As the conversation continued,

I began to fear losing one of the most interesting women I had met, but I persevered, explaining my sensitivity to power relations, which had emerged from my interest in gender and women. Ayelet raised her final question, directing it toward my own identity, inquiring: "Are you a feminist?" Surprised and unsure what the "right" answer might be, I said yes, simply delivering the truth. To my relief, Ayelet responded, "well done." This type of researcher-researched role reversal was enacted by some of the participants with subtlety, seemingly inspired by sincere curiosity, while others approached it with a sense of challenge, to gauge whether I was worthy of their time and trust.

Such challenges to hierarchical observer-observed power relations were also expressed by the interviewees' knowledge regarding my appearance and behavior. Complicating the nature of knowledge and knowing associated with sight and light (Schillmeier 2006), interviewees put me under the theoretical spotlight of women's appearance as well. Participants commented on my voice, touch, shape, and smell on several occasions during interviews. At one point, Aviva responded to my voice, saying: "You sound to me like a very delicate girl, so maybe I'm too honest for you." Rinat, a forty-four-year-old visually impaired writer who also facilitates group sessions on sexuality and embodiment for young girls and women, made a similar remark during our interview, addressing my tone: "I'm sorry, Gili; I'm being really honest with you, and it sounds like it embarrasses you. But this is the topic you chose." In other situations, such as my meeting with Orly, a thirty-year-old congenitally blind woman, I received a comment on my smell, a compliment on the pleasant aroma coming from my hands. This remark was surprising to me since it didn't occur in the context of my questions about appearance and femininity but happened after I took a break during our interview to use the restroom, and when I came back, Orly commented on the smell of the soap I had used. From that point, I became highly aware of my body scent, making sure to carry hand cream to interviews and paying much more attention to these concerns than to how I looked.

At times, comments I received from interviewees were directed more specifically to my visual appearance. During the interview with Anat, a thirty-four-year-old congenitally blind woman, I asked, as usual, about her feminine grooming. Anat talked about her preference for a casual look that is in-between femininity and masculinity, and described being aware of visual norms of appearance, of colors even, and of the ways she was culturally socialized into possessing visual knowledge as a blind woman. In this context, we discussed the reasons she does not wear makeup and her choice to avoid it. To this question, Anat replied: "No, I don't. But we also haven't talked about why you're not wearing any." A similar discussion occurred during my interview with Roni, a twenty-seven-year-old congenitally blind woman, whom I met at a coffee shop in a bus station. Because we met in a public location that was not familiar to Roni, when walking to the elevator, maneuvering the station, and entering the coffee shop, she put her arm on mine, holding her guide dog in her other hand so that we could get to our destination faster and more easily maneuver the crowded building. The messages our hands convey came up when discussing the fact that Roni considers herself fat. When I asked about the ways she developed this notion without seeing herself and others, she addressed my own appearance and explained:

> People told me [I'm fat], and . . . I don't know, I found out. There were these insensitive people who told me so, but I also found out [ . . . ] in your case, for example, when I took your hand I could tell that you're really skinny. As soon as I gave you my hand, I felt that you were . . . very slim. You see, and this is without actually seeing you, only because I took your hand [laughing]. . . . Yes!

I was surprised to hear this comment—a surprise Roni probably felt and so continued to explain:

> I'll tell you another thing. Many people make fun of me, even today, because when I'm combing my hair, I stand in front of the mirror. Yes. [ . . . ] I don't know [why]; I can also distinguish between light and darkness, so many times I turn the light on, and people tell me "but you don't need to, you can't see." But I do need it, it comes naturally; I don't ask myself why. And sometimes I stand in front of the mirror and say, "Wow, how pretty I am," because I feel it from the inside.

Roni's account reveals how complicated definitions of blindness and sight are. On one hand, Roni interpreted and commented on my looks and shared that she even uses a mirror. At the same time, she does not refer to herself as sighted and relies on touch, sound, and inner sensations in gaining visual knowledge. Her experiences demonstrate the richness of sensations and feelings research participants expressed in our dialogues, integrating visual and blind culture and challenging binary distinctions such as visual and corporeal, external and internal, and feelings and looks. Somewhat similar to Colligan's (2001) work with Karaites in Israel, in which she learned from the ways her informants spoke of and handled her own body, my experiences in the field transformed my body into an "open book," in Colligan's words, making me aware of the subtle messages I deliver through body scent, tone of voice, or my hands and touch. This understanding delineated knowledge as created from multiple positions and produced within a *dialogue*, problematizing common understandings of researcher-researched relations as fraught with unequal power relationships, while at the same time adding new dimensions to discussions of authority and voice, considerations central to disability studies (Colligan 2001; Oliver 1992; Shuttleworth 2001).

## II. Sensory Ethnography and the Researcher's Body

I would urge contemporary ethnographers of the senses to be more explicit about the ways of experiencing and knowing that become central to their ethnographies [ . . . ] and to acknowledge the processes through which their sensory knowing has become academic knowledge. (Pink 2009, 2)

In addition to the ways my sighted position made me aware of the nonbinary power relations of blindness and sight, the research process revealed the importance of what I refer to as "sensory knowledge" in the field, that is, knowledge drawn from the sensory experience of bodies and objects in space. My study can be identified as belonging to what Ophir (2016) calls, in her work with dance teachers in Israel, research of an "increased embodied dimension." In such studies, Ophir explains, the researcher's body becomes a tool and axis of knowledge through which the researcher knows and interprets the field. While Ophir refers mainly to work within dance studies, I would identify my study as having an "increased sensory dimension" derived from my participation in activities that incorporate and emphasize the lived body. This sensory dimension fashioned my sensory body into a "vehicle for bonding and a vessel for the transmission of knowledge" (Colligan 2001,119) through the collection and interpretation of data, developing my sensitivity to the sensory dimensions of qualitative inquiry and the possibility of articulating the process through which "sense-making practices" (Vannini et al. 2012, 17) are produced in research.

First, the sensory knowledge developed in my study exposed the "sensoriality" (Pink 2009, 83) of the ethnographic interview, contributing to what Forsey (2010) identified as "engaged listening" in ethnography, and to what Bendix (2000) called an "ethnography of listening." During the course of my work, I discovered the importance of nonvisual gestures while interviewing a blind person, as well as the use of words, sounds, and touch in research observations. While the typical interview method involves visual cues (Almog 2011, 36) such as facial expressions and body language, interviews with a blind woman emphasize a nonvisual interaction. My research participants compelled me to verbalize my presence, responses, questions, and feelings, and to pay attention to acoustic dynamics during the interview. Nonvisual communication was also important in the observations, where blind participants identified me mainly by hearing my voice and body movements, as the participants' ability to recognize me was not taken for granted but indicated a familiarity I had developed with people in the field.

Next to sound, touch played a central role in my interactions with research participants, who at times created an unexpected body proximity and personal intimacy, such as when interviewees held my hand or sat very close to me. Almog (2011) described a similar experience in her research with blind students in higher education, discussing how walking *anagage* (arm in arm) with a visually impaired interviewee created a "rather unusual situation of getting into someone's personal space, on the basis of such a short relationship" (37). It is important to mention, though, that the kind of touch and bodily intimacy created in the field does not express stigmatized-romanticized notions of the "blind touch," which assumes blind people's congenitally heightened tactile ability, and their habit of regularly touching others' faces, even those of strangers, as a way to learn what others look like.[12] Research participants were respectful of my personal space, and our bodily intimacy was created in specific situations, such as when I requested a participant's opinion on a clothing item, or when participating in a physical activity that involved the lived body, such as practicing massage techniques or riding a tandem bicycle. Such intimacy was, of course, made only with mutual permission to touch, and physical contact occurred only on the participant's terms. In these instances, touch served as a platform for attentive relations with research participants and access to a nuanced sensory knowledge, expressing the kind of intimacy Classen (2007), an anthropologist of the senses researching the historical and cultural meaning of touch, identified as inviting "intimate engagement" between people and between objects and people, "providing information not accessible to the eye" (90). This kind of physical proximity, "fleshly companionship," in Wacquant's (2005, 450) term, occurred, for example, in my interview with Tamar, a twenty-four-year-old congenitally blind woman, with whom I met and walked through, as with Roni, a large central bus station as she held my arm with one hand and her guide dog with the other, while entering the elevator, the restroom, and the coffee shop. Our familiarity compelled a more intimate exchange of bodily information than I usually experience upon first acquaintance, such as skin texture and body scent.

Bodily intimacy also occurred in research observations, most explicitly in the medical massage course, which trains blind and visually impaired participants as professional masseurs. After three months of observing the group of twelve students, I moved from observer to participant-researcher when I agreed to pair with one of the students who needed someone to practice on. Exposing my half-naked body to her hands felt unusual; however, it not only created an intimate bond between us as a "massage pair" but also allowed me access to knowledge about the ways blind people learn anatomical nuances. I learned through this experience about the multilayered nature of touch as a physical encounter consisting of complicated haptic sensations (Hammer 2017).

The sensory awareness I encountered in interviews and research observations compelled me to consider my body as the location through which I inquire into, inhabit, comprehend, and interpret the field. This attentiveness developed, for example, through conducting a research "observation" with my eyes closed while visiting a guide dog center in 2009,[13] when at the request of the guide who gave me the tour, I remained blindfolded for the entire visit. This allowed me to study the center through my senses other than sight, exploring its dorms, hallways, front desk, yard, and auditorium, aware of the smallest nuances of the tactile and sonic information I was using to detect the shape and features of the spaces I walked through. I started paying attention to the tactile marks on the floor, for example, which I had not noticed when entering the building, as well as to the shape of the walls as I searched for a corner to stand in or a banister to hold, and to the echoes and other sonic qualities created by the shape and size of each space. In response to my guide's question regarding my feelings when standing in the middle of a room versus in a corner near the wall, I told him I felt safer where I was able to orient myself in relation to the tactile experience of a wall or corner. This practice served as an important lesson about nonvisual spatial experience and offered me knowledge I used when guiding blind people I met later in my research. At the end of the tour, we went outside to the large outdoor space where an integral part of the guide dog training takes place. As we exited the building, my body was struck by a strong light that I also sensed through my closed eyes, causing me to reflect on the problematic aspect of the term "total blindness." Even through my closed eyes, I could see the change in shadows and lighting, especially when stepping outside into the early spring sun.[14] The experience was also meaningful from the perspective of gender. As a woman led by a blind man, I was conscious of my gendered body but in a different way than I usually am. I was less aware of my visual appearance and instead was aware of my sense of powerlessness and vulnerability caused both by the fact that I was deprived of my ability to see and I was being led by a man—a man who had to occasionally touch my arm and to whom I had given my trust as I followed the sounds of his deep, confident voice. The guide's behavior toward me was respectful, but I was reminded of stories interviewees had told me about their vulnerability and exposure to sexual harassment, as they are often much more dependent on a partner or even someone they have just met on a first date than they might otherwise choose to be (a subject I will refer to in chapter 5), which creates difficult dilemmas around whether or not to ask for help.[15] While the sensory knowledge I gained in this tour was not intended to offer an understanding of how blindness feels, it made me aware of the dynamics of sensory knowledge during research observations, generating a deeper understanding of the topics of gender and blindness I was studying. The guide dog center and the many sensory details my body gained during this "observation" will remain as a tactile presence in my memory, reminding me of what Seremetakis (1996) calls the "memory of the senses."

On other occasions, the experience of sensory knowledge did not require the elimination of sight altogether. While conducting observations in life-skills classes, for example, I learned about the many ways the body is experienced through the different activities of the program and in mundane tasks such as using a knife in the kitchen, crossing a street in a neighborhood, and learning techniques for distinguishing the differences in currency notes when using a bank's ATM. In a class devoted to sewing, the teacher integrated both touch and sound, instructing the participants in how to thread a needle without having to see the eye but instead just feeling and listening to it. On another occasion during a class in which students learned kitchen skills while making pizza, sensations of temperature, weight, shape, smell, sound, taste, and touch were all involved, as the participants read the Braille labels on the flour package; felt the weight of the cheese, the shape of the eggs, and the texture of the olives; smelled the oregano and the basil; listened while opening a can of tomato sauce; and tasted the salt. This class indicated the ways knowledge is acquired through multiple senses and that employing multiple senses and bodily sensations while performing such tasks can actually make them easier to accomplish. To this day, I continue to use a simple recipe for gnocchi I learned in the life-skills class, one that relies mainly on the sense of touch and can be made relatively easily without relying on sight. The class, then, offered me sensory knowledge I can literally feel in my fingertips and utilize when conducting research and interpreting culture.

Observations in the medical massage course also developed my sensory awareness. The teachers' use of verbal metaphors when explaining visual maps and diagrams of the muscles and the human body raised my awareness of the importance of words in the teaching process and in the acquisition of knowledge, informing my understanding of a more integrated approach to body and mind I later discuss in chapter 5. The class also sharpened my awareness of my surroundings in general, as during the year of observing it, I became more aware of the different shades of green through the classroom window; the texture and incline of the sidewalk; the composition of the bulletin board in the training center; and the changes of wind, light, and temperature at the sports institute from one visit to the other. In a context so sensitive to the lived body and the smallest anatomical distinctions, these nuances became integral to the research observation and the knowledge I gathered in the field, helping me absorb and capture the experiences that informed my analysis of the medical training, including experiences of pain, hunger, discomfort, confusion, embarrassment, and exhaustion. Whether I was cooking, sewing, folding laundry, or shopping with participants in the life-skills class or learning physiology, anatomy, and orthopedics in medical massage training—my body was the locus though which questions regarding gender, blindness, and culture were examined and scrutinized, offering a nuanced account of the ethnographic inquiry as a sensory endeavor.

These sensory aspects of research observations allowed me to incorporate into the analysis the "sensoriality and sociality" (Pink 2008, 175) of shared experiences with research participants, addressing my "embodied ways of knowing" (Sanders-Bustle and Oliver 2001, 509) in interpreting the activities I observed. This type of bodily experience in interviews and research observations contributes to the field of "sensuous scholarship" (Vannini et al. 2010, 63), indicating the ways sensory meanings are expressed by visible sounds, voices, sights, and tastes the ethnographer experiences, challenging the ways the "peripheral" senses other than sight have been commonly placed in opposition to the rationality and objectivism of the eye (Macpherson 2009). These descriptions also allow enriching the researcher's understandings of the role of her body within the collection and production of knowledge, and the analysis of how "the gendering of the senses" (Vannini et al. 2010, 32), or sensory classificatory thought, occurs.

## Epilogue: Tango Class, or the Dance of Ethnographic Research

My research process offered a deeper understanding of the ways the researcher's body is intertwined not only with those being researched but also with the space around her and with autobiographical bodily experiences. One of the most memorable events in this process began at the end a long day after my first month of observations in the medical massage course. As we all began to gather our belongings and prepare to leave, Anna, a visually impaired woman in her forties, approached me unexpectedly and declared: "And now, a private class! Tango!" In addition to her training as a medical masseur, Anna is a tango instructor, who in an earlier conversation had told me she had mastered the dance by relying on her sense of movement, touch, space, rhythm, and sound. Now, without giving me any time to consider her offer, she grasped my arm and held up her iPhone, from which the unmistakable sound of tango music began to play. She explained:

> The tango is a dance in which the woman doesn't need to see. It's even better not to see. In this dance, the woman has to give up all control. The man decides everything, every move, every direction. You need to give up control. You know, judging by your body, it looks like it would suit you.

Unconvinced, I grumbled back, "I'm not interested in having a man telling me what to do." Still, Anna beckoned me, and I realized that she was actually inviting me to release sight as my dominant sense, not literally asking me to follow a man's orders but opening a doorway into the sensory experiences that create her world of meaning. Suddenly, a private dance class was indeed in session, transforming the institutional classroom—a dull, grey fluorescent-lit room replete with massage beds and metal lockers—into a classical dance ballroom. With the music playing on her phone, Anna explained the steps and created the atmosphere, and we danced back and forth across the room while the others formed a circle around us, encouraging us, enjoying a welcome respite from the exhausting and stressful day. Soon, additional students joined us, embracing each other in the classic tango posture while Anna gave instructions on how to move within an imaginary triangle; how to hold our arms at sharp angles, tight in the air; and how to keep the correct distance between ourselves and our partners. Surrounded by these dancing bodies, I was taken back to the struggles of my adolescent years, of the war I had held with my body back then, and I remembered how I had hated all five years of the dance classes I had taken, half by force, half in an attempt to be like the other girls. I thought of how awkward and clumsy I had felt, struggling futilely to stretch my leg higher over the bar or my chest closer to my knee during warm-ups, hobbling gracelessly across the floor, incessantly stumbling along while painfully aware of the laughter in the background coming from the other girls. In those moments, and many other times during those years, I had felt invisible and out of place, always too quiet, too tall, and too skinny.

"How different this evening's tango dance was," I wrote in my journal afterwards. It not only broke down a barrier between me and the group, bearing significant methodological meaning on the knowledge I gathered in the field, but it also symbolized a dynamic taking place among the participants themselves, dancing their ways within and around the different backgrounds and approaches to body, intimacy, and touch they brought with them and with which they were confronted at the institute. As though exposing their bodies to each other's hands twice a week was not enough, affiliations such as gender, age, ethnicity, nationality, religion, profession, and language had created additional layers of intricacy only further complicated by the presence of blindness, raising questions such as: Who can touch whom? What body parts can be exposed? In which ways should one touch the other? And which social restrictions on touch should be accommodated and which not?

Dancing the tango with my massage school classmates marked a milestone in the development of my relationships with the group members, whom I continued to watch as they mastered the medical massage profession, altering their bodies, postures, hand movements, and appearance as they progressed through the course. Holding my body upright as I danced the tango that evening, feeling confident, and putting myself completely in Anna's hands, I remember thinking to myself, "This is the tango dance of ethnographic research," a revelation that buoyed me even as I journeyed outside the institute and into the windy night, and remained with me as I traveled back home, elated, feeling the spirit of the dance embedded in my body.

## Section I

# Blind Women's Gender Identity

---oᴈᴈo---

I don't know how you express femininity when you're sighted [ . . . ] I don't know how you do it with sight. But I can tell my friends "I really feel like looking like a million dollars tomorrow," so I'll do it, you understand? I'm preoccupied with it; I play with it. (Aviva, twenty-seven years old, blind from age six)

Within traditional cultural imagery, femininity is so tightly bound to seeing and the visual that being feminine, to a degree, requires being able to see and be seen. Femininity is "a way of being seen," Berger (1973) reminds us in his seminal analysis of the gaze, inspiring numerous researchers to explore the implications of the woman being the object of the gaze of another—a phenomenon defined by Young (1980), for instance, as "The basic fact of the woman's social existence [ . . . ] a major source of her bodily self-reference" (148).[1] The "ocularnormative system," Bolt (2014) similarly explained, rendered crucial that "man can look, stare, and/or gaze," and that "a woman can see that she is the object of the look, stare, and/or gaze" (53).

The prevalence of this linkage between femininity and the visual was first evidenced to me in the early stages of my research when describing my research topic to interested acquaintances, colleagues, and friends. I noticed that simply putting the words "gender" and "femininity" in the same sentence with "blind women" elicited surprise and curiosity from both men and women. The topic seemed to prompt people to immediately ask themselves, "How can blind women know anything about beauty and femininity?"

This bond between seeing and being feminine not only links gender with the visual but also serves to exclude blindness from the realms of beauty and femininity. Kleege (2001) tackles this point in her magazine article, *Beauty and the Blind*, addressing the ways blind women are typically perceived in popular culture:

> Blind women in movies are usually beautiful [ . . . ] but their friends seem to feel that beauty is wasted on the blind woman because she is so unconscious of it. She cannot see her reflection in the mirror or the impact her appearance has on others, so her beauty is somehow muted or defected. (48)

Blindness, as Kleege describes, is typically depicted as a negation of, or at least a powerful barrier to, beauty. In his article on the history of sex education for the blind, White (2003) offers a similar line of thought, explaining the reason the intersection of blindness, sex, and gender has attracted so much attention among educators. "Why is there so much at stake for the authorities here?" White asks. "The answer is that blindness, by its very existence, poses a significant challenge to orthodox understandings of sex, gender, and desire" (140).

If processes of gender socialization have typically been associated with sight and the visual, assuming a "sighted subject," in White's words, what can we make of blind women's narratives of their gender performance, and of Aviva's assertion in the opening quote of this chapter that she doesn't know how to "do" femininity *with* sight? These are the questions I discuss in this section, arguing for the ways Aviva's and other blind women's narratives offer a radical stance on gender and blindness. Their descriptions bring blindness into the realm of appearance and femininity, not only demonstrating that blind women indeed participate in visual culture but also *how* visual culture affects them.

This section explores these arguments through three chapters, each respectively addressing a central theme: socialization, appearance management, and romantic relations. In chapter 3, I describe *the socialization processes* of blind women into visual norms of gender and femininity, addressing the varied ways through which blind women receive visual information regarding feminine appearance. Blind women's narratives of their route into visual knowledge are helpful in explaining the multiple sensory mediums through which appearance norms are absorbed and transmitted, as well as the centrality of visual appearance for both blind and sighted women living in visual cultures.

Chapter 4 focuses on specific *practices of appearance management*. Within feminist research of women's bodies in modern-Western cultures, appearance has been discussed as an inseparable component of the performativity of personhood and gender identity (Butler 1990; Featherstone 2003; West and Zimmerman 1987) and as influential in multiple arenas of women's lives, such as health and employment, affecting women's social, cultural, and economic status.[2] Situating blind women's appearance management in this theoretical context, I offer a microanalysis of the ways blind women perform appearance in their everyday lives. I describe not only a wide range of feminine grooming activities within which it is practiced but also appearance management's dual role. On one hand, blind women's appearance management functions as a site of discipline of the female body, exemplifying the production of what Foucault called "docile bodies" (1977, 135), integrating disability and ableism into "the disciplinary project of femininity" (Bartky 1997, 100), and demonstrating the multiple senses through which socialization processes of docile bodies occur. On the other hand, blind women's appearance management serves as an important tool of stigma management and social inclusion, contributing to understanding "stigma resistance" (Frederick 2017, 132) conducted through appearance by other marginal groups countering stigma related to sexuality (Hutson 2010), disability (Frederick 2017), age (Slevin 2010), religion (Kaya 2010), class (Krumer-Nevo 2006), race (Crockett 2017), and gender (Frith and Gleeson 2004; Rudd and Lennon 2000). Blind women's appearance management is also targeted toward providing personal sensory pleasure, as will be discussed in chapter 8 of this book.

Chapter 5 turns to discuss the intersection of *blindness and romantic relations*, demonstrating the ways blindness may simultaneously preserve and challenge traditional gender roles in the realm of dating and intimacy. While the topic of sexuality will also be part of the discussion of chapter 6 in this book, in the context of the gaze directed at blind women, here I focus on blind women's everyday experience of dating, exploring the ways blindness is stigmatized in this context but also offers an opportunity to challenge traditional gender roles and to shift the focus from visual appearance to the other senses.

Blind women's narratives in this section as a whole allow examining the impacts of blindness on gender socialization, women's embodied practices, and sexuality, offering a better understanding of dilemmas specific to blind women, as well as new perspectives on visual gender norms and feminine practices applicable to social study of the gendered body in general.

*Three*

# Socialization toward Visual Norms

During interviews, blind women offered descriptions of the varied means through which they gain visual information regarding gender norms. Neta, a thirty-six-year-old congenitally blind woman who is a professional singer and musician, described her awareness of the visual during our interview at her home in the center of Israel. At the time, Neta was newly married, and I asked her questions about visual standards, how she developed visual knowledge regarding her own appearance and femininity, and her expectations and wishes regarding her partner's appearance. In responding, Neta repeated the word "bubble" a couple of times, arguing that blind people do not live in a bubble and are not disconnected from visual norms and social expectations regarding appearance. She explained:

> I know how people talk; I don't live in a bubble. I know what society says about certain kinds of people; I'm here! The fact that I don't see doesn't mean I don't know what's going on [ . . . ] I don't know why it isn't obvious. I think people need to understand that blind people with normal intelligence know what's shown on TV; they know what their friends look like and what they look like in comparison to their friends. It's not like "Wow, I just discovered I'm not blonde!"

In this assertion, Neta described her knowledge of visual norms as understanding "what's going on," indicating that she and other blind people she knows are well aware of images projected by the media, their friends' styles, and their own style. Neta also understands that people are judged based on their appearance ("I know what society says about certain kinds of people"). Other women I talked to expressed not only awareness of visual culture but also an interest in it. "I can say that I'm really interested in how people look,"

Aviva, whom I mentioned in the introduction to this section, said. "When a new lecturer arrives to teach a university class, my friends make sure to ask me, 'Aviva, did someone already tell you what he looks like?'" Aviva's curiosity about the visual is also directed at what she wears. Describing her choices regarding her clothing, she said, "It's important for me to know how it looks to the eyes, not just how it feels [on her body]. After all, I live among sighted people." Aviva, who emigrated from Ethiopia as a child, also emphasized the importance of receiving feedback on her look. "Sometimes my sister would make remarks about clothes that I'd wear, asking 'What's wrong with you? Look at you! Have you just come from Ethiopia?!' I even had a time when I wanted to check if people might ask me 'What's wrong with you? Where did you buy these clothes? What happened to you?'" Other women also talked about their interest in knowing not only how an outfit feels on the body but also how it looks. Rinat, for example, a forty-four-year-old visually impaired woman who works as a mentor for girls and women on issues of sexuality and gender, argued for the importance of "visual feedback." "For someone who doesn't know how she looks in certain kinds of clothes," she said, "she needs to rely more on feedback from the people around her. So I have to work a lot with the people around me, to know what's more flattering to my body." Talia, thirty-one years old, blind from age three, also referred to the importance of how an item looks on her body, mentioning a day we spent shopping together. "It's like when you and I went to choose clothes," she recalled:

> I can be excited by something, and you'll tell me, "Talia, it doesn't look good; it doesn't suit your body well." Sometimes I can take something and say "OK, this suits me well," sometimes I can judge by myself, but I can't always see myself from the outside and know exactly how it makes my body look. And it can be problematic. I wouldn't want to choose an outfit that shows something I'd rather hide.

Yael, twenty-six years old and blind from the age of four months, also expressed her interest in knowing what people look like, mentioning, however, that she "feels uncomfortable asking, because it's a bit strange that I can't see but still want to know how people look." Similarly, Dvora, a thirty-year-old congenitally blind woman, explained her curiosity about the visual. "It's interesting to me to know how I look to others." "I ask people," she explained, "mainly close friends and relatives. I'm especially interested in my facial expressions and body language. Or others' reactions to me."

Blind women's awareness of visual culture is primarily gained through formal and nonformal socialization mechanisms, which include education and rehabilitation programs such as the "beauty care class" for blind and visually impaired girls I observed. The class offers instruction and practice in beauty care of the skin, eyebrows, nails, and hair. "We're taught how to put on makeup," a visually impaired sixteen-year-old girl enthusiastically explained to me. "We work on hairdos, clothes, dressing up, what's in style, what goes with shirts or pants." Such socialization work was also part of the life-skills class I observed, which included occasional discussions about appearance, as well as about wider social norms of acceptable behavior. Although the training did not focus specifically on beauty, the topic of acceptable appearance came up during conversations between Hanna, the instructor, and her students. For instance, on one occasion Hanna asked one of the female students about the reactions she got to the makeup Hanna had taught her to apply in the previous class, and another time Hanna helped a female student apply nail polish (at the student's request) and attempted to explain to her the ways others might interpret the message of the color she was using. During the class about laundry folding and clothes sorting, Hanna offered some advice about fashion and appearance, explaining which clothes would be considered "elegant" and which should be kept on hangers to keep them from wrinkling.

Blind women's understanding of visual standards regarding beauty and femininity is also gained through informal input absorbed from their surroundings. Tova, a congenitally blind woman in her sixties, explained:

> Many times people describe clothes to me, my husband, friends—it's important to them that I know about what they wear; so a friend might come and tell me "you won't believe it, I highlighted my hair today," or "come and see the new shirt I bought," or if someone on the street is dressed really badly, people might describe him to me.

Tzila, a fifty-nine-year-old congenitally blind woman, described herself as "a real pain in the ass," who constantly inquires about fashion. "I ask a lot! And I ask people to read fashion sections out loud, and if something's shown on TV, like the next winter collection, I immediately ask 'what color are they, what are the shoes like?'"

As indicated in Tzila's mention of the TV, blind women are also exposed to visual norms through the media: by hearing radio, TV, and Internet ads and articles through devices that feature talking software, as well as through books and magazines in large print, Braille, or audio. As Neta explained: "I hear the commercials [ . . . ] It's in the tone of the words in the commercials;

it's in the way the woman speaks or when someone talks about the woman or to her." Anat, a thirty-four-year-old congenitally blind woman, also spoke about the commercials she hears:

It's this irritating sound, and this blonde, I know she's there and that her breasts are exposed, because I know commercials [ . . . ] I'm involved; it doesn't matter that I don't see it. I know that . . . this woman opened her jacket and her breasts were out, or that she leaned her breasts on the car. All kinds of nonsense that you hear or read about.

Yael also addressed the media she was exposed to through recorded teen magazines she received as an adolescent:

In adolescence, you start receiving all these teen magazines on tape. They [the library for the blind] recorded and printed [them] in Braille, and they had references to all types of things in sighted society—modeling, models, celebrities, how people look. They didn't modify the text to accommodate blind [readers]; they just took the sighted society's magazine and recorded it, to make it accessible.

Haya, a fifty-seven-year-old congenitally blind woman, spoke about the role of the radio, saying: "Unfortunately, you can't not be exposed [ . . . ] believe me, the radio is doing a good job in completing the picture for me."

Mothers, sisters, teachers, and members of the wider community also operate as mediators in this process. Similar to the ways sighted women are influenced by social mediators who conduct cultural work of visual appearance socialization, blind women receive advice about fashion and appearance from peers, parents, and other women. Noa, a twenty-six-year-old congenitally blind woman, explained how she learned through her mother's and sister's descriptions of clothes: "I developed all kinds of images according to what they said, like 'this makes you look more feminine.' It was in their words; 'This looks religious, this looks like a grandma,' and saleswomen used the words 'sexy, young, feminine, hot.'" Einat, a twenty-seven-year-old congenitally blind woman, mentioned the help of her mother and teacher. "My mom always made sure I dressed normally and looked good," she said. "Makeup I learned from my mobility teacher. We worked really hard on it because I wanted to be able to leave the house without anyone's help. Now I put on makeup in two minutes."

Along with hearing other people's advice, the sense of touch plays a role in acquiring knowledge about appearance. Dvora said: "I touch myself and others in a non-intimate way [ . . . ] while walking down the street, for example, if I hold someone's arm, I can sense his height and weight, or when hugging a friend." And Daliya, fifty-six years old and blind from age sixteen, acknowledged:

> I'm a person who likes to touch. When I speak with people, I touch them all the time [ . . . ] when friends approach me, I immediately hug them, and say "what an interesting shirt you have on," or "did you gain weight? Or lose some?" And it [the hug] gives me plenty of information about the person in front of me. You [Gili] can see, so you don't need it [touch], but I do; and I want to know if she gained weight, or lost it, and how her hair looks, so I touch a lot.

While it is an opportunity to critically consider whether sighted women indeed gather visual information without the need to use touch, Daliya's comment is also useful in conveying the centrality and necessity of tactile information for blind women in forming visual understanding, emphasizing non-intimate, functional aspects of everyday usage of touch and indicating the relation of touch to the other senses (Paterson 2009).

The variety of mechanisms through which blind women receive visual information and the interconnectedness of sensory modes were evidenced during my interview with Aviva, when I happened to become involved in a conversation between Aviva and her sighted friend Zoharit. Aviva and I had met for our interview in a quiet room in a service center for the blind, and about an hour into our conversation, Zoharit, who didn't know about the interview, popped her head in, looking for her friend. Aviva took the interruption as an opportunity to ask for her friend's help with my questions. "Zoharit, please come in and explain to us how, as a blind woman, I understand what I like [to wear]." Zoharit obliged her, and after making sure I was aware of the fact that Aviva can see colors to some extent, she explained: "So, she [Aviva] sees colors and checks for them." "You also check the fabric," Zoharit said, turning to Aviva, "And how it [the clothing item] sits on your body." "I don't stand in front of a mirror though," Aviva hurried to add. "So how do you know without a mirror?" I asked. "There's no mirror!" Zoharit said, "She touches them [the clothes on the body]. [She does the same to] Me as well." "I sometimes tell *her* what to wear," Aviva added. "She consults me when she has a job interview. 'Is this okay or not?'" "Today, for instance," Aviva continued, turning to Zoharit, "I like how you're dressed. You're not wearing those pants you got, thank God." "I don't always agree with her," Zoharit answers. "So, yes," Zoharit concluded, returning to my initial question of how Aviva gains visual information:

> I think you [Aviva] check the material, and . . . the shape. And stitching. And . . . colors. Sometime she drives me crazy, "wait a minute, what exactly does it look like?" "No, no, wait a minute, what do you see exactly? What's sticking out? Which color stands out most? Does it look childish? How does it look? Festive? Does it look funny? Will I look strange?"

Aviva had to agree with this. "She's right. I'm really a leech," she admitted. On this humorous note, Zoharit left the room so that we could get back to the interview.

This conversation, and other descriptions regarding blind women's various means of gaining visual information, challenge the visual dominancy of gender socialization and demonstrate the multiple modes of visual knowledge acquisition. Women mention touch and kinesthetic sensations, as Aviva checks how the clothes "sit" on her body, noting elements of shape and texture and the way clothing feels on Zoharit's body and on her own. Sound and verbal communication also play a part in this process, with Aviva pummeling her friend with questions about how she looks, and Zoharit taking the role of cultural mediator. Aviva's visual capacity also informs her, as she does have a limited ability to see colors.

Ultimately, the conversation demonstrates what scholars of blindness identified as the inner position of blind people within visual culture (French 1999; Kleege 2001; Michalko 1998), arguing for blind people's awareness and knowledge of the visual world. As Kleege (2005) emphasized: "The blind grow up, attend school, and lead adult lives among sighted people. The language that we speak, the literature we read, the architecture that we inhabit, were all designed by and for the sighted" (180). Indeed, Aviva takes an active role within visual culture, even offering consultation to her sighted friend on the proper appearance for a job interview, for instance.

Blind women I talked to were not only aware of visual norms but also critical of them. As Neta, a woman who defines herself as overweight, said:

> I think the [beauty] standards are impossible. I think many women don't feel good about themselves because of the fashion norms. It's really sad, what's going on [ . . . ] constantly facing an impossible

standard. And women have to suffer so much to fulfill it. It's cruel, what they publish today [ . . . ] my friends tell me, my friends who are single and on dating sites, that the guys' messages are like this: "I'm looking for a woman between this and this age, and thin." It doesn't matter if she's educated, smart, good, loyal; no, she needs to be thin. And that's how we all live today. We're all under that threat of "I'm not thin enough." [ . . . ] So I also feel like that. And . . . when you asked me how I feel about my femininity, all my insecurity comes from *these* things, not because of my disability. All my insecurity comes from being overweight and from what the market wants you to be, even though I'm married and not looking [for a partner]; it doesn't matter. You're still required to fulfill some impossible standard.

Neta's thoughts express her awareness of the ideal standard of female beauty in the Western world, which is based on "thinness, attractiveness, and fitness" (Rudd and Lennon 2000, 152). She positions herself "in the same boat" with sighted women who do not satisfy this "impossible standard," arguing that the oppression she experiences as an overweight woman is similar to those faced by other women, whether sighted or blind. In this, Neta expresses arguments made by Mollow (2015), who, in her article *Disability Studies Gets Fat*, identifies the parallels between oppressive systems of ableism and anti-fat prejudice (211). Indeed, Neta argues that both blind and sighted women are aware of what society expects their bodies to be and are negatively affected by it. Yael also criticized the feminine ideal presented by the media and its "twisted" messages regarding femininity:

Femininity has become very twisted [ . . . ] You see all these commercials on TV; you see all those models [ . . . ] Femininity has become very twisted [ . . . ] You know what? Take ancient Greece, the Middle Ages, the Renaissance, women weren't supposed to be as thin as they are today. So a woman was full! The feminine image was of a full body, wide hips [ . . . ] Today femininity has become very flat, because of TV, because of commercials, because of newspapers. It's about twisted messages society delivers to women.

Yael's acknowledgment of the "impossible standards" that women face echo the widespread feminist critique of visual culture and consumer culture as sites that not only oppress women but also present her body as a spectacle (Peiss 1996; Weitz 2001). Semadar, for example, a thirty-two-year-old congenitally blind woman, offered her personal experience of this phenomenon, acknowledging her awareness of the additional stereotypes regarding blindness and disability. "I think society judges women by the way they look. Their shape, size, their femininity. All this applies to me, plus the fact that I'm blind. So if it isn't enough that I'm a bit full, not really a model, I also can't see."

Blind women, therefore, indeed operate as inner, gendered agents in visual culture and make active choices regarding appearance, based on familiarity with gender norms, perceptions, and expectations. But how do they translate this knowledge into practices of appearance management? And what are the purposes of these practices in their everyday lives?

*Four*

# Practices of Appearance Management

———⊷⊷⊷———

Feminist scholarship has addressed women's appearance management as including different activities and behaviors, such as "eating disturbances, fitness and body shaping regimens" (Rudd and Lennon 2000, 154) and "the use of clothing, cosmetics, and/or cosmetic surgery" (Tyner and Ogle 2007, 88). I use the term "appearance management" to refer to a wide range of practices blind women exhibit through bodily gestures and expressions, and through the use of material culture, such as clothes and cosmetics. These practices include *a spectrum* of attitudes and approaches toward body care, fashion, and the performance of femininity, from highly elaborate and stylized means such as laser hair removal, color identifier devices, and Braille labels for clothes, to approaches focused on minimizing time and effort spent on appearance, such as buying clothes in neutral colors or emphasizing comfort and simplicity over fashion. This variety of choices contributes to a broader understanding of women's agency in visual culture when negotiating appearance norms.

## The Spectrum of Feminine Grooming

Women who practiced highly groomed feminine appearance described their efforts to "look good," challenging the supposed inherent contradiction between feminine grooming and blindness. As Aviva noted: "I have jewelry in different colors. I want my hair in a certain way; I have my own clothes that I choose for myself." Grooming was discussed by blind women as an expression of their interest in looking "good," "fashionable," "pleasant," and "attractive." Karin, a forty-five-year-old visually impaired woman, explained: "I'm not addicted to fashion, but I like to look good; so I won't wear a really unfashionable outfit because I want people to look at me and say 'what a babe.'" Practicing highly groomed femininity includes careful attention to cosmetics and clothes, as expressed, for example, by Einat. "Visual appearance is very important to me," she said. "I pay lots of attention; I have sighted friends who don't care as much as I do." In response to my question, "What do you mean by 'paying attention'?" Einat replied: "My clothes, my hair, I get a haircut exactly once a month, and remove my body hair every once in a while, even if I don't see that it has grown." Assiduously composed feminine appearance was also expressed by Miri, a forty-nine-year-old woman, blind from age fourteen:

> I really like grooming [ . . . ] It's important for me to dress nicely, to wear spotless clothes. It's important for me to put on makeup, powder, eye shadow, rouge, and lipstick before leaving the house. It's important for me that my hair is washed [ . . . ] I buy jewelry, and I really try to match it to my clothes.

Roni, a twenty-seven-year-old congenitally blind woman, also indicated how important her look is for her, arguing that grooming can be achieved without relying on the mirror. "I make sure to groom myself. Because, no, I can't see myself in the mirror, but it's important for me to look good. So, you know, like going to the esthetician, plucking my eyebrows, even going to the hairdresser to highlight my hair." Neta also accentuated the gendered aspect of her appearance management, identifying her practices as "feminine pampering," which includes wearing makeup and having facial treatments, manicures, and pedicures.

On the other side of the spectrum, blind women's appearance management includes the desire to minimize the time and effort spent on appearance. Dvora noted: "There are blind girls that wear makeup and nail polish, and they look good; but I don't pay much attention to appearance. And it's comfortable for me this way." Talia expressed a somewhat similar view, saying: "I know a lot of blind women who are obsessed about clothes, so they sew Braille labels on [their clothes] so they know what color they are and divide the closet in a certain way, but I make my life easy." Women who identified themselves as "not caring much about appearance," described it as "not really on [my] mind," and referred to themselves as women who "don't like to dress up," or who "never really cared about fashion rules." These women emphasized employing casual and relaxed feminine practices that allow less concern regarding appearance, sometimes replacing makeup with the use of perfume or simple hair styling, as Talia described:

Instead of wearing makeup, although I was taught how to do it, I'd rather go and dye my hair red in order to have color in my face and for people to stop telling me "you look pale." I prefer this rather than worrying all the time about putting on lipstick and blush. I'm happy not being obsessed with the hair dryer in the morning [ . . . ] And you know, I wake up in the morning, I simply comb my hair, and I don't need to put hours into it. I don't feel like it. I have no patience for that, no energy; it's not natural to me.

Talia's narrative emphasizes the fact that her casual attitude toward appearance is a matter of a rational, conscious choice rather than a condition driven by lack of knowledge. Her preference to avoid makeup is not due to her blindness but to her personal choice of not putting much effort into her look.

Women who seek to minimize the role of appearance also employ strategies such as buying clothes in neutral colors and choosing "easy to match" outfits such as jeans. Roni, for example, told me: "Usually, I'm in jeans, and jeans match everything. So . . . that's it; I take whatever jeans I want and any shirt I feel like." Talia also expressed a similar attitude, choosing off-white as the dominant color of her wardrobe:

All my pants are in neutral colors, jeans, or black, or off-white [ . . . ] and the shirts are colors that I like; and my shoes are always black. And my socks are off-white; the more off-white, the merrier. And that's it! I don't have to question seventy times if it's good or not; the only thing I need to know is which shirts need a white bra and which shirts don't.

Hani, a twenty-six-year-old congenitally blind woman, described not only her use of neutral colors but also her refusal to spend time and effort using a color-identifying device:

I mostly buy clothes in neutral colors that go with everything, even though there's a gadget that can tell me the color [ . . . ] but I can't bring myself to use it. That gadget, it's a matter of importance, the way you organize your priorities. So if I decided to use it more often, I'd also waste more time in the morning.

By choosing comfort over fashion and refusing to use "gadgets" as a way to distinguish colors, Hani also provides a point of resistance to the formulation of blindness as a technical problem requiring technical solutions. In addition, Talia, Hani, and other blind women's choices can be read as a challenge to dominant cultural discourse encouraging women to invest time and money into appearance. Tyner and Ogle (2007), in their analysis of dress-related rhetoric within issues of *Ms. Magazine*, identified such examples of the selection of functional clothing as a "counterpoint to the material and embodied oppression inherent in following fashion for fashion's sake," a choice that they framed "as a means through which one could resist dominant cultural discourses about the body and gain empowerment through personal appearance" (89).

Blind women's appearance management is also mediated by and related to social affiliations such as age, class, and religion. Research participants' age range produced a spectrum of attitudes toward fashion, which highlights changing priorities regarding appearance, as older women were more concerned with, for example, when and how to color their hair or whether to consider plastic surgery; economic class impacts blind women's appearance mainly by affecting their ability to purchase fashion, hygiene, and beauty products. And in Israel, where traditional Jewish imagery and modern commercialism are constantly juxtaposed (Sered 2000), blind women's appearance management is also influenced by religious affiliation. Religious women included in their appearance considerations the edicts of the religious authority and the discourse of the pure and modest female body, contemplating, for example, whether or not to cover their head and the style of the head scarf, whether to wear pants or skirts and the length and width of the skirt, or whether to use cosmetics. Tamar, for example, a twenty-four-year-old congenitally blind woman who is Orthodox religious, expressed her opinion regarding the "appropriate" appearance of the modest body:

> Right now, I don't like wearing long skirts [ ... ] I hate it. I don't find it comfortable [ ... ] In my opinion, pants are much more modest because with a skirt I need to sit down carefully [ ... ] Pants are much more modest, and believe me, if the rabbi said so, everyone would wear them.

Aviva also expressed her dilemma regarding wearing long skirts. As a "traditional-observant" woman who emigrated from Ethiopia, Aviva is aware of the symbolic effect of her long skirt. In the Israeli context, a cultural stereotype labels Ethiopian Jews as religious; therefore, her skirt is assumed to express her gender, religious, and ethnic identities simultaneously. Aviva explained with frustration that people usually associate her long skirt not with her feminine style but rather interpret it as a mark of her assumed Orthodox religious identity. "I don't want people to affiliate me with a group I don't belong to," she said. "If they see me with a [long] skirt, no one would look at it and think, 'OK, she wants to be feminine.' No, they would say 'That one, she's religious.'" These narratives reveal appearance management issues that blind women on the religious spectrum must consider, exemplifying that religious concerns do not reduce the cultural emphasis on normative appearance; rather, they function as an additional set of rules concerning the female body.

Blind women's appearance management, then, is not uniform in application and is influenced by a range of social contexts, as well as personal priorities and taste. It is varied not only in relation to the ways it is practiced but also in the circumstances and purposes for which it is done. "I dress differently for every occasion," Rinat explained. "So if you see my closet, it has the entire spectrum, from miniskirts to long ones, from very modest clothes to tank tops. I mean, it's not like I can tell you 'this is the only way I dress.'" During interviews, blind women mentioned multiple contexts that influence their decisions about appearance, including their work environment and the nature of their job, after-work activities, or romantic events, while different occasions also inspire different goals of appearance management, such as to achieve a "comfortable," "attractive," or "sexy" look. This variety of appearance management practices blind women describe is useful in understanding aspects of agency in relation to appearance norms women negotiate, indicating the ways women resolve tensions about appearance and make decisions regarding use of material culture and adornment of their bodies (see also Guy and Banim 2000, 325).

## Conducting "Skilled Work" to Achieve a "Normal" Look

The spectrum of blind women's decisions regarding appearance brings to mind what Guy and Banim (2000), in their article on women's relationship with clothes, called "skilled work"—situations that require of women a high degree of knowledge about dress (323). Either practicing a more casual feminine appearance or a more meticulous one, blind women in this research indeed perform "skilled work," making an effort to actively and consciously interpret and implement visual norms. Alongside the diversity of feminine grooming within blind women's appearance management, the importance of "normal" or "decent" appearance was repeated in women's narratives across the board. This aspiration functions both as a discipline tool of the body as well as an instrument of stigma resistance, reflecting Guy and Banim's (2000) assertion that "The effort involved in these situations had both positive and negative aspects for the women." "Effort may sometimes be concerned with the labour of body discipline [ . . . ] but it is an active, skilled process [ . . . ] [an] efforts to be recognised and positively valued!" (323–24).

Blind women's skilled work of appearance management can be read through this dualism: expressing a labor of the body, as well as a deliberate choice to create a certain type of look. In this case, the effort blind women put into appearance is aimed at achieving a "normal look." Kleege (2001) describes this aspiration, linking it with the messages blind people receive from society regarding appearance:

> From childhood we, and our caretakers, are bombarded with advice about the need for good grooming, physical fitness and tasteful attire. But for us, the goal is not merely to make the most of whatever attractions we might possess but to make ourselves visually appealing to others in order to dispel the expectation that the blind are always indigent and helpless. In other words, we are encouraged not to become more beautiful but to look less blind. (48)

Similar to what Kleege described, in most cases, blind women I talked to highlighted the significant role of appearance not as a means to look attractive but to being perceived as a "normal" woman and even as "human"—in the workplace, in academia, and in their children's environments.

## Resisting Stigma

"Attractiveness," therefore, is only one component of blind women's appearance management, which in most cases is targeted toward claiming a more general human subjectivity. As Aviva explained:

> It's important for me to look good [ . . . ] because I walk down the street and people look at me, so I want them to see something that looks good, not neglected. Like everything else, it started from "I don't want them to pity me; I don't want to be the poor blind woman" [ . . . ] so [people] won't go and say, "Well, what can you expect? She's blind."

This wish to "look good," in Aviva's words, serves women in negotiating the stereotypes and dehumanizing attitudes they encounter, such as beliefs that their blindness denies them the ability to speak for themselves or that it negates their feminine and maternal abilities, beliefs expressed through questions such as how can you help your son with his homework? how do you match socks? or even, how do you know you got your period? As Aviva related: "For people who don't know me, I'm the 'blind woman' [ . . . ] it's like they just see me and immediately dismiss me." Such dehumanizing attitudes are typical of the ways society treats people with disabilities in general, as occupying "ambiguous personhood" (Murphy 1990), "nonperson status" (Gill 2001, 361), or "humanity in doubt" (Whyte and Ingstand 1995, 10). Within these social dynamics, blindness is typically associated with failure, defeat, bitterness, and passivity (Kudlick 2005, 1590). Appearance management, therefore, plays an important role in negotiating stereotypical notions and is used by blind women as a powerful instrument in their struggle to defy the cultural labels of "blind" and "disabled," by attaining a "respectful," "pleasant," "ordinary," "communicative," or "decent" look. Hani, who typically dresses casually, pointed out: "It's important, of course, to dress in clothes that fit well [ . . . ] God forbid that I should walk around in stained clothes or something like that." Haya also pointed out the need to follow social norms. "I want to look normal," she said. "I don't want to look like Miss Universe; I want to look decent." Ayelet, a thirty-three-year-old congenitally blind woman, also addressed the need to look decent:

> I want people to look at me and say, "She's ok. Her being blind doesn't make her ugly, and it's not like she doesn't take care of herself" [ . . . ] I arrive at work with a neat shirt and wear makeup and earrings. I don't need them to think I'm pretty; that's really not the issue. What matters is that they look at me and don't see a damaged and ugly person. A person should give a good impression; a person should be put together.

In our interview, Ayelet emphasized her desire not only to maintain an appearance that will pass as "decent" but also to deliver a specific "un-damaged" feminine look, through practices such as wearing makeup and jewelry and removing her body hair. Michal, a twenty-six-year-old congenitally blind woman, expressed a similar notion, illustrating the ways in which appearance can be used as an expression of both a collective and a feminine identity that indicates her desire to be accepted as "part of society." "It's important for me to be feminine in order to be a part of society," she explained. "And it's also important for me because of my partner, so he won't feel like he's walking around with a small child, but that he's walking around with a woman!"

Women's use of appearance as a practical strategy in reacting to the degrading ways in which they are perceived was expressed by women across economic classes. Interviewees from lower economic classes reported the effort to achieve a "normal" or "decent" appearance, though limited by their financial means. Shoshi, for example, a sixty-nine-year-old woman who has been blind from age thirteen and who immigrated to Israel from an Islamic country as a child, described her childhood and adult life as one of ongoing economic strife, and explained the importance, as a blind girl, of her appearance. Recalling the years she attended a boarding school for the blind, she related the prioritization of appearance in blind women's education, as mothers, teachers, and friends recognized the value of the "right look":

> I was a cute girl, and my mother always made sure to send me clothes from home, even though the school provided clothes for us. But she was always sending me clothes so I would look good [ . . . ] It was really important at home that no one would ever think that since the girl is blind she's missing something—on the contrary. My mother really cared about the way I looked.

Blind women's emphasis on the importance of displaying a "good" look, in Shoshi's words, expresses their attempts to "unspoil the spoiled identity" (Goffman in Brueggemann et al. 2005, 20) and disabled women's negotiation of normalcy. This can be situated in a broader context of what Frederick (2017), in her research on mothers with disabilities, calls "stigma resistance," "that is, how marginalized individuals challenge stigma" (132). A few scholars have attended to the specific role of appearance in this process, identifying the ways groups experiencing oppression on the basis of age, sexuality, class, race, or disability use appearance practices to resist stigmas. Participants in Slevin's (2010) research on the management of the aging body, for instance, use diet, exercise, and cosmetic surgery in order to keep a younger appearance and resist ageism; racial minorities negotiate stigma through what Crockett (2017) calls, in the context of consumer culture, "politics of respectability"; mothers with disabilities in Frederick's (2017) research project a "professional appearance" and use what she calls "respectability politics" to defy negative stereotypes of incompetence and danger (133); and disabled men practice hyper-masculinity to offset disability status as weak and dependent (Murphy 1990; Sparkes and Smith 2002).

Within this context, blind women's appearance management operates as a mechanism that delivers messages regarding ability and disability, as well as gender and femininity to the wider society, and is tied to the contradictory intersection of categories that delineate where women with disabilities exist. Disability as a social construct is patriarchal and thus labels disabled people with "feminine" traits such as subservience, helplessness, childishness, and dependence (Limaye 2003; Lonsdale 1990; Morris 1991; Saxton 1987; Shakespeare 1996). While disabled men are also labeled with these characteristics, adopting "masculine" traits such as competitiveness, leadership, aggression, and ambition can create opportunities to avoid the stigmas of the disabled. However, the aesthetic discourse of the feminine body demands conformity to a narrow description of accepted female appearance, a construct that does not include the use of aids such as a wheelchair, white cane, guide dog, or artificial limbs, leaving disabled women to face a paradoxical situation, as they are accepted neither on the masculine side of the equation, because of their femininity, nor on the feminine side, because of their disability. Moreover, in their appearance work, blind women also need to negotiate the social expectations of the aesthetic discourse of the feminine body as well as those of visual culture, which is saturated with images of the feminine body as a sighted subject, assuming blind women to be ignorant of visual norms. Thus, unlike blind men's practices, blind women's appearance management is targeted toward claiming a feminine identity, negotiating the "blind" label in order to claim their place in society as women, mothers, and romantic partners. And different from sighted women's practices, blind women's appearance practices are also aimed toward refuting labels such as "pitiful," "miserable," and "helpless," and the assumption that they are ignorant (of visual knowledge).

Yet, unlike other forms of what Goffman (1963) called "stigma management," blind women's appearance management is not targeted at passing. Their negotiation of gendered visual norms is not aimed at hiding blindness or at passing as sighted. In contrast to findings in earlier studies about, for example, practices used by people with disabilities to pass as not disabled (see Brune and Wilson 2013), strategies employed by women with disabilities in an effort to be treated as "normal" (Williams and Nind 1999, 668), or actions aimed at passing as younger among men and women negotiating their aging bodies (Slevin 2010, 1013), blind women's narratives indicate that the purpose of their appearance management is not to enable them to pass as sighted or as non-blind. Rather, blind women's appearance management is an attempt to deliver complicated messages regarding the possibility of displaying femininity and personhood *alongside* blindness and disability, at the same time and in the same body. This type of stigma resistance shares some similarities with the strategy Siebers (2004) calls a "disability masquerade," which "counteracts passing, claiming disability rather than concealing it" (19). Blind women's negotiation of stigmas through appearance is also reminiscent of the type of appearance management Tyner and Ogle (2007) identify in their analysis of feminist perspectives on dress and the body, which may include women feeling empowered and self-actualized as a result of their appearance management choices, acting as savvy feminine performers (89).

Blind women's appearance management carries an additional role in the context of Israeli society, in which individuals must prove their membership in and contribution to the national project in order to gain an "entrance ticket" into the collective. In this context, individuals gain membership through specified sites: masculine militarism (Rapoport and El-Or 1997; Sasson-Levy 2007, 484); feminine fertility (Berkovitch 1997; Gooldin 2002); the display of modernity among Mizrahi Jews, who were historically stereotyped as uncivilized and uneducated Easterners (Khazzoom 2008); or a "proper" Jewishness among immigrants from the former Soviet Union, who were seen as a potential threat to the Jewish collective nature of the state because of the large number of non-Jews among them (Cohen and Susser 2009; Kravel-Tovi 2012). Blind women's appearance management also serves as an inclusion mechanism into the wider society. Since blind women are exempt from military service and therefore cannot "enjoy" the social glory associated with disabled veterans, the display of "normal" femininity and human subjectivity can be used in this setting as an alternative route into the "public collective" (Lomsky-Feder and Rapoport 2001). In addition, the mastery of a normative look allows blind women to claim their belonging to a feminine "ideal" of womanhood and motherhood, an extremely important characteristic in the Israeli context as a mark of normative identity, while also proving their involvement in Western beauty discourse, which has increased during the past two decades as a result of a shift toward capitalism (Carmeli and Applbaum 2004). Therefore, blind women's attempt to display "personhood" paves a pathway toward inclusion within Israeli society and an escape route from social marginality.

## Disciplining the Body

While the display of a "normal" feminine appearance functions as a tool of stigma management and social inclusion, it also exacts high costs from its practitioners, exposing the interconnections between normalcy and beauty norms as two disciplinary mechanisms (Garland-Thomson 2002, 10) operated upon the bodies of women with disabilities.

The display of a "normal" and "aesthetic" look requires a hyper-aware feminine performance and a rigorous control of the body. This came up in my interview with Karin, a forty-five-year-old visually impaired woman whom I mentioned earlier. Karin, who is of European origin, described herself as caring about her appearance, but she also feels somewhat conflicted by the joy she feels when grooming herself on one hand and the anxiety of being constantly aware of her appearance on the other. In our interview, which took place in her apartment, she described how her appearance mediates her relationships at work, in dating, and in her everyday life. For example, because Karin's right eye does not function, she needs to pay meticulous attention to her body movements and facial expressions, controlling the right side of her face, keeping her eyebrows at the same height and her eyelids in the same shape, and coordinating the movement of the lens of her eyes with the turn of her head. "I pay lots of attention!" she explained. "I really do a lot of work on it. It requires energy; it requires focus! Intense focus, all the time! Could you be so focused all the time? This is what it takes of me. It's not that I can't do it [ . . . ] but it's hard!" Karin and many other women described their appearance management as demanding a tremendous effort: scrupulous use of body movements as they move their bodies, stand, sit, or walk, and highly controlled facial expressions, with specific attention to the area surrounding the eyes (the direction of the gaze, the movement of the eyes, eyelids, and eyebrows). Talia described directing her attention to sitting upright and to the way she walks. "When I was ten, I used to walk with my legs in this Charlie Chaplin walk," she remembered. "And my mother told me not to. 'Why not?' 'It doesn't look good.' 'What do I care?' 'You care! You want to look normal, right?'"

Blind women's control over normative appearance emphasizes appearance work that the sighted are also required to engage in, yet blind women's descriptions reveal a self-reflective awareness of practices that sighted women might take for granted. Talia, for example, described her attempt to avoid "blind mannerisms" such as rocking back and forth, scratching her eyes, or playing with her fingertips. The importance of avoiding "blind mannerisms" was also expressed by Neta, who identified it as "acting blind." "If you don't act blind," she explained, "or have blind people's mannerisms, rocking or doing all kinds of stuff, then people forget, and you're a person like anyone else, and the blindness isn't important." Some of the women mentioned not

only avoiding "blind mannerisms" but also choosing to perform bodily practices that are pleasing to sighted society, although they are inimical to more
practical and comfortable behaviors—efforts such as directing their gaze to
the speaker's eyes or moving their hair from their eyes. This effort can be
read through McRuer's (2010) term "compulsory able-bodiedness," a cultural
discourse McRuer named following Adrienne Rich's concept of "compulsory heterosexuality." Compulsory able-bodiedness operates as a system of
exclusion that, similar to the way compulsory heterosexuality works, seeks
to normalize or assimilate disability and the non-normative sexual/disabled
identity. We can think of blind women's emphasis on a "nondisabled" appearance as reflecting the domination of "compulsory able-bodiedness" in which
women with disabilities display a nondisabled appearance in order to match
the normalcy standards of a healthy and whole body.

Blind women's "stylizations of the body," in Butler's terms (in White 2003,
138), also occur within socialization processes blind women are exposed to,
processes that outline the boundaries of femininity as a unified and "natural" way of being and attempt to mold blind girls' "bodily gestures, speech,
movements, grooming practices, and styles of various kinds" (White 2003,
138) to a normative ideal. Such practices were evident in the beauty care class
I observed, where blind girls are taught about beauty and feminine appearance. Beauty standards were learned by practicing the use of cosmetics and
through the instructor's comments on the girls' looks and her advice regarding "decent" appearance. "Remember when you used to have something on
your face every morning when you arrived at school?" Ilana, the instructor,
jokingly reminded one of the students. The kind of appearance work practiced in this class was presented as a uniform set of rules, applicable to all
women and achieved through hard work, even suffering at times. This was
evidenced when a student, apprehensive about a facial treatment, recoiled
and said "yuck" after Ilana dabbed her cheek with facial cream. In response,
Ilana replied, "What do they say? You have to suffer to be beautiful, right?"
and later on included me in the beauty standard consensus as well:

> I also use it [facial treatment] once a week. Gili does it, too, prob-
> ably, right, Gili? Every woman needs it, to clean her face. And we also
> learned at the beginning of the year about clean and suitable clothes.
> The appearance, you saw the older girls; they're already aware of it.
> They dress up, match colors, and wear jewelry.

In addition to cosmetics, the class addressed body size, emphasizing thinness
as the ideal. In one of the classes I observed, a conversation about weight took

place, with Ilana praising a student who had lost weight. "I've become very thin," the student concurred, "You see how my skirt is falling off?" "Did you want to lose weight?" I inquired. "Very much," she replied, "and I want to lose [even] more. I want to be like my aunt; you haven't seen her, but she's really thin." "Why do you want to be thin?" I asked. "Because . . . it's more comfortable, walking [around], with less weight, and it's more fun to find clothes." In response, I asked Ilana if they talked about weight in class. "Sure," she said, "about food, about eating lots of vegetables."

This class and blind women's narratives are useful in framing blind women's appearance management within modern "projects of docility" (Foucault 1977, 136), offering an insight into Foucault's view of the body as a site of modern disciplinary practices that employ "subtle coercion of [ . . . ] movements, gestures, attitudes, rapidity: an infinitesimal power over the active body" (137). Ilana's work in the beauty care class hearkens back to the effort made by sex educators for the blind in earlier times—a "labor" White (2003) described as done "under the burden of explicitly teaching the blind what is normally learned naturally and effortlessly through everyday experience" (141). This vigilant discipline of the body to conform to a narrow range of accepted behaviors and looks has negative effects for women, such as limited opportunities for spontaneity or nonchalance and a large investment of time and attention to simple tasks. Women expressed anxiety and talked about the lack of naturalness, changeability, and freedom inherent in their attempt to master a "normal" feminine look. "I'm always and all the time in some kind of . . . readiness," Karin said, "awareness." "I can't just simply run downstairs and choose clothes; it's not that easy. It's not casual [ . . . ] Most of the time, I'm paying attention." Ayelet also described the constant tension that accompanied her feminine practices as a blind teenage girl, referring to her adolescence:

> Your body is changing; all of a sudden you're supposed to behave like a woman and not like a girl [ . . . ] Listen, you get your period! And you say, "Hold on, am I different from everyone else? Am I more developed or less developed, or like everyone else?" Maybe you suddenly don't wear your bra right, everything bounces around, I don't know [ . . . ] Some of the girls in school will say things; others will laugh at you [ . . . ] A sighted woman can see herself in the mirror and what everyone else sees, she sees herself.

Even though sighted women may also feel a type of stress similar to what Ayelet describes, Ayelet's comment is helpful in distinguishing one of the challenges visual culture can impose on blind women, who cannot rely on the confirmation of the mirror and are dependent to some extent on feedback from others.

Ayelet's and others' examples also reveal the ways disciplinary practices of what Foucault (1977) called "micro-physics of power" (222) affect blind women, compelling a focus on body movements, facial expressions, and clothes. Blind women's appearance practices offer a nuanced discussion of the disciplinary norms operated on women, who, feminist literature tells us, "manipulate the body through continuous dieting, plucking, shaving, cutting, and constricting" (Odette 1994, 41). They allow integrating blindness and disability into feminist discussions of docility, contributing to feminist disability theory's critique on appearance and the medicalization of subjugated bodies. As Garland-Thomson (2002) explains:

> Feminist disability theory suggests that appearance and health norms often have similar disciplinary goals [ . . . ] The twin ideologies of normalcy and beauty posit female and disabled bodies, particularly, as not only spectacles to be looked at, but as pliable bodies to be shaped infinitely so as to conform to a set of standards called normal and beautiful. (10–11)

Such disciplinary processes, blind women's appearance practices demonstrate, do not necessarily rely on vision or require a sighted subject. The power of the Panopticon comes not just from seeing visual power regimes but from self-monitoring due to being systemically institutionalized into gendered norms. As Foucault (1977) described: "He who is subjected to a field of visibility, and who knows it, makes the constraints of power play spontaneously upon himself; he becomes the principle of his own subjection" (198). In attempting to achieve a "normal" and "aesthetic" look, blind women indeed participate in the docility project, controlling and monitoring their appearance even without the physical ability to see themselves and their surroundings. Disciplinary mechanisms, therefore, are expressed and experienced not solely through visual, panoptic practices but through the entire sensorium. Participants in the beauty class, for instance, internalized social visual norms by feeling the temperature and texture of the cream on their faces, sensing its smell, and listening to the instructions regarding its use; and blind women's narratives describe numerous bodily sensations accompanying their beauty practices. These experiences demonstrate the ways socialization processes of docile bodies occur through multilayered sensory experiences and not merely through the sense of sight or through a visual regime.

Blind women's embodied descriptions of the use of their senses within the processes of applying and achieving appearance norms also bridge the concepts of appearance and embodiment. Hutson (2010), in his research on gay and lesbian individuals' appearance choices, explained that the term "appearance" has been broadly understood as "the way one's body is adorned" and as a tool of stigma and identity management (218). Appearance has largely not been approached from an embodied perspective, and the body was understood in the context of appearance management to function as a "social object." Blind women's emphasis on the use of their senses within appearance management and the discipline of the body does not allow a separation between embodiment and appearance, emphasizing the embodied aspect within appearance work and aspects of gendered and feminine docility.

*Five*

# Dating and Intimate Relations

⸺⸙⸺

In addition to practices of appearance management, dating and intimate relations were mentioned by blind women as an important site of gender performance in which blindness plays a central role. Somewhat similar to the duality accompanying blind women's appearance management, blind women's experiences in the realm of romantic relations expose the different facets of blindness, which on one hand carries stigmatized notions of women and gendered roles, and on the other hand carries subversive potential that challenges the role of beauty, for example, in social relations as well as in traditional gender roles.

Love and blindness make a productive cultural pair, found at the center of stories, poems, folklore, and movies, typically serving as fertile ground for expressing stereotypes eroticizing blindness with a heightened sense of touch or treating blind women as incapable of fulfilling traditional domestic roles. Nevertheless, the sociological question of how blindness affects everyday experiences within intimate relationships has garnered little scholarly attention (with the exceptions of Deshen's 1992 study of the lives of blind people in Tel Aviv, and Frame's 2004 research on communicative performance of visual impairment in relationships and social interaction). The few studies on sexuality and visual impairment offer a more psychological focus, discussing mainly sex education and the experience of adolescents (Kef and Bos 2006; Pinquart and Pfeiffer 2012). During my interviews with blind women, the topic of romantic relations came up again and again, as women addressed their challenges concerning dating, recalling the lack of sex education they received, and the hurtful attitudes expressed toward them by romantic and sexual partners during their adolescences and into their adult lives.[1] At the same time, conversations with blind women about this topic pointed out blindness as a source of alternatives to the social order, challenging the centrality of sight and traditional gender roles within romantic relations.

## The Stigma of Blindness

The issue of the inferiority of being blind is expressed most markedly in matters concerning women in the marriage market. (Deshen 1992, 46)

Why is blindness perceived as such as threat to romantic relations and sexuality that dating is identified by blind women as a main site of struggle? Kent (2002), in her article about her experience of being blind and becoming a mother, pointed to the stereotype of blind women as "unfit" for the role of wife or mother as one of the reasons for the adversities blind women experience in this arena. As she explained:

The public generally regards blind girls and women as unlikely candidates for motherhood. First of all, we are often perceived as asexual, uninterested in dating, and unattractive to potential partners. Second, we are considered helpless, incompetent, and unable to care for ourselves, let alone tend to small children. (82)

In her writing, Kent addresses both the roles of mothering and parenthood, conflating stigmatic attitudes toward dating, sexuality, and partnering. These roles are not identical, since blind women may be stigmatically seen as more tactile and dependent, for example, making them socially acceptable as sexual/romantic but unfit as mothers. However, in what follows, I address both the roles of being a mother and a sexual partner as related to the realm of romantic relations. I do so for two reasons. First, women I talked to referred in one breath to their experiences as mothers and romantic partners, and to stigmas they encounter in both realms as related to the issue of dating. For instance, women talked about the hardship of finding a partner due to stigmas about their inability to function as mothers. Secondly, in the Israeli context, which, as mentioned earlier, is characterized as pro-natal, femininity is tightly bound with fertility (Berkovitch 1997), and the role of a wife is actualized through motherhood.

Women in my study recalled being the target of assumptions similar to those described by Kent, expressing their frustrations concerning stigmatic attitudes toward blindness, factors they believed contributed to their difficulty finding a romantic partner. Talia, for example, who was dating a blind man at the time of our interview and with whom I had evolving conversations around the topic of romantic relationships, offered her experience of men's reactions to her blindness on dating sites. "[E]ven on the Internet," she said,

If I give my details, you know, open a profile on J-date or something, these weird questions always pop up. It starts with "What do you mean when you say you're blind?" "Um . . . let me think!" It can be really stupid, and it can even end up with . . . you know, setting up a meeting somewhere; and sometimes they don't even have the courage to come up and say "Listen, I don't like you," or they call me from their cell when I'm already sitting there waiting, saying "I saw you, and you don't suit me." [ . . . ] And I just don't have the energy to get hurt anymore; I'm really tired of it.

Talia's blindness, therefore, poses a challenge within romantic relations even in the online sphere, raising dilemmas regarding how to introduce herself online and what to expect in a face-to-face meeting. Talia also talked about the lack of knowledge about her disability, which she has encountered throughout her life:

[T]hey [men] don't have this insight that being with someone blind doesn't necessarily mean something different than being with a sighted person, in terms of . . . the things you do together, you know. There's always this cliché, that . . . like, "What, can I take her to a movie?" Of course, you can; you're welcome to go to a movie with her. By all means. I mean, there's no problem with that. And then, it's like, "but will I have to explain everything? Will I need to do this and that?"

The stereotype of blind women as weak and dependent can cause some potential male partners to become fearful of having to take "feminine" roles in the relationship, such as being in charge of domestic responsibilities and child care. As Talia further explained: "Most men would prefer to date a sighted woman [ . . . ] They assume that a sighted woman doesn't need help with anything; you don't need to check for stairs in front of a restaurant when going out, or if there's an elevator, and you don't need to guide her."

The "inferior stereotyping" (Deshen 1992, 43) of blind women, based on both their blindness and femaleness, gives birth to social expectations of blind women to "marry downwards," "compromising in terms of the physical and social attributes of the groom" (44–55). Although more than twenty-five years have passed since Deshen's study, women in my research indeed expressed their understanding that society expects them to be with someone who is socially "damaged." "It's really difficult to meet a guy when you can't see," said Liron, a single, thirty-year-old congenitally blind woman from a traditional religious background. "All the matchmakers, what they brought, they brought guys who weren't okay in the head [ . . . ] and, of course, I didn't want them. I don't need someone like that." Adi, a married, twenty-five-year-old congenitally blind woman from a religious background, described being confronted with similar attitudes regarding her marriage options before her wedding:

> Society-wise, it was obvious that first of all, they needed to look for someone who had some kind of a problem and then to consider whether we're suited to each other or not. And it really pissed me off. Really! Because I don't think this should be our common ground. And I was once offered a divorced 40-year-old, thanks a lot! Not that I think they're less than me, but I wanted us to have other things in common.

Neta, who is married to a blind man, also addressed her initial reluctance to have a blind partner, making blindness what they share in common. "At a certain age and at a certain period," she said,

> I felt that being with a blind man would be a compromise, a failure. That he'd pick me just because he's blind and I'm blind; he wouldn't pick me above all other girls. I said, "What, just because I'm blind and society expects me to be with a blind person, I'm going to be with a blind person? I won't! I'll be with a sighted person."

Liron's, Adi's, and Neta's experiences narrate their encounter with the medical model of disability, which treats blindness as a "problem," and as such, something that should serve as "common ground" in a relationship between people labeled as socially inferior. On one hand, women's narratives reveal a continuum of social stereotypes of blindness but, on the other, also illustrate a change in blind women's negotiation of these stigmatic attitudes. While Deshen (1992) reported that blind women frequently accepted the "feeling of inequality of the blind in relation to the sighted in a marital context" (45–46), women I encountered rejected the notion that only a "blemished" sighted person would marry someone who is blind, and challenged disparaging attitudes by either rejecting such proposals made by people in their surroundings or looking for a sighted partner.

An additional reason for blind women's challenges in establishing intimate relationships can be found in women's descriptions of the difference in attitudes toward disability among men versus women. In this regard, interviewees described women as being more open and accepting of a partner with a disability in a romantic relationship than men are. "Blindness is very intimidating," Dvora, a thirty-year-old single mother, explained, "especially for men [ . . . ] walking with me down the street, they might feel embarrassed; introducing me to their family, they might feel embarrassed." Neta expressed a similar understanding:

> I think sighted women accept a blind man more easily than the other way around. Women can hold and contain more than men. It's more rare [for men] to understand that a [blind] woman can be independent. That really, you don't have to take care of her only because you can see and she can't. That she's not the weak person in the relationship.

Other women expressed similar notions, arguing that women are more tolerant, compassionate, and willing to accept the "other" in general, including a blind partner. "I think that women are more ready, by their nature, for a marriage with a blind or disabled man," Haya, a fifty-seven-year-old congenitally blind woman and a mother of three who is married to a sighted man, said, "they're more willing." "Women are more tolerant, more accepting," Semadar, a thirty-two-year-old congenitally blind woman who is divorced and a mother of one, added, "[They're] more willing to accept someone who's a bit different. So [this is why] blind men find it easier to have a sighted partner." And Roni, who is single, described: "More sighted women are willing to marry a blind man than the other way around. Because . . . women are more compassionate, more . . . I don't know. Men find it [blindness] intimidating." This belief was also expressed by Rinat, a forty-four-year-old visually impaired woman who is divorced and a mother of one, addressing the differences in the social pressures placed on men versus women regarding their romantic partner, and women's capacity to accept disability in their romantic relations:

> I think it's easier for blind men [ . . . ] because women are caregivers in their soul. A woman is under less social pressure. She'll marry someone blind or with another disability; she's more capable of handling social pressures. There're a lot more sighted women married to blind men than the other way around [. . . .]

Even though such descriptions of women as more "compassionate" and "tolerant" may be critiqued as essentialist, they express important sociological notions about gender and romantic relations. When blind women describe hardships in finding a partner due to men's difficulty accepting blindness and being seen with a blind woman, they express awareness of traditional perceptions of women as fulfilling the caretaker role. When Neta and others say that "sighted women accept a blind man more easily," they refer to a double social paradox in blind women's location within romantic relations. On one hand, blind men would rather not date a blind woman due to a fear that her disability would put them in the role of the caretaker, a phenomenon established in previous studies indicating that "a wife's or mother's illness or disability imposes the greatest risk to family functioning, possibly because the husband or father may be inexperienced at care giving" (Rolland 1994 in Frame 2004, 65). On the other hand, when blind women indeed express independence, they may be perceived as not "feminine" enough, creating dissonance between "social expectations and the behavior of the disabled individual" (Frame 2004, 66). Frame (2004), a visually impaired psychologist, addressed this conflict, sharing her personal experience that men find her confidence and independence intimidating, not feminine enough, but also found her "physical neediness" (67) as a disabled woman undesirable.

Blind women's descriptions of men's avoidance of an assumed caretaker role in a relationship with a blind woman also illustrate specific hardships blind women face within the Israeli context. Rinat, for example, addressed the differences between blind women and blind veterans:

> Take for example IDF [Israeli Defense Force] disabled or blind men— many of them are married to sighted women. Many. How many totally blind women or visually impaired are married to a sighted man? Maybe, maybe, maybe. . . . I'm talking about astronomical percentages, about a huge gap. That's rare [ . . . ] [When] a woman goes out with her [blind] husband, with [his] guide dog, [she] will say, "Hi, meet my husband." A man who walks out with a [blind] woman with a guide dog, [will say], "I'm helping her."

Rinat's description echoes a challenge blind women face in the Israeli context, where they negotiate not only stereotypes associating blindness with weakness but also a social system that classifies a "legitimate" disability as one associated with a heroic contribution to society (mainly of IDF veterans).[2] Deshen (1992) addressed this in his study, describing the "superior social and material status" of blind [army] veterans in the marriage market (44). Therefore, despite the evolution of the Israeli "family system" Deshen (1992) recognized as expecting both the ability and willingness of women to perform servile domestic roles in marital life and of men to be successful breadwinners (43), stigmas about blindness and disability have indeed remained and continue to play a role in blind women's romantic relations in this context. They are intertwined with what Mor (2006) identified as "Israeli ableism" (82), which has excluded deviant bodies and idealized the strong, masculine, healthy body of the pioneer, the sabra, the soldier, and the worker (Weiss 2002), creating a differentiation within the disability community (Mor 2006; Rimon-Greenspan 2007) between disabilities associated with heroic contributions, such as those of disabled veterans, and "general disabilities" (Feldman and Yahalom 2004).

Blindness and disability raise additional dilemmas for blind women in romantic situations, and women talked with frustration about "moments of blindness"—times when, because of their disability, they are dependent to some extent on their partner or companion, sometimes more than they would like to be, or in a way that could be misinterpreted as a desire for intimacy. This is linked with what Mingus (2017) terms "forced intimacy," "the common, daily experience of disabled people being expected to share personal parts of ourselves to survive in an ableist world." Blind women addressed this type of "forced intimacy" as a component they need to negotiate within romantic relations. Aviva, who is in a relationship with a sighted man, mentioned this in reference to maneuvering unfamiliar public environments; for example, she might need help locating the toilet in an unfamiliar restaurant and may need someone to accompany her in places she doesn't know, even if she doesn't want the help. "Say last week I had a fight with him [her boyfriend]," she said, "and I didn't want to hold hands while we walked! I didn't want him to come with me, but I don't know the place! You understand?" Karin, a single mother of one, described the frustration of being forced to hold onto a man when walking around or carrying out certain tasks. "[When] I need help, it weakens me," she said:

> When I need to walk around with a guy [ . . . ] or when I need to get something done, and at some point I need his help walking, or other stuff; because he's a man, the first thing he thinks is that I'm hitting on him. Even if I make it clear and say, I'm holding your hand because I can't see; I'm not hitting on you. Even if I've made it clear, in the subconscious [it doesn't matter], a physical contact was made. Touching is forced on me. You understand? [ . . . ] and it drives me crazy. It brings out the feminist bitch in me . . . and it gets out of proportion.

Rinat also described the complexities in meeting a potential partner or when going on a first date. "When you go out with someone who picks you up in his car," she said,

> And you're going, let's say, just to have coffee, on a first date, so, will you take out your cane? Will you go out with a dog? Or, alternatively, will you ask him for help? It [his help] creates this intimacy that I don't think is right for a first date, and maybe not even for a fourth, a fifth, or a tenth; it really depends on the person.

Rinat's example indicates the intricacy of her situation: if she chooses to take out her cane or to use her guide dog when meeting her date for the first time, she will have to negotiate the stereotypes associated with blindness and disability. In addition, she might not need the cane when riding in his car to a familiar place. However, if she chooses not to use the cane, she will be more dependent on her date, which also means being in a physical proximity that could signal unintended messages about intimacy and boundaries.

Rinat's description once again signifies the hardships in the sphere of romantic and gendered relations for blind women, who are perceived as dependent on others and in need of care. While this experience may be common to women with physical disabilities in general, blindness also raises specific adversities in the realm of sexual relations. The visual imagery equating erotic desire with eyesight has associated blindness with physical and symbolic castration, labeling blind people part of a "culturally constructed group," "placed beyond erotic desire and vice versa" (Bolt 2014, 53). While women did not describe social castration directly, they expressed fear of not being able to adequately fulfill their partner's desires and the challenge of not being able to communicate through visual messages. Talia, for example, described her concerns about not being "enough" for her (sighted) partner because of her inability to look at him and offer visual feedback. As she explained:

> It [blindness] also raises questions in the relationship I'm in now; it raises additional questions, because suddenly there're these moments when I say to myself, "He won't be able to stay with me because he'll never be able to please my eyes. And he'll look for it; he'll look for me enjoying the way he looks" [ . . . ] because one day it won't be enough for him to show me with his hands, to show things and explain them to me. Sometimes I have this feeling. Because he'll need his partner to enjoy the way he looks, at least the way he dresses.

Alongside their exclusion from the realm of sexual desire, blind women are also in danger of being hypersexualized as a result of the cultural fetishizing of blindness as an intensified sexuality (Rodas 2011), the association of blindness with a supranormal sense of touch, and blind sexuality as "dangerous" and uncontrolled (White 2003). Confrontations with these kinds of exoticized notions of blindness were expressed by blind women, who recalled instances in which people assumed their heightened sense of touch, as will also be discussed in chapter 4 of this book. Karin talked about the myth that blind people have a sixth sense, something she hears a lot in her work as a physiotherapist. "There's a wonderful myth that we poor blind people have a sixth sense," she said:

> It's a great myth. "You probably feel intensely!" [ . . . ] "She can't see but she can probably feel." If that's what they think, I [typically] don't ruin it for them. If it's someone I know better, I explain that it's a nice myth, but just a myth. That there are sighted people who have excellent sensory abilities, and blind people who might not feel a thing— that it's a matter of whether or not you've developed this sense. It's nonsense to think that our senses of touch or hearing are better [than sighted people's]. It's a myth because if you're blind, it doesn't mean you have this skill automatically. I, for example, can interpret a lot, really a lot, from someone's breath and voice. But this is my own development, and there might be other people who can do this as well.

While the topic of dating and romantic relations came up during interviews as a site of struggle and discrimination, interviewees also discussed blindness as offering an *opportunity* within the realm of romantic relations for rethinking traditional gender roles, such as the female caretaker, and untying the association of sexuality and romantic attraction with visuality and sight.

### "Love at First Handshake"

Conversations with women reveal that blindness allows them to challenge traditional gender roles within romantic relations by shifting the focus from visual appearance and by resisting normative social expectations about the roles of wife and mother.

First, women described the advantages of experiencing romantic relationships from the prism of multiple and rich sensory experiences. Hani, who is single, described, for example, the advantages and disadvantages of not putting much weight on her appearance or that of her partner:

In a romantic relationship . . . looks are a lot less important to me [ . . . ] I'm attracted to someone not by his looks but according to other things, tone of voice, touch. But with sighted people, it's different; they're attracted physically to what they see. Obviously, that's not all of the appeal, but it's a significant dimension of it. On one hand, it's an advantage that I really don't judge people according to their appearance, and I come from a more "clean slate" place character-wise. On the other hand, it's also a disadvantage in that it takes me more time to know whether I'm attracted to someone or not.

De-emphasizing visual appearance and instead placing value on someone's "character," in Hani's words, is interesting considering the central role of appearance management I discussed earlier in this section. This indicates that appearance has different meanings in different contexts, and that women take different notice of their own appearance versus the appearance of others. This also diverts the focus of romantic relations from sight to other dimensions, opening the door to experiencing romantic relations and sexuality from a prismatic "theory of multiple senses" (Kleege 2005, 187). Somewhat similar to Hani's subjugation of visual appearance, Talia challenged the importance of appearance in her choice of romantic partner, and when I asked her about her attitude toward her date's looks, she said, "The truth is, I don't care much," and offered as an example, "According to my friends, my second schmuck looked like a monkey wearing a sweater. And I told them that was also true when he was naked—he looked like a monkey wearing a sweater. And . . . it doesn't sound very pleasing, but, you know, I loved him for who I thought he was." "It took me a while to understand," Talia elaborated,

> That I don't need to go along with social conventions, only because society says something. When I was young, I had this thing about wanting a blond guy with blue eyes, you know. It sounds cool, but it wasn't something that came from the inside. And you know, this is what I'm happy about today, that I really don't care if his eyes are brown or green or blue or gray or black. He can have purple eyes for all I care. It really doesn't bother me.

Talia, thus, not only indicates how visual appearance became less important to her regarding her partner's looks but also that her blindness allows her to challenge social expectations of beauty when it comes to choosing a romantic partner. Similar to Talia, many blind women described their focus in sexual and romantic experiences on senses such as touch, hearing, and smell, emphasizing haptic sensations, scent, and tone of voice. When addressing touch, women included interpretations of sensations such as body heat, sweat, strength, and the nature of the touch (the handshake, the caress), addressing this sense not as a substitute to sight nor simply as a means of gaining an understanding of their date's visual characteristics, but as a somatic experience of romantic and interpersonal connections. Roni said: "The relationship wasn't in the eyes but in the hands. Let's say, [hand] shakes, for example; first of all, you hold a person's hand It's a connection, you [can] feel it; it's the touch." Talia seconded this concept: "When I meet a man, I shake his hand; and by the touch, I already know if I like him. Love at first handshake!" On another occasion, she added that she has a negative reaction to the feel of body piercings:

> It . . . doesn't sit well with my hands. I don't know, not in my head and not in my hands [ . . . ] But what I'm really attracted to are a man's hands. I knew this guy who kept asking me all the time to give him a chance and all that, and I just couldn't, because his hands were sweaty, and . . . clammy, you know, really unpleasant to touch; and just to imagine having those hands on my body . . . it really wasn't attractive in my imagination. What's more important to me is what I touch.

And Marla, a twenty-one-year-old single blind woman, said that what she likes about her boyfriend is "his warm body." Sonic experiences were also central in blind women's choice of a romantic partner. Many women mentioned their partner's vocal qualities as what made them attracted to them or curious to know them, describing having a "weakness" for certain types of voices. "Voice means a lot to me," Roni said. "A person's voice means a lot. Um . . . conversation, this simple chemistry, it's something you just can't explain. It's this tension in the air, and this click that happens." Yael, who is single, also mentioned the importance of a person's voice, even directly challenging the centrality typically given to sight within cultural imagery. "It's the voice," she said. "[He] needs to have a pleasant voice. There're men that I can't go near just because of their voice. I'm very sensitive to the intonation. I can read meanings in people's voices. You know what they say—that the eyes are the mirror to the soul? I think that's bullshit!" Women also addressed smell and aroma as important in this sensory alignment and testified to the importance of cleanliness and aesthetics. Dina, a congenitally blind nineteen-year-old single woman, mentioned smell when asked about what is important to her in her partner: "If he's stinky or doesn't smell good, I could die." And when asked the same question, Rinat said, "The smell and aesthetics are very important to me; it's very meaningful to me. If someone smells a bit off, he's immediately out of the question."

In addition to referring to sensorially enriched romantic relations and sexual attraction, women talked about blindness as allowing an alternative marital path from that of their sisters, or peers from the same social background, and offering a certain amount of freedom from expected gendered roles. "If I were sighted, today I would be married, plus three," Ora, a single twenty-nine-year-old woman who has been blind from age three, told me. Ora, who comes from a traditional Ethiopian family, emphasized in our interview that given her ethnic and religious background, her blindness freed her from social expectations around marriage:

> On one hand, it's good that I can't see, because the culture I'm from [ . . . ] it's good I'm in this position because I have a lot of choice. There're plenty things I've done that my sisters couldn't [ . . . ] like . . . I've been freer although I'm blind; not although, *because* of this situation, that's what came out [of it].

While identifying blindness as a way out of traditional gender roles, women also addressed it as a way *in*, delivering the message that a woman can be blind and sexy or function as a mother if she chooses to. Anna, for instance, a thirty-year-old single mother who has been blind from age four, said that she didn't hesitate about her wish to become a mother and went against society's and even her partner's opinion on that matter. Dvora, who is also a single mother, mentioned similarly how she had to fight the authorities in order to be in control of the assistance she received as a new mother.[3]

Blindness also challenges assumptions about disability within romantic and social relationships more broadly, with women using it as a test, in a way, a means to find "real" love. As Neta said: "I've been with a few sighted people who theoretically had no limitations, but God help me! What bullshit and what demons they have in their heads." Women expressing this approach treated blindness as an opportunity to deliver the message that there are important things other than sight by which romantic and social relationships can be judged. "There's plenty of sighted people I know who can't see a thing!" Aviva said:

> I'm sorry, I know a lot of people who . . . see with their eyes but can't read their environment; [that] don't get it, dumb. And . . . I wouldn't go

out with them [just] because they're sighted. Definitely not! Like . . . not everything begins and ends in the eyes.

Adi concurred with this notion, recalling something her sighted husband once told her when she was occupied with the effect of her disability on their relationship. "[People] always treat blindness as . . . something special," he said. "But there's blindness in every relationship."

# Conclusion

## *Performing a Feminine–Blind–Personhood*

The analysis presented in this section explored the dualities embedded in the intersection of blindness and gender. While social assumptions treat the integration of femininity and blindness as a paradox, blind women's narratives reveal not only that being blind and feminine is not an oxymoron but also that blindness allows an opportunity to "redefine" femininity, using Rosemarie Garland-Thomson's (in Brueggemann et al. 2005, 15) words. They allow rethinking the topic of stigma management and women's agency, revealing the various ways in which women negotiate acceptance, assimilation, and subversion within modern visual cultures.

Women's narratives express an awareness of visual culture as an ability to perform, enact, and decipher the visual norms of sexuality, beauty, and femininity, and point out feminine appearance as a powerful tool within stigma management that allows them to be actively involved in the ways they are perceived. Through appearance management, blind women seek to challenge stigmatizing attitudes by resisting the "normative" script written for them as blind women, revealing the existence of a female subject who actively chooses how to manage her appearance and romantic relations. Visual culture then, with its norms regarding femininity and gender, is a system central within everyday interactions, one women participate in regardless of being sighted.

Blind women's femininity, as diverse as it is, also offers an alternative approach to the social order, since it questions what counts as "disability" within social and romantic relationships and deconstructs taken-for-granted socialization mechanisms and gender norms typically silently operating through the visual. The docile feminine body, blind women's narratives reveal, is also socialized through senses other than sight and is linked not only with beauty norms but also with discourse of normalcy. In addition, resisting stigma through appearance is not necessarily an attempt at passing or concealing the disabled look but can be a means of linking disability with femininity, for example, or blindness with personhood.

Further, blind women's gender performance reveals the complicated nature of blindness, which functions as a disciplinary mechanism operated upon women's bodies and at the same time disrupts expectations and imbues agency. While third wave feminist studies have indeed argued that women find embodied discipline practices both empowering and oppressive (Weitz 2001, 668), blind women's experiences reveal a subtle attempt to negotiate the stigmatizing dynamics of blindness, gender, and disability from an unapologetic standpoint. Through appearance management, blind women endeavor to reclaim subjectivity as a feminine-blind-person, not to "escape" their blind identity or to become sighted; and within the realm of romantic relationships, blind women use their blindness to facilitate an association among blindness, disability, and sexuality. In this, blind women's performances demonstrate the feminist argument that "women are savvy to cultural pressures about the body and may use this awareness to their advantage, seeking power through the exploitation of cultural scripts of female beauty" (Tyner and Ogle 2007, 78). This standpoint also contributes to the debate between the constructivist "social model" approach to disability, which emphasizes social barriers and limitations (Oliver 1996), and the "essentialist" approach, which recognizes the material reality of actual pain and illness in the everyday lives of people with disabilities (Thomas 2002). Within this debate, blind women reveal their simultaneous negotiation of *cultural prejudices* about the roles of "women," "the blind," and "the disabled," and of *embodied sensations* such as the tactile, auditory, and olfactory experiences that accompany their everyday performance. "After all," White (2003) assured us in his article, "blind sexuality is not really a problem at all. It is a political opportunity" (144).

# Section II

# Blindness and Visual Culture

*The Dynamics of Gaze, Staring, and Display*

—❦—

> Visual culture entails a meditation on blindness, the invisible, the
> unseen, the unseeable, and the overlooked. (Mitchell 2002, 170)

The *phenomenon of display* is central within the relations between blindness
and visual culture: the display of blind women on the street and the display
of blindness and, I argue, of sight, in a museum exhibit. By attending to the
theme of display, I offer a reading of the types of gazes blind women experience in their everyday lives and of the staring mechanisms society directs
at blindness as a cultural category. When using the term "visual culture," I
embrace W. J. T. Mitchell's (2002) definition of this field as not limited to the
study of images or media but rather "the study of all the social practices of
human visuality" (174), extended to "everyday practices of seeing and showing" (170).

My research has indicated to me that blindness is a useful site from
which to rethink those practices Mitchell calls "seeing and showing." During the course of this research, the subject of staring and the gaze was not
only central within women's narratives as told in interviews but was also an
issue I experienced when walking around with research participants or during research observations. For example, when we walked down the street
arm-in-arm, people commonly stared at us, giving me a look of admiration
for helping a blind person. I remember a time when I was walking down
the street with Talia, a research participant who became a good friend. Talia
had come to visit me at my new apartment and held my arm as we walked
down the crowded street on our way to have lunch. My partner joined

us, and I gave him my hand, with my free arm. He happened to be wearing sunglasses, and we suddenly noticed that people were looking at us as
though I was leading two blind people, one on each arm. I received stares
of admiration and empathy while people gazed at my partner and at Talia,
not knowing that my partner could see them. On other occasions, people
thought I was blind myself and allowed themselves to stare at me. This
happened, for example, on some occasions during my fieldwork with the
tandem cycling group of blind and sighted participants. As I will explain
in chapter 9 when discussing this research site, I usually participated in the
rides as the rear rider—a position typically occupied by a blind person. As
a result, people who did not know me or the group were led to think that I
was blind or disabled. The stares I received were indeed useful as a research
tool but unpleasant on a personal level. People looked at me inquisitively,
as if checking to see what was wrong with me, and sometimes talked to me
very loudly and very slowly.[1]

In this section of the book, I expand on these kinds of notions and stares,
arguing for the ways blindness can lead to rethinking how we see and what
we see, offering insights into questions such as what are the differences and
similarities between different types of gazes directed at blindness? What are
the agentic possibilities of blind women occupying the role of the staree? And
what are the conditions and consequences of the (blind) Other looking back?

I address these questions through two research sites. In the first chapter
of this section (chapter 6), I discuss blind women's negotiation of staring and
the gaze in their everyday lives, addressing different types of gazes directed
at them, including the normalizing gaze, which pathologizes their condition and erases their sexuality, and the masculine gaze, which eroticizes their
sexuality. In chapter 7, I offer an analysis of the way blindness is displayed in a
dark museum exhibit where sighted visitors are led by blind guides, addressing the orientalist and colonizing gaze, which exoticize blindness. This section as a whole presents an overall analysis of the ways society sees blindness
and of the ways blind people look back. The two chapters of this section offer
different interpretations of the politics of the gaze and of scopic regimes. The
first presents blind women's experiences and negotiation of staring, which
challenge the common notion of "being stared at" as consisting primarily
of dynamics of objectification and dehumanization. These incidents indicate
that staring-back practices are possible for blind women, and that the gaze
can work as a site of intersubjective communication. The dark museum exhibit, on the other hand, enacts the gaze as an act of domination, an orientalist gaze that constitutes the native (blind) Other versus the modern (sighted)

self. As in the rest of the book, chapters 6 and 7 create a dialogue with each other, presenting a conversation between blind women's daily experiences (as well as sighted people's understanding of the categories of blindness and sight) and representations of blindness, demonstrated by the ways blindness is displayed in the exhibit. Together, the two chapters allow asking about the conditions in which looking at the other takes the form of power relations versus the instances in which gazing functions as a mutual exchange that can serve to challenge social boundaries.

My impression that blindness is a site relevant to the research of visual culture, and more specifically for the study of dynamics of staring and display, stems from the dialogue among scholars of visual culture who have discussed the intertwining relations of blindness and sight. Kleege (2005), for example, addressed the need to investigate seeing and the visual from the standpoint of a blind person, moving beyond the "simple blindness versus sight binary" (188); Elkins (1997) argued for the ways blindness happens alongside seeing—"that is, it happens while we are seeing" (205), disputing the notion that blindness is the opposite of seeing; Jay (2012) addressed sight as an apparatus that not only consists of moments of visual clarity but also of "fuzzy haze," "natural limits," and "spatial blurring" (221); and Mitchell (2001) explained how vision and blindness coexist. "It is not that there is 'normal seeing,' clear, uninterrupted, and transparent," he writes. "Such a seeing would in fact be blindness. Normal seeing is intermittent, jumpy, interrupted, and blinkered" (394).[2]

My research has shown additional ways in which blindness and sight coexist and different reasons for thinking about visual culture through blindness. First, because blind people are typically being stared at and serve as the object of the gaze,[3] blind women's experiences are a significant source from which we can learn about the position of the staree, the experience of being seen, and the tasks involved in negotiating different types of gazes. Blind women may be considered by sighted people "safe" to stare at, typically assumed ignorant of the looks directed at them as outsiders to this visual exchange. But as discussed in chapter 3 of this book, blind women are actively involved in visual culture and manage their appearance to display a specific feminine look. The misconception of blindness as a position external from visual culture further emboldens the male gaze when directed toward blind women, "a position of privilege in social relations which entitles men to look at women and positions women as objects of that look" (Garland-Thomson 2009, 41). While experiencing hypervisibility then, as the object of the gaze, blind women are also commonly placed by society outside the realm of femininity, and thus are subjected to a normalizing gaze that tends to erase their

gender and sexuality. Blind women's position within visual culture is therefore complex, consisting of hypervisibility *and* invisibility, and thus useful for
the study of the relations among different types of gazes and of the experience of the staree.

Secondly, blindness is important for the research of visual culture since it
challenges the taken-for-grantedness of sight. As Michalko (1998) noted: "I
came to understand that thinking about something natural required a disrup-
tion to that naturalness [ . . . ] my blindness provided me with the 'sight' necessary to read the story of sightedness" (113). Indeed, blind women's responses
to the gazes they encounter disrupt the typical power relations between the
starer and the staree and ask sighted people looking at blind women to reflect on the way they see blindness, disability, and gender. Similarly, encounters with blindness and blind people in the dark museum challenge visitors'
taken-for-granted sightedness. And although these encounters do not dis-
mantle stereotypes of blindness, as I demonstrate in chapter 7, they can teach
us about the mechanisms of the orientalist gaze.

Thirdly, blindness is important to the research of visual culture since, as a
social category, it is part of visual culture's logic of "ocularcentrism"—a set of
attitudinally generated social practices that privilege vision and debase blindness (Jay 1993). Within this vision-generated, vision-centered interpretation
of knowledge, truth, and reality that characterizes visual culture,[4] vision is
cast as not only dominant but superior to other ways of knowing (Omansky
2011), while blindness is perceived as the opposite of reason. Therefore, when
blind women stare back, or when blind guides are put in a position of authority in the dark museum, ocularcentrism is challenged. Ocularcentrism is
also tackled when the narratives of blind people teach us that blindness and
sight are not distinct, binary categories, but coexisting, and consist of multisensorial mechanisms that are engaged even when eyesight is prevented, as
in the dark museum.

Finally, it is important to note that in employing blindness to learn about
the visual, I do not take an "anti-visualist" stand. While previous research
has tended to challenge the dominancy of vision in modern Western culture
by ignoring vision at the expense of sound, smell, touch, or taste,[5] I ask to
*reexamine* the visual experience as consisting of blindness *and* sight. Therefore, rather than joining a "recent commitment in anthropology to making a
case against vision" (Willerslev 2009, 24), by examining the experience of the
visual among blind and sighted research participants, I ask to contribute to
what Grasseni (2009) called the "anthropology of vision," investigating the
"actual processes of visual training that engender certain kinds of sociality,
ideology, and standards of practice" (5).[6]

Embracing this call to investigate the processes of "visual training," in this section, I employ blindness to examine the socialization processes instrumental in forming a person's sighted or blind identity, his/her ability to stare back, and the formation of visual relations as consisting of both domination and subjectification. In this, I ask to problematize the concept of the gaze, demonstrating (a) that visual relations function not only as a panoptic framework but also a rich field of meaning in which individuals assumed to hold a subjugated position can express agency and activity; (b) that visual relations consist of contradictory dynamics of gazing based, among others, on gender and disability; and (c) that the "gaze" is a broad concept, consisting not only of direct visual observation but also experiences and ideas that can be employed through senses other than sight.

*Six*

# Blind Women's Negotiation of Staring and the Gaze

⸺∘≋∘⸺

[S]taring can be a mutually vivifying visual dance in which starers and starees engage one another. (Garland-Thomson 2009, 5)[1]

Although it is an uncommon way to describe starer-staree power relations, "visual dance" is a term surprisingly fitting to describe the relationship between blind women and the gaze. Through conversations with blind women, I learned that the experience of being stared at and serving as a spectacle is central in their everyday lives. The experience of serving as a spectacle and being aware of the gaze is not unique to people with disabilities and has been acknowledged by feminist scholars and researchers of visual culture (Tyler 1984; Classen 1998; Kleege 1999) as relevant to women in general. This experience is also fundamental to people with visible disabilities, resulting from the curiosity, fear, and discomfort the disabled body prompts. As Garland-Thomson (2005a) described:

> Despite the ubiquitous admonitions not to stare, even children learn very early that disability is a potent form of embodied difference that warrants looking, even prohibited looking. Indeed, the stare is the dominant mode of looking at disability in this culture. (31)

While blind women indeed share the experience of being stared at with other women, and particularly women with visible disabilities, blind women, being both blind and women, are the object of numerous types of gazes, including the male gaze (directed at the female body) and the normalizing gaze (directed at the disabled body), while also being assumed safe to stare at, blind to the gaze. These factors related specifically to their blindness, in a way, posit blind women as the ultimate subject of the stare, as they are not only visibly different (when walking with a cane or a guide dog) but also assumed unaware of their visibility, ignorant of the gaze directed at them.

However, blind women are not only aware of the gaze and of the liminal characteristics attributed to their location, but they also employ sophistication, creativity, and agency when responding to the gaze. As I demonstrated in chapter 3, blind women are indeed involved in visual culture; they hold visual knowledge regarding beauty and femininity and employ strategies of appearance management that allow them to be actively involved in the ways they are perceived. While in chapters 3 and 4 I discussed blind women's involvement in visual culture in relation to feminine performance, in this chapter I focus on how blind women participate in the gaze, taking an active part in this visual dance. Their responses to the gaze allow examining how *different gazes operate*, and the similarities and differences between the terms "gaze" and "staring," contributing to a broader understanding of women's agency in visual culture.

## "You Feel Like Some Kind of Poster":
## Blind Women as the Object of the Stare

> Beautiful people complain that potential friends and lovers are intimidated by their looks and that potential employers doubt their intelligence. They should spend more time with the blind because we have much in common. We too know what it's like to create a sensation when we walk down the street. We know how it feels to be judged for our appearance alone. (Kleege 2001, 48)

As Kleege ironically describes, the experience of living with blindness is very much about learning to "manage staring" (Brueggemann et al. 2005, 20). Women I interviewed shared in common the experience of being stared at and attested not only to their awareness of it but also to actively reflecting on the meaning implicit in staring. These narratives underscore the fact that even though one can imagine blind women may not be aware of people's stares, staring is a dominant component of their daily lives. This came up in my conversations with Einat, a twenty-seven-year-old congenitally blind woman I met at one of my observation sites and also interviewed on the topics of gender and femininity. Einat works as a coach and consultant and conceptualizes herself as a culturally sighted person. "My parents decided to raise me like an ordinary girl. Not from a place of denial—I know I can't see—but I'm living my life as a sighted person in every aspect." When we discussed her visual knowledge, Einat also addressed her awareness of her visuality, acknowledging that even though she cannot see others, others indeed look at her. As she explained:

> You can't ignore the fact that human interaction starts with the first impression, and you have to be aware of it. Now, to say "I don't see, so I'm exempt from this," I think it's not right, on the contrary! It means that when you don't see but give a message that you're well-groomed and wear makeup, you make people want to talk to you and take an interest in you. I don't think that if you can't see, then others can't see you either. It's not true. It's true only in a room full of blind people, and then all you have to do is wear perfume, if you even care.

In this, Einat expressed her awareness of several topics. First, that visual impressions, especially first impressions, have a crucial impact on people's perceptions of others in our visual culture. Second, that her appearance is a means of communicating with others and delivering messages regarding her personality, ability, and skills ("to make people want to talk to you"). And third, that even in a room "full of blind people," some sort of judgment of each other will take place, maybe by smell rather than sight.

Other research participants reiterated Einat's awareness, acknowledging that they are highly aware of others looking at them, and that the stares are often accompanied by verbal comments, whispering, and gestures such as finger pointing. Aviva, a twenty-seven-year-old woman who has been blind from the age of six, described her awareness of people's reactions to her blindness:

> I know that people see me and look at me; I understand that when I stand at a bus stop with the cane, people look at me [ . . . ] Today I went on a bus, and someone was whispering: "Wow, she really can't see?" And her friend tells her: "Yeah, she really can't see, but look how nice her hair is." And the other one says: "Shh . . . be quiet so she won't hear us." I wanted to tell them that I already had!

In our interview, Aviva not only addressed her awareness of the way people look at her as blind and a woman but also as a person belonging to an ethnic and racial identity. Aviva immigrated to Israel from Ethiopia as a girl and mentioned in the interview that she is also aware Ethiopian Jews in the Israeli context are considered as belonging to a low economic and social status; and that because of her skin color, when she goes to the theater for example, people who do not recognize that she is blind have assumed that she is the cleaning lady, rather than an audience member.

Adi, a twenty-five-year-old congenitally blind woman, also spoke of comments she receives. An Orthodox Jew who was newly married when we met, Adi addressed her awareness of the ways she is judged as a blind married woman, sharing her experience of the gaze in the context of her marital status, and her anxieties about her husband's feelings regarding staring:

> I was concerned that my husband would be intimidated by the stares we get from people in the street, because it's really—really irritating. You feel like some . . . I don't know, like you're some kind of poster; and it's clear to me that they stare, and they don't even bother to hide it, you know. They come up and ask questions, like: "What, are you dating?" And I think, "What do you care?!"

Adi's anxiety has to do with the stares she receives not only as a blind woman using a cane but also as a blind woman displaying a relationship with a sighted, non-disabled man. This echoes my discussion in chapter 5 regarding blind women's challenges within romantic relationships and society's expectation of blind women to date disabled or blind men.

Women also addressed comments their cane or guide dog attract, comments that convey the message they are a "stareable sight" (Garland-Thomson 2009, 21). Tamar, a twenty-four-year-old congenitally blind woman who uses a guide dog, noted, "When I walk around with my dog, I attract lots of attention. Sometimes my friends tell me they're sick of the stares. I don't know if people are staring at me or the dog." As I mentioned in chapter 2, I experienced such stares myself when walking around with Tamar in a central bus station where we conducted the interview and as we navigated together the elevator, the coffee shop, and the entrance to the restroom. And Neriya, a visually impaired woman in her forties whose vision has gradually deteriorated, described the attention her cane attracts. "[When I use my cane] people treat me as though I've been blind from birth," she said. "[They think] I've never been able to see, I have no idea what colors are, [that] I know nothing about appearance, I have no sense of orientation." Neriya's cane marks her as blind in the stereotypical sense with people, upon noticing her cane, wrongly assuming that she is congenitally blind and ignorant of visual knowledge.

Women also conveyed that they know they are being stared at based on their experiences while accompanied in public by a sighted person. Family or friends sometimes remark on the fact that sighted people stare, and in some cases, that they stare back. Aviva related that she and her friends have their own private language and "code words" about staring situations, having "all kinds of terms for staring." And Anat, a thirty-four-year-old congenitally blind woman, described the "evil eye" her partner and mother give people who stare at her. "My partner started to stare back at people who stare at me like I'm a monkey in the circus; staring back at them with a look that says 'what are you looking at?' My mother calls it the 'evil eye'—shooting sparks at them." Anat, who identifies as a lesbian, also talked about the social gaze she experiences as a blind lesbian woman among blind people, as well as in the LGBT community, both communities treating her with restraints and exclusion.

Some women spoke of experiencing the normalizing gaze, an expression of the ableist perspective of "physical normality" (Wendell 1996, 88) that infantilizes blind people and considers their need for help a burden. Noa, a twenty-five-year-old congenitally blind woman, described encountering this in school. "I hated when people wanted to see me as a childish person or something like that," she said. "I had to . . . approach [my teacher] for everything, and I felt that she was treating me like a little girl, asking me what I needed; and it really irritated me that she didn't get it." Noa described the gaze as not restricted to her interactions with sighted people. "Even among blind people, I felt blind," Noa explained. "[It felt like] I was being measured by others, just like I was measuring them." Noa's experience of the gaze among her blind peers indicates once again that blind people participate in visual culture. This demonstrates that the gaze is not really about sight but is a phenomenon rooted in cultural beliefs and values; therefore, as cultural citizens of visual culture, blind people participate in it, too. As Adi, Avivia, Neriya, and Noa describe, staring is commonly accompanied by words and gestures blind women indeed hear and feel. This recognition allows expanding the concept of the gaze from that of an act employing the eyes to an act that makes use of additional sensory and bodily experiences. This broader understanding of the gaze is important in order to better describe the relations of vision to the other senses, as well as to language. It refutes a simplistic division of sight and the other senses, as well as of sight and blindness as binary, separate worlds of meaning, offering a more complex interpretation of the many ways blindness and sight, and sight and the other senses, are interdependent. That some are surprised blind women are indeed aware of the gaze and possess visual knowledge is in itself evidence of commonly held, bifurcated definitions of sight as opposed to blindness, and visual as opposed to nonvisual communication. The gaze, therefore, can be defined more broadly, as not simply people looking at blind women, but people projecting the stigmatizing cultural conceptions of blindness and disability through staring and through verbal reactions to blindness.

## Gender and Disability, The Gaze and Staring

Blind women's perpetual awareness of being stared at resonates with feminist interpretations of the objectifying gaze as one that places women in the passive role of spectacles who serve as "an object of vision, a sight" (Berger 1973, 47) under the dominant male gaze. Aviva, for example, conveyed frustration about her inability to control the gaze:

> It upsets me that people can look at me and stare at me [ . . . ] but I can't suddenly look back and take someone's eyes off me. It's like, "OK, you can see that I don't see, that's enough! Stop staring at me." And I'm not hallucinating. I'm not . . . paranoid. It's real. I'd like to be able to decide for people how much they can or cannot look at me. I don't feel like having people stare at me. And it's not that I have something to hide, no, I just want to be able to control it like every other person. I just know they stare all the time; "enough people, snap out of it. You understand what's going on, who this girl is, that's enough."

Aviva's description shares similarities with feminist interpretations of the gaze as a power mechanism directed upon women in visual culture. However, feminist theory of the gaze might not agree with Aviva's notion that if she were sighted, she might be able to resist and control the gaze. Her narrative actually resonates with feminist theorization of the gaze as constituting a female subject that internalizes the gaze, constantly watching herself being looked at, regardless of whether she is sighted or blind.

While Aviva's and other blind women's descriptions of their experiences share similarities with feminist interpretations of the gaze, they do not produce a simple parallel between "the gaze" and "staring." Located in a precarious position where sexuality, gender, and disability converge, blind women's position in relation to staring and visibility is complex. On one hand, blind women's visibility is intensified, attracting stares and serving as a spectacle under both the male and the normalizing gaze. On the other, blind women's visuality is simultaneously erased, as they are often perceived as marginal subjects since their disability raises doubts about their ability to fulfill the role of wife and mother, or that of a sexual partner, as I illustrated in chapter 3.[2]

Ayelet, a thirty-three-year-old congenitally blind woman, described this duality between visibility and invisibility and argued that the stares she receives result from her disability rather than her femininity. "I'd like to walk down the street without attracting any attention," she asserted. "But because I'm blind, I get the attention anyway, and not because I'm a woman; and it's not fun." Ayelet emphasized that her wish to be more anonymous or unmarked as a blind woman does not express a desire to hide her blindness, nor does it mean she is ashamed of it. This was evident even by the location Ayelet chose for our interview: a public park near her apartment. As she said: "Not that I want to hide my blindness; you see, I'm here, sitting with you in the park."

Ayelet thus emphasized that she feels invisible as a woman but visible as a blind person. In his article, *Seeing Disability*, Mitchell (2001) addressed this duality of hypervisibility—"being remarked, noticed, stared at," and its "dialectical twin: invisibility" as "crucial to the experience of disability" (393). Mitchell discusses this "dynamic of exchange and transformation between the visible and the invisible" in relation to stuttering, deafness, and mental illness, and writes about the parallels of disabled people's hypervisibility/invisibility and that of other marginal, marked groups. He mentions, for example, Ralph Ellison's novel *Invisible Man*, in which "Ellison's man is not literally invisible. His problem is that his racial markings as an African American are hypervisible, and so his identity as a human being and a speaking subject is rendered invisible" (2001, 393). Blindness is extremely relevant to this duality of visibility/invisibility and especially the position of blind women, who negotiate staring directed at them as both blind and women, simultaneously experiencing an intensified visibility as the object of the staring and a denial of their public and personal visibility as fully human and sexual beings.

The position of blind women reveals a disparity between gender and disability systems of constructing identity through the gaze (Sandahl 1999; Samuels 2002; Garland-Thomson 2005b), not only because of their negotiation of invisibility/hypervisibility but also because of their experience of being considered as asexual. While women typically experience the gaze as one that constructs them as sexual objects for the pleasure of male spectators, some of the women in my research described the experience of being perceived as asexual, experiencing staring that placed them outside the realm of femininity and (heteronormative) sexuality. (It is important to note, however, that while stigmatized as asexual, disability intensifies the risk of sexual assault and violence [Curry et al. 2001].) Talia, thirty-one years old, blind from age three, spoke of her "invisibility" as a woman and sexual being, referring to her adolescent years. At the age of sixteen, she felt transparent in terms of her sexuality:

> I felt like air, I felt like . . . the boys weren't looking at me as a girl; I was . . . a *person*. And I was literally a girl in every sense, you know, but I didn't feel like they were looking at me as a girl who had the potential to be interesting or anything. I felt like they looked through me. Just through me. The boys, I mean . . . I wasn't treated as a woman or as someone who belonged to a specific sex.

Importantly, while offering this narrative in Hebrew, Talia used the English word *person*, emphasizing the gender-neutral way in which her peers looked at her and her feeling of being sexually invisible. It underscores an experience many women conveyed to me. Anat expressed a similar notion also in a non-heterosexual context. "When I went to events [in the LGBT community], I was like air. Didn't talk [to me], didn't pay attention, nothing. And I tried to hit on girls, and they evaded with all kinds of excuses."

This social perception of disabled women as asexual has been widely discussed by disability studies and feminist scholars,[3] and as demonstrated here, it is also relevant to blind women. As Deborah Kent (1987) describes:

> People may pity the disabled woman for her handicap, or admire her for her strength in overcoming it, but she is too unlike other females to be whistled at on the street. If men don't make passes at girls who wear glasses, what chance does a blind girl have, or one in a wheelchair, or a woman with spastic hands? (82–83)

Scholars of blindness, disability, and sexuality explain different possible reasons for the exclusion of blind women from the realm of sexuality. When Omansky (2011), for example, writes about societal stereotypes of blind women as asexual (12), she cites White's (2003, 134) discussion of heterosexual beliefs that construct sexuality as a visual process, which, as a result, frames young blind people as sexually underdeveloped. Indeed, a common belief regarding sexuality "is that only through vision one can see a man/woman to whom one is attracted" (Limaye 2003, 95). Others argue that the perception of blind women as asexual may also be based on the cultural association of blindness with castration (Bolt 2014, 51) and of romantic love and sexual arousal with sight and the eye (Kleege 1999; Rodas 2011). As Kleege (1999) writes: "The act of seeing plays a large part in male sexual arousal [ . . . ] what you can't see, you can't want. And don't forget: masturbation will make you blind" (24).

Paradoxically, while experiencing invisibility to the male gaze, blind women indeed experience staring and are sexualized in other ways. Talia, for example, alongside feeling transparent to the gaze as a woman, also acknowledged being stared at. She recalled a boy at her school telling a friend of hers that, "The guy who goes out with her will be really lucky, because she'll need to touch him in order to know what he looks like." After hearing this, "I just sat there on the sidewalk bursting with laughter," Talia said. "Because it was really funny to me, you know, it's like . . . they really didn't know anything about blindness." Talia's story—of feeling on one hand "like air" and on the other learning she is the topic of conversation—reveals the contradictory ways blind women's femininity and sexuality are perceived. While her blindness and disability make her invisible to the male gaze, distancing her from the realms of heteronormative femininity and sexuality, it also fetishizes her as being imbued with an intensified sexuality (Rodas 2011). The stares she receives, then, acknowledge both her femininity and disability, enfolding her "freakishly disabled body [ . . . ] into the freakishly gendered body" (Samuels 2002, 63).[4]

During an interview, Talia told me another story that demonstrates blind women's paradoxical location between visibility and invisibility, and the complexities of visual systems of staring and the gaze. While walking down the street with her cousin, whom Talia describes as "a very beautiful girl," Talia recounted:

> Suddenly, my cousin said, "I'm sick of it! [ . . . ] I'm sick of the staring." "It's because you're beautiful," I told her. [And my cousin said] "No, Talia, it's because you're blind." [So I asked her] "Ho, ye? What's there to look at?" And she answered, "I don't know; they stare 'cause you're blind."

In this occurrence, Talia and her cousin shared the experience of walking through life visible and exposed. Yet while Talia knows that her cousin attracts the *gaze*, an observation and appreciation of her body as human and sexual, Talia's cousin recognizes that Talia is the object of *staring*, an assessment of her body as asexual and medically different. This difference resonates with Garland-Thomson's (2005a, 32) analysis of the gaze directed at the female body and staring directed at the disabled body:

> The male gaze produces female subjects; the normative stare constructs the disabled. While both are forms of visual marking, gazing trades on a sexual register and staring traffics in medical discourse. Both visual exchanges prompt narrative. Gazing says, "You are mine." Staring says, "What is wrong with you?"

Talia's story also indicates, however, the ways in which staring and the gaze, rather than discrete binary functions, are in fact intertwined. The stares Talia received result from both her disability and her femininity, as blind women present an "unexpected body" (Garland-Thomson 2009, 58) in the public sphere. Being a woman and blind, Talia experiences both staring *and* the gaze, as her blindness intensifies her visibility, placing her under the dominant male gaze that addresses women as spectacles and also under the normalizing gaze, which pathologizes her appearance. Moreover, the gaze not only marks her identity as an anomaly but also "defines and legitimizes the normalized" (Garland-Thomson 1997, 17). Therefore, the beauty associated with the stares Talia's cousin attracts stands in contrast to the otherness attributed to Talia, indicating the ways asexuality, gender, and disability converge.

Blind women's paradoxical location between invisibility and visibility was expressed by other women as well. Ayelet described the ways her blindness intensifies her visibility: "I'm exposed [to staring] both because I'm a woman and because I'm blind [ . . . ] a woman is by definition more exposed. And then, if you're blind, you're more exposed because you don't see them, any of them, but everyone sees you." And Neta, a thirty-six-year-old congenitally blind woman, addressed the challenges she has to cope with as blind and a woman, and in our interview, criticized the visual norms and beauty standards women are compelled to follow, which apply to her as well.[5] The stares blind women attract, therefore, indicate their location as both *women and blind*, as evidenced by the comments they receive such as "What, are you dating?" as Adi described earlier, or "Look how nice her hair is," as Aviva mentioned.

## "If They're Going to Stare, At Least I'll Give Them a Good Reason To": Blind Women Staring Back

Goffman (1972) noted decades ago that staring challenges the unspoken "ease" of "public relations," often motivating the individual being stared at to put on a show. And indeed, in reaction to their complicated and contradictory position as the staree, several blind women described putting on a type of a "show," taking the role of an active performer. This active role challenges feminist interpretations of the gaze that have typically considered a woman's role as that of a passive spectacle. As Mitchell (2001) explains, "politics of the gaze" automatically assume power to be held by the spectator and associate the position of the visual object with powerlessness and victimization (393). Visual culture in general has been identified as consisting of scopic regimes where vision and visual images are expressions of power relations in which the spectator dominates the visual object and images, and their producers exert power over viewers (Mitchell 2002, 172).

Blind women's experiences of staring reveal their position as *active subjects* in staring relations, negotiating the meanings attached to their social positions to turn staring into a site of communication in which messages are exchanged between the starer and the staree. Aware of their position as social spectacles, on different occasions blind women embrace these situations as an opportunity to address the stares, spontaneously or deliberately.

In some situations, blind women employ nonverbal reactions to staring and the gaze, juxtaposing the overly theatrical with the everyday aspects of social performance, as in the case of Talia, who embraces the position of an active agent in reaction to the ways she and her blindness are perceived. The first thing I noticed about Talia when she opened the door to her parents' house, where we met for our first interview, was the amusing statement on her T-shirt: "If you can read this, you're standing too close," expressing her awareness of the visual and her attempt, by wearing it, to communicate with people looking at her, claiming her role in visual culture. On some occasions, Talia uses a written medium to address staring, as in her blog posts; in other instances, she responds nonverbally to the staring she attracts. This happened on the occasion mentioned earlier in which Talia was stared at while walking down the street with her beautiful cousin. In response, after learning she was being stared at, Talia started to dance. "Yes!" she said, when I responded with surprise to her story. "And my cousin asked me, 'What are you doing?' and I said, 'Well, if they're going to stare, at least I'll give them a good reason to!'" By dancing in the street when being stared at, Talia simultaneously collaborated with the situation by attracting people's gazes, and ridiculed it by dancing.

Other women relayed different accounts of performances they engaged in as reactions to their presence in the visual realm, in these cases a more direct and pedagogical approach to staring. Neriya, for instance, described her reaction to the gaze as an attempt to create change in society's attitudes toward blind people and people with disabilities, advocating in particular for blind women and mothers. Neriya responds verbally to the gaze and people's comments, initiating direct communication with the starer. For example, when exposed to the stereotypes that associate her disability with asexuality, incompetence, and congenital blindness, she offers her personal story to defy the stigmatization of her blindness, complicating the "inherent" notions of what blindness is. "I always explain to them that I'm a mother, that my pregnancies damaged my sensations, so I can't learn Braille; I tried to, but I can't. I became blind during my adult life; I've learned and gotten used to it." Educating the starer through conversation, Neriya challenges the common exclusion of women with disabilities from the realms of sexuality, femininity, and motherhood by integrating the worlds of blindness and motherhood in her narrative. On other occasions, she claims her voice and her right to move freely in the public sphere as the object of the stare by approaching people she hears and sees. As she described:

> If I'm walking with my cane and a mother warns her child "be careful, a cane, a blind person, be careful," she gives him the feeling that a blind person with a cane is something horrible. But I hear this, and I stop, and I say "Hi, darling, hi, mama, I'm also a mother and have a child your age. Come, look at my cane, look at how it folds and how it opens by itself like magic." And then, the mother sees that I have a human face, and I'm not something from outer space. But I come back home exhausted because I put out so much effort, and it hurts me [ . . . ] Even being successful, and good looking, and someone who easily connects to people and all that, in my opinion, at the end of the day, I'm the "blind woman."

Exposing her identity as a mother while using her cane as a prop in her performance, Neriya bridges the social differences between herself and the sighted mother who is the audience of her improvised show, negotiating the view of her blindness as a threatening otherness. While this strategy allows her to temporarily reclaim her "subjectivity and autobiography"—traits diminished by the medical gaze directed at people with disabilities (Eisenhauer 2007, 18)—she also describes paying the price in energy and effort, while still being forced to acknowledge the ways she is perceived. In addition, by choosing to respond in the way that she does, Neriya walks a fine line between "over-normalizing" herself (through her attempt to erase her difference by emphasizing her motherhood) and empowering herself (through claiming her identity as blind and disabled).

While some women engage in spontaneous performances in response to the gaze, others may do so through carefully planned performances in which they invite staring. This was the case for Noa, who cultivates reactions to her position through her art as a musician, manipulating the looks she receives while on stage and in her everyday life. Describing her life as balancing between the world of the blind and that of the sighted, Noa embraces the identity of an artist, which allows her to be eccentric and different regardless of blindness. She attended high school at a prestigious school for the arts, which offered her an environment where everyone was a bit different. Music became Noa's means of reflecting on and accepting her identity as a blind woman and responding to the ways she is perceived. It offered her a means of critically exploring her identity as a blind artist and the representations she negotiates as a blind woman. "And here comes the story of my costume," Noa said, referring to an incident in which she used her music to invite a dialogue with the way she is perceived, this time calling upon perhaps the most haunting image of blindness, the blind beggar.[6] At the age of seventeen, Noa decided to embody this image during her high school's Purim festival (a Jewish holiday that includes the tradition of wearing costumes). In response to my question of how she came up with this idea, Noa said that when walking around the city, she occasionally encountered blind beggars, and that, "It was something that was the most embarrassing thing for me, a misery that I didn't feel any empathy for," she said, "and felt totally contemptuous toward, and pissed off by. And yet, because it was so different from me, and also a bit similar, I decided to dress up that way." Noa's costume was carefully planned from head to toe, and included "socks with holes in them and all kinds of clothes that didn't match, and sandals." "And I had a small tin can in my hand, with 'I'm a blind woman, stricken by fate, pity me' written on it. And I held out my hand [ . . . ] while playing a melodica." "It [the costume] had two goals," Noa elaborated:

> First, to examine society's attitude to this situation; I mean, to ask myself and others how far they're willing to go, cooperating with this act of social banishment, exclusion, examining their relationships with me [ . . . ] And it also had another goal, of taking this misery, which I didn't like, to an extreme, asking myself, "Am I really like that? Am I really similar to all kinds of blind people whose behavior I couldn't stand? Those poor people who highlight their misery?" So I could really test everyone. I mean . . . it was a costume used as an indicator of my status in this system. And so I sat there [on the floor at the entrance to the faculty room] and began playing the melodica.

Performing her figurative blindness, Noa's choice of the costume objectified and disoriented the stereotypical cultural images of blindness (and gender)— images of helplessness, dependency, misery, loneliness, darkness, and ignorance. Her act raised questions regarding gender, disability, and class, challenging her classmates, her teachers, and herself to rethink the prejudices, anxieties, and social stereotypes blindness evokes. In the context of Purim, Noa took the opportunity to stretch the social order one step further, daring to perform not the regular reversal ceremony of the carnival, in which she is expected to move away from her disabled identity, but rather to theatrically re-embody her physicality, asking spectators to reflect on the ways they perceive gender, blindness, and disability. Creating a mischievous invitation to participate in the gaze, Noa simultaneously embraced and played with it as a blind woman artist. In so doing, she employed staring-back strategies discussed in relation to visibly disabled performance artists (such as Mary Duffy, Carry Sandahl, Petra Kuppers), who, by walking on stage with a visible disability, employ their bodies as a "critical aesthetic medium" (Garland-Thomson 2005a, 33), "holding up a mirror" to their audience's voyeurism, saying, "So you want to look, do you? I'll give you something to look at" (Duffy in Eisenhauer 2007, 182).

To conclude, blind women's narratives not only express the complexities inherent in women's reactions to and negotiations of the ways they are perceived, but also illuminate less discussed aspects of visual relations. First, in their descriptions of negotiating and managing the multiple gazes directed at them, blind women's narratives demonstrate the ways various visual dynamics intertwine, overlap, and contradict each other. Secondly, blind women's active role as the staree exposes the agency of allegedly weak individuals. Their responses to the gaze emphasize a creative dimension of the complexity inherent in women's agency in visual culture in general and of blind women's spectatorship in particular, as women who are typically dismissed from the act of looking. In this sense, blind women use "tactics" in the art of what de Certeau (1984) called "making do"—a modality of action in which individuals who are usually considered passive creatively challenge the culture imposed on them by a dominant order. Moreover, when staring is intersubjective and functions as a dialogue, the stare can serve as a possibility to acknowledge the other rather than normalize or objectify her. Participating in the gaze, blind women do not collaborate with a gaze that denies or erases social differences, but rather in visual relations that explore the conflicts and paradoxes inherent in them, perhaps casting the starer and staree as mutually vulnerable subjects. Participating in the gaze by employing a wide range of linguistic and bodily performances, blind women perform staring-back practices that have been identified by Sartre (1966) as inseparable from the visual. In his discussion of "The Look," Sartre posited the possibility of the other to look back at us at the heart of vision, addressing the Other not as the object of the dominating stare but instead as a potential threat to the self, given the opportunity to stare back. As Mitchell (2001) explains: "For Sartre, seeing the Other is the glimpsing of a wound in the world; being seen by that Other is the threat of being swept into that wound, swallowed up inside the body of the Other" (394). Therefore, blind women staring back and participating in the gaze "threatens witnessing the self as staree." "The Other looks at me, and as such he holds the secret of my being, he knows what I am [ . . . ] the Other has the advantage over me" (Sartre 1956, 473, in Garland-Thomson 2009, 44). As did Noa when wearing the costume of the blind beggar at the age of seventeen, Neriya when advocating for blind women and mothers, and Talia when dancing in the street when being stared at as an adolescent, blind women claim their bodies as their own territory in response to medical discourse, embrace their identity as blind in response to normalizing discipline, and assert their role as active agents in response to the male gaze.

Finally, blind women's awareness of and responses to the gaze allow a conceptualization of visual relations as a rich field of meaning, tangled with nonvisual mechanisms such as linguistic performance and body language. The visual has been typically identified in terms of power relations, with scholars arguing for the violence carried by methods of visual surveillance (Feldman 1997) or as the objectifying, classifying, and orientalist gaze (Garland-Thomson 1997; Hyndman 2000; Said 1978) exercised on the Other. However, blind women's responses to the gaze allow conceptualizing spectatorship as an interactive and relational field. "Being stared at," as Mitchell (2001) argued when discussing what disability contributes to the research of visual culture, "may be more than mere objectification, dehumanization, or reification. It may also be a sign of curiosity, wonder, empathy, surprise, or acknowledgment" (393).

*Seven*

# Visual Dynamics at the Dark Museum Exhibit

∞

One of the reasons this exhibit is so successful is because people want to experience something different, something . . . challenging. As a guide, I take them and say, "OK, I'll give them a different kind of tour." What's so special about this tour? That you can't see a thing. This tour is about using your senses. So all of a sudden the experience is unique, different, challenging, experimental. (Moshe, a blind exhibit guide)

A different site in which the gaze is directed at blindness is the dark museum exhibit: a site in which Othering dynamics are simultaneously challenged and reconstructed. While blind women's experiences of staring indicate how the object of the gaze can look back, the encounters taking place at the museum demonstrate how staring at blindness can take the form of the orientalist gaze directed at the blind Other, even in the dark. The gaze directed at blindness in this space expresses some of the inaccuracies in the ways much of society understands blindness (perpetuating the blindness-as-total-darkness myth); hence, scrutiny of this site allows learning about the ways society sees blindness, as well as about the ways blind and visually impaired guides working in the museum experience the display of blindness in this space, and their negotiation of it.

The exhibit, which offers visitors an interactive educational encounter with blindness in the dark, is part of an international enterprise of exhibitions and workshops in a variety of formats, yet all in total darkness. Found in twenty-one countries in Asia, Australia, Europe, North America, and South America, these exhibits attract millions of visitors every year. Each invites visitors, led in small groups by blind and visually impaired guides, to navigate a series of simulated environments such as an urban park, a ferry ride, a noisy city street, and a bar.[1] As part of my research, I conducted interviews with twelve exhibit guides (five visually impaired, four blind, and three sighted people), the exhibit coordinator (who is visually impaired), and the museum director (a sighted person). My research also included conversations with sighted visitors, observations of the instructions visitors receive from guides before and after the tour, and my experience of the exhibit as a tour group member.

The interviews and observations revealed the exhibit to be an important site from which to learn about visual culture, seeing, and the gaze. As Moshe described in the quote above, the exhibit indeed offers a "unique, different, challenging, experimental" experience. If we consider visual culture to be, as I mentioned in the introduction to this chapter, the "everyday practices of seeing and showing" (Mitchell 2002, 170), we can think of the exhibit as an opportunity to examine what happens to visitors' understanding of themselves as sighted in this space. The encounters between blind and sighted people in the exhibit reveal that visitors are indeed affected. While becoming aware of their senses other than sight as means of knowledge production, they also develop a gratitude for their sightedness, understanding blindness as a condition of helplessness and dependency, which can lead to a sense of pity toward blind people. The encounters between sighted visitors and blind guides in the museum are useful for discussing visual culture also because they allow learning of a mechanism typically associated with the museum space, history, and design,[2] that of the orientalist/colonizing gaze, the gaze that turns the unfamiliar into the exotic (Said 1978). The colonizing look, Garland-Thomson (2009) explains, "marks its bearer as legitimate and its object as outsider [ . . . ] it occurs at myriad collective social staring rituals such as museums, freak shows, and the pages of *National Geographic*" (42). While the museum has previously been discussed as a site dominated by vision and the (colonizing) gaze (Bennett 1995 in Losch 2006, 224; Garland-Thomson 2009), the dark exhibit allows considering whether the orientalist gaze is present when eyesight is prevented.

The answer to this question is complex. In some aspects, the orientalist gaze distinguishing the sighted "self" from the blind "other" is challenged in the exhibit, with visitors experiencing what Losch, in her analysis of the Margaret Mead Hall of Pacific Peoples at the American Museum of Natural History, calls "sensory immersion," engaged in a "sensescape, a particular imaginary sensorium" (224)—in this case, of a sensory reality not governed by sight. In this liminal sensory reality, borders between us and the Other become more flexible, and a temporary "communitas" with the Other is formed. In other aspects, the orientalist gaze is recreated in the dark, with visitors placed in the role of the able-bodied outsider looking in at the disability of blindness. This duality in the exhibit allows broadening the way we conceptualize the gaze from that of a direct visual observation of people, objects, and images to a set of experiences and ideas that can be employed through the other senses as well.

## Challenging the Gaze through a Sensory "Communitas" in the Dark

If we think about the dark exhibit in relation to classic museological experiences, which are typically governed by sight, it is clear that the dark exhibit provides a unique sensory environment. It posits a challenge to the orientalist gaze by provoking a dialogue with blindness that raises awareness of bodily difference and modes of perception other than sight, inviting the visitor to go through somewhat of a sensory rite of passage in the dark. This exercise initiates a sensory "communitas"—an experience Turner (1990) identified as bringing participants onto an equal level through disrupting stable identities and affiliations and, as a result, creating a temporary in-between event. Somewhat similar to sensory-oriented communal experiences taking place within sacred or festive environments (Kapchan 2008), the "communitas" offered by the dark exhibit challenges the boundaries around senses, social identities, and ability/disability power relations. It fosters the development of "alternative social arrangements" (Turner 1974, 14) that integrate sonic and tactile awareness along with exposure to disability and alternative embodied experiences. As Adams (2012) wrote in her review of the dark exhibit that opened in Manhattan in summer 2011: "It [the dark exhibit] offers the opportunity to experience the world in completely new ways" (856).

Sensory communitas is evoked in the exhibit first and foremost by compelling a nuanced use of the sensory body, through which visitors experience a more acute awareness of their sonic and tactile sensations. Such heightened attention to the senses was evidenced in the visitors' impressions I documented. "It's a tour that compels you to use your senses, without sight, to listen, to feel," one said. "You really need to sharpen your senses, of smell, of hearing—it required effort," another maintained. "The tour makes you concentrate more on your hearing," another visitor commented, "you're more attentive; you hear things you wouldn't hear otherwise. Sounds directed my way. And also the smells, the smell of soil, and the gravel."

This sensory emphasis is present throughout the tour of the exhibit. Upon entering the museum, visitors (organized into groups of ten) are instructed to leave their possessions, including visual devices such as watches and cell phones, in locked cabinets, and to keep only some change with them to use at the snack bar waiting for them in the dark. Next, a sighted instructor presents each visitor with a white cane as the new means of navigation they will use and then leads them through a tutorial on its proper use. Finally, visitors enter a corridor into darkness so absolute that sight is instantly eliminated, forcing an immediate shift to sensory methods of navigation based on tactile, auditory, and kinesthetic inputs, and to proprioception. At this point, they are joined by their guide, whose voice will provide not only information but a means of orientation; and while running one hand along the corridor wall and tapping the white cane with the other, they slowly sense their way into the main exhibit area.

Throughout the tour, each of the separate stations of the exhibit stimulates numerous sensations, offering differing combinations of sound, touch, smell, and taste. At the stop replicating a park, for example, which includes trees, bushes, a stream, a bench, a bridge, and a tiny wooden house, visitors are offered the opportunity to use tactile senses to experience varying temperatures (the colder park versus the warmer house), to feel liquids and solids (water, trees, and bushes), and to navigate changing terrains (a gravel trail, soft grass, muddy soil, a wooden floor), as well as feel the shape and texture of different objects (the table, pot, tap, sink, kettle, silverware, and chairs in the house). In the absence of light, auditory skills are highlighted, as visitors not only listen for the sound of the guide's voice but hear various additional sounds (other visitors' voices, water, frogs, toads, crickets, and birds). The kinesthetic, too, becomes a conscious practice, as visitors' corporeal experiences are both intentional (sitting on a bench, bending to feel the water) and inadvertent (bumping against trees and bushes, moving up and down while crossing the bridge).

This variety of sensory stimulations recurs throughout the tour; on the ferry boat, visitors feel its movements and the splashes of water, and run their fingers along the name of the boat carved in its wooden hull; at the market, they concentrate on olfactory sensations as they distinguish between the fruits and vegetables through smell and touch; in the music room, visitors sense the carpet underneath them, sitting on the floor while listening to music and recordings of everyday sounds; and at the snack bar, the audience operates its sonic, tactile, and gustatory awareness, attending to the guide's and other people's voices while tasting the sugary drinks and salty snacks, and when paying for them, feeling the shape, size, and weight of different coins in order to determine their value. Heightened sensory awareness is also invigorated by the guides, who through verbal instructions encourage the group to investigate and explore their environment, to navigate location and direction. Accordingly, the notes from my own tour are full of somatic descriptions, among them: the chilly park, colder than the corridor leading to it, the feeling of grass under my feet, and the disorienting feeling of moving up and down in space while crossing a wooden suspension bridge. I recalled my sense of the hustle and bustle of the market through the cacophony of sounds there, including cars, bikes, and vendors' voices; the density of the space, occupied by street lights, garbage cans, mailboxes, bikes, and cars; and its atmosphere, saturated with the aromas of fruits and vegetables, foods I identified through touch as potatoes, eggplants, cabbage, onions, peppers, and tangerines. I also noted being intrigued by the floating sensation I experienced in the music room while resting on the floor, listening to music in the dark.

The exhibit's emphasis on the senses, inviting visitors to touch, shake, and even taste the objects inside the exhibit, expresses an unconventional approach to museum design, replacing the visitor's traditional role as a distanced viewer with that of an active participant. Engaging the senses of touch, sound, or smell, and encouraging behaviors such as eating, drinking, and talking, the exhibit also challenges the valuation of seeing and hearing as primary senses for the production of rational knowledge, forcing visitors to actively and attentively utilize their other senses when identifying objects, navigating space, and deciphering their experience. Eli, a blind guide at the exhibit, addressed this subject and said that by raising visitors' awareness of their senses other than sight (asking them, for example, how they would handle an electrical blackout), his aim is to construct sensory experiences as *shared* by both blind and sighted people, rethinking cultural boundaries between the sensory-blind experience versus the non-sensory-sighted one.

The exhibit's sensory emphasis not only makes visitors more aware of nonvisual ways of being-in-the-world but also transforms ability-disability hierarchies, and hence, typical orientalist relations of "us" and the "other," as guides are placed in the role of both facilitator (leading visitors through the exhibit and operating its facilities) and counselor (helping them cope with the anxieties and fears darkness evokes). As Moshe explained: "I, as a guide, have the upper hand; I know the place. I lead them [the visitors] to their seats; they're in my hands." This proximity and intimacy that darkness fosters was also identified by Adams (2012) in her analysis of the dark exhibit in New York, arguing that, for sighted visitors, one of the most "valuable" aspects of the exhibit may be "the unprecedented experience of proximity to and dependence on a blind guide" (857). This is important in a broader context, Adams explains, in order to indicate the ways "we are all dependent on others." The transformation of power relations during the tour directs the interactions not only between visitors and guides but also among the visitors themselves, who share a common "liminal status" that stands in contrast to the structured hierarchies and statuses outside the exhibit. Saerberg (2007), in his analysis of the dining in the dark phenomenon, identifies this dynamic of the dark space as constituting "equality, change in perspectives, role-reversal, and role exchanges." "In darkness," he argues, "sighted people are separated from light, from their 'normal' status in society, and are led into a liminal state of existence." Moshe also related this liminality among visitors, explaining:

> What I like about the dark is . . . that hypothetically we're all in the same boat [ . . . ] there're no barriers, and everyone's equal. And it doesn't matter if someone's a father, or a mother, a boy, or a girl; no one has any advantage in the group, even if he's already been here before.

This "being in the same boat" experience Moshe describes applies to the heterogeneous audience of visitors from a wide variety of backgrounds coming to the exhibit, including adults, school children (above the age of nine), and organized groups, who eventually form the egalitarian community created in the dark. Having abandoned their material personal possessions and the ability to look at each other outside the exhibit, visitors are stripped of their visual signs of status, and guides' and visitors' visual labeling and affiliations based on race, nationality, age, and ethnicity are delayed. While darkness, of course, does not eliminate all social differences or backgrounds, as linguistic performance can also signal racial, gender, and ethnic affiliations, it suspends the immediacy of visual labeling and raises doubts about social identities. Aviel, for example, a blind guide of Ethiopian descent, described visitors' surprise when discovering his identity at the end of the tour. "I don't always tell people [that I'm Ethiopian]," he said, "and many times they don't even know. Many times, they think I'm actually Ashkenazi." "When I sometimes hear comments about Ethiopians I don't respond; only at the talk at the end of the tour, and then they're shocked."

This sensory communitas the exhibit produces engenders a dialogue with the other, expanding the audience's sensory (and visual) self to include rich and nuanced sensations and experiences. Touch, for example, becomes a broad somatosensory experience, with visitors translating tactile sensations of temperature, shapes, textures, and surfaces, as well as kinesthetic ones, into knowledge of their environment. Visitors must also notice a wide range of auditory experiences, including the sounds of objects (e.g., motor vehicles; an approaching car, bus, and train; metal touching metal), animals (dogs, frogs, toads, crickets, and birds), humans (calls of vendors in the market, recorded voices in the music room, the guide's and other visitors' instructions and verbalizations), and music (jazz, classical, rock, and pop in the music room). Simultaneously touching and being touched, hearing and being heard, the visitors embody an experience Merleau-Ponty (1968) identified as an intimacy of myself with others, emphasizing that daily experiences in and outside the museum are both seen and felt.

## Reconstructing the Gaze: The Exhibit as a Classificatory Encounter

Alongside the communitas the exhibit engenders and the challenges it offers to visual othering processes, darkness in this context recreates dynamics belonging to the orientalist encounter typically associated with vision and the gaze. Situating the educational encounter with blindness in the dark, the exhibit constructs blindness and sight as separate worlds, establishing both categories within a binary *and* hierarchal system, raising in the audience not only an awareness of but also an appreciation for its sighted identity that is reestablished as they return to the light. "Thank God I can see," visitors commented at the end of the tour when returning to a lighted space. "I'm so lucky to be sighted." "I've learned to appreciate every morning we wake up and see," a visitor said when exiting the tour. Such impressions were also described by Moshe:

> If the first thing a visitor says when he goes out to the light is "blessed (is he) who gives sight to the blind," I've failed in my work. That's what I think. I mean, the message didn't go well. Every person has the right to think whatever he wants, that a blind person is miserable, OK; but if the first thing he says to me once I go back to the light with him is, "thank God I can see," somewhere along the line something went wrong.

Moshe expressed regret not only regarding visitors' feelings of relief at regaining their sight but also regarding the misperception of blindness as total darkness that the exhibit engenders, and the reactions he occasionally receives about his blindness:

Sometimes visitors ask us, "Wait a second, do you guys live here?" So I tell people, "Hey, I don't live in this darkness [ . . . ] If you really want to know how it feels to be blind, it's not what you've had here [ . . . ] Here you experienced something short, temporary, maybe a little taste of blindness. But only very briefly; 'blindness-light,' I call it, a piece of cake." I'd like my life to be more like this exhibit; it would be much easier, you know?

Moshe describes then the way visitors learn to associate blindness with darkness (and even with the enclosed space of the museum, asking him if he lives there), as well as the inappropriateness of the dark exhibit as a simulation of blindness. In this, he echoes the common disability studies' critique of simulation exercises (Burgstahler and Doe 2004; French 1992; Siebers 2008) as experiences that may offer participants the wrong impressions about disability. As Burgstahler and Doe (2004) explain:

[M]ost disability-related simulations are designed to result in negative feelings. By disabling participants and simulating problematic experiences . . . participants learn how difficult it is to maneuver a wheelchair, how frustrating it is to be unable to hear or read, how frightening it is to be visually impaired, or how impossible it is to participate in activities without the use of their hands. They focus on what people with disabilities cannot do rather than on what they could do with appropriate access, technology, or skills (11).

Opposing the exhibit's function as a simulation of blindness, Moshe tries to explain to visitors that using a cane for a short amount of time, in a safe space, does not simulate the reality blind people cope with outside the museum, in which the environment is typically not only inaccessible but also fraught with stigmas and stereotypes of blindness.

Other exhibit guides mentioned similar questions and comments they received from visitors expressing an ill-informed understanding of blindness. In one incident, for example, a group of visitors complained, after learning that their guide was (only) visually impaired and could perceive some degree of sight, that they wanted "a real blind guide." This incident demonstrates the ways questions of authenticity are present in the exhibit and intertwined with orientalist othering processes reminiscent of "primitivist tourism" (Stasch 2015), in which visitors typically arrive to *see* and consume the authentic "native." In the case of the dark exhibit, the blind guide is, in a way, cast in the role of the "native," and the event as a whole constitutes a form of "disability tourism" (Adams 2012, 851). The artifact most representative of the blind "native" in this case is total darkness, and once this representation is in doubt (as in the case of the group receiving "only" a visually impaired guide), the exhibit's authenticity is at risk and visitors protest.

That the meeting with blindness occurs in total darkness establishes a tension between visitors' expectation they will have the opportunity to experience what blindness feels like, and the exhibit's and guides' goal of avoiding a simulation of blindness. The exhibit, for its part, calls itself a "journey through darkness" rather than an experience of blindness, and the guides I talked to emphasized this idea. "I tell visitors not to fall into the trap that they can learn what blindness feels like," Moshe explained, advising his groups to address the experience as "a lack of sight" rather than a simulation of blindness. Aviel explains to visitors that they're "not here to experience blindness," emphasizing the temporary nature of the exhibit. And Sarit, a visually impaired guide, expressed her hope that visitors would not assume that, "I went into the exhibit, now I know how blind people feel." "Even I," she said [as a visually impaired person], "don't know how blind people feel." Despite these intentions, visitors typically leave the exhibit under the impression that it serves as a representation of blindness, a notion also reinforced by media and scholarly reports. A review in *The New York Times* (Rothstein 2011), for example, addressed the exhibit as a "genius presentation" of being "really" blind, and Adams (2012) pointed out the ways the exhibit encourages visitors to "believe they have experienced life as a blind person" (851). Similarly, visitors I talked to exited the tour assuming that what they experienced was a representation of the blind experience, which is characterized by a complete, constant darkness. "A person who's never seen light in his life," a visitor replied in response to my question about the message he received from the exhibit, "I'd like to ask how it feels to wake up in the morning and stay in the dark."

These impressions visitors leave with nourish the "simple blindness versus sight binary" (Kleege 2005, 188) criticized by scholars of disability and visual culture, a binary that associates blindness with a sudden, congenital, and total absence of light. The physical experience of blindness (and sight) is in fact much more complicated, including a "vast spectrum between 20–20 and total darkness" (Kudlick 2011, 2) and different degrees of "light perception," "visual sensation" (Rodas 2009, 118), or "light, color, form, and movement" (Kleege 2005, 187). Even the legal definition of blindness is extremely broad, incorporating two factors: visual acuity of 3/60 or less, and/or a visual field of not greater than 20 degrees (Kurssiya and Gleitman 2009). Each legally blind person, then, experiences a degree of visual acuity and/or visual field, which results in a large variety of visual impairments, including night/day vision loss, peripheral/tunnel/central vision, blur, compromised color perception, and more, initiating an endless diversity of abilities and needs, as some legally blind people are able to read large print, for example, but need a cane when navigating public spaces. Moreover, the vast majority of legally blind individuals are not congenitally or totally blind and experience the loss of vision as a gradual process, often later in life (Kleege 2005; Omansky 2011; Rodas 2009).

The pitch-dark space also reinforces the orientalist gaze toward the other through evoking fear and anxiety among visitors in their encounter with blindness (and in this case, with darkness). Such impacts of simulation exercises have been identified by Burgstahler and Doe (2004), who asserted that "rather than dismantling stereotypes [ . . . ] participants in disability-related simulations may even become frightened by the experience" (11). This aspect of the exhibit was present in my observations and interviews, with exhibit guides and visitors referring to the experience of darkness in words such as "traumatic," "torture," "a difficult experience," and "survival," and as an experience provoking emotions such as stress, hysteria, panic, fear, and anxiety. These feelings connect blindness and disability with the realm of the mysterious and threatening—a dynamic demarcating us and the other and associating blindness with incompetence, as visitors could link their own fear of the dark with the way a blind person would be helpless out there in the world.

In addition to the total darkness of the exhibit, its design, and the activities in which visitors participate, the exhibit also categorizes blind people as the exotic Other through locating blindness within a simulated reality different from everyday life outside the museum. The exhibit's engaging environments (such as the boat tour and the music room), the behaviors it encourages (feeling, touching, squeezing, and shaking objects, bumping into people and objects), and the roles in which blind people are placed (tour guides, bartenders) are quite different from the everyday lives and behaviors of blind and visually impaired people, relegating the exhibit to the category of entertainment (Mathur 2001, 492)—a dominant feature of past ethnographic exhibits of the other. Limited information about the use of accessible technologies, such as Braille watches, typing machines, and books, is provided at the end of the exhibit tour in Israel, yet at this point, visitors are typically focused on sharing their experience of exiting total darkness and reentering light, as well as seeing their guide for the first time. In this sense, the tour resembles more a "participatory theater," as one of its critics wrote (Rothstein 2011), than a realistic representation of blindness. A lack of attention to social aspects of blindness and disability also results in situating blindness solely within the individual's body rather than within a wider social, cultural, and spatial context as well. This is expressed most strongly when visitors have the opportunity to ask the guides questions during a conversation that occurs in the last stop of the tour, a conversation typically focusing on the guide's personal history; his/her history of blindness or visual impairment, and his/her "overcoming" narrative, offering the "normal" life course of studies, dating, and hobbies. Dramatized by the dark, the story told by the guide functions somewhat as a "confessional performance" (Terry 2006) of blindness, "leaving broader social structures fundamentally unchallenged and unchanged" (209). The exhibit guides with whom I spoke reported commonly encountering ignorance during this talk, as visitors glorified the guides' normative activities and statuses such as studying, traveling, getting married, and becoming a parent.

By constructing blindness as a homogenous experience separated from the everyday life outside the museum, the exhibit reduces the liminality and ambiguity associated with corporeal otherness in general and with blindness specifically (Kudlick 2011; Omansky 2011), establishing a "safe" space in which visitors can encounter (and gaze at) blindness. Therefore, while Saerberg (2007), in his analysis of dark restaurants, claimed that the dark environment eliminates "staring at the other" since oral communication "tears down barriers that are often constructed visually," I argue that the classificatory dynamics of the dark exhibit recreate spectatorship typical of the colonial encounter and the orientalist gaze, establishing a "new pattern of reality" (Douglas 1966, 38) in which the "ambiguous or anomalous event" has a place.

To conclude, the representation of blindness in the dark museum exhibit allows investigating the cultural meanings this experience reflects upon visual dynamics and the gaze in the context of a public display of blindness. On one hand, the orientalist gaze is challenged in this space by offering visitors a sensory experience that suspends the boundaries around blindness and sight, us and the Other. Challenging visual dominancy by engendering a liminal experience of sensory communitas, this public engagement with blindness initiates a temporary communitas of mutuality, sharing, and equality among visitors and guides, evoking sonic and tactile intimacy, as visitors experience a reversal in ability-disability power relations, and an alternative to visual social interaction and perception. On the other hand, the orientalist gaze is reconstructed in the exhibit by exoticizing blindness as total darkness. By portraying blindness as a world of absolute darkness, a world from which visitors exit (re)appreciating their sighted selves, the exhibit functions as a classificatory encounter exercising the orientalist gaze that preserves cultural boundaries between blindness and sight, indicating that power relations typically associated with visual mechanisms can be generated in the absence of sight through auditory and tactile experiences.

This duality allows reflecting on the ways contradictory discourses may operate within visual politics of power relations. Somewhat similar to the ways in which blind women's experiences of staring reveal the work of different, contradictory gazes directed at them, the encounters of blind and sighted visitors in the dark exhibit reveal that visual politics of meeting with the Other may include discourse both of *sensory immersion*, as well as of *distant viewing*.[3] This contradiction allows understanding darkness as a component of visual culture and revealing the role of sight and the other senses within classification processes relevant to additional sensory arenas in which we encounter bodily difference in the public sphere and in everyday life.

# Conclusion

## *Rethinking the Gaze through the Prism of Blindness*

⸻⸱⸎⸱⸻

Disability will have to work through its own relation to visual culture—and, even more important, challenge the very notion of what it means to look at other people or see things from their point of view. (Mitchell 2001, 393)

As Mitchell suggested, disability in general, and blindness in particular, allow rethinking the act of seeing and, I add, the phenomenon of the gaze. The narratives in this section demonstrate that there are many ways to see and varied ways to experience and react to being seen. Blind women's negotiation of staring and the construction of blindness and sight in the dark museum exhibit offer a story of how we can rethink seeing and the gaze, and the visual logics of sexualizing, disabling, and othering. They allow reexamining two main dynamics (or traditions) of visual culture: first, the active-passive binary, which has typically characterized the relations between the starer and the staree; and secondly, the notion that vision is the hegemonic sense of visual culture. Blind women's experiences of the gaze and the encounters at the dark exhibit indicate the active role of the staree, as well as the specific relations of vision to the other senses, especially hearing and touch.

First, the discussion presented in chapter 6 allows conceptualizing staring as a dialogical encounter. Blind women's creative and agentic responses to the gaze disrupt the typical power relations between the starer and the staree, challenging the idea of the gaze as a one-sided power mechanism relying on an active starer and a passive staree. These responses to the gaze not only reveal that the staree can take the role of an active agent who can negotiate a paradoxical position between visibility and invisibility, but also that staring can be considered an intersubjective dynamic of communication that may insert surprises into the social order. Garland-Thomson (2009) addresses this aspect of the visual:

> [S]taring affords a spontaneous moment of interpersonal connection, however brief, during which two people have the opportunity to regard and be known to one another. So while social rules script staring, individual improvisation can take the staring encounter in fruitful directions. Staring, in other words, makes things happen between people. (33)

Discussing the potential communicative aspects of staring, Garland-Thomson (2009) also addresses the agentic possibilities of the staree. "Being a 'staree,'" she notes, is "to show a starer something new, to catch a starer off-guard with an unfamiliar sight" (7). Blind women responding to the gaze indeed show something new, dismantling traditional cultural images of blindness and, rather than embodying mainstream disability narratives that revolve around tragedy or inspiration, reclaiming their voice and presence in the public sphere. The look, they reveal, can also carry an ethical component when exercised with humanity, acknowledging the presence of another person and of bodily difference, and potentially inviting a conversation.

Second, the intersection of blindness and visual culture reveals how staring operates through the other senses, understanding the gaze as a sensory and social phenomenon. While blind women's active role as a staree can be interpreted as staring-back practices, the encounters in the dark museum exhibit do not leave much room for the other to stare back. Paradoxically, when eliminating sight altogether, rather than rejecting the orientalist gaze and cultural othering, the dark space recreates the colonizing look that subordinates its object. This follows Edward Said's point (1978) that "the ability to observe without being observed is emblematic of the colonial encounter" (in Garland-Thomson 2009, 42). If we consider the orientalist look as a gaze that ascribes to the staree the identity of "the exotic, outlaw, alien, or other" (Garland-Thomson 2009, 42), then the dark space produces exactly this. Sighted visitors experience blindness as exotic and their own sightedness as legitimate and normal (even something to be grateful for). The orientalist gaze sighted visitors operate functions as a tool of domination, a type of staring Garland-Thomson (2009) identifies as "fixing" a person in gender, race, disability, class, or sexuality systems (42).

In addition, while it is common to think of cultural othering as dependent upon looking as an act of domination, the encounters at the dark museum indicate that the gaze can indeed rely on senses other than sight and that the whole body may participate in gazing. The operation (and suspension) of the orientalist gaze at the dark exhibit and the ways blindness is individualized and exoticized in this space suggest that classification systems are not governed only by visual dynamics. This understanding contributes to former discussions of how the Othering process takes place through the senses. Haldrup et al. (2006), for example, developed what they called "practical orientalism," which is established through bodily practices; Ameeriar (2012) articulated the concept of the "sanitized body" through which the dominant culture imposes itself in order to institute new ideals of bodily comportment through smell; and Classen (1992) acknowledged "olfactory codes" as "pervade[ing] classificatory thought, not only in 'exotic,' highly olfactory-conscious societies, but even in our rather 'deodorized' Western society" (133). Othering practices taking place in the dark broaden this discussion to also include the role of tactile and auditory experiences within colonizing dynamics. The ways blindness is exoticized in the dark allows understanding the orientalist gaze through a sensory standpoint, while also thinking about tactile and auditory experiences through a visual prism. The ways this sensory engagement with blindness exoticizes blindness demonstrates what Classen and Howes (2006) argued regarding the "open-air" museum or exotic theme park, that "mere tactile engagement with an artifact will not necessarily deepen one's understanding of its cultural role [ . . . ] sensory content would need to be placed in cultural context" (219). In order to challenge visual domination, then, or, for staring to become about a communicative dialogue (as in the case of blind women staring back), a mere meeting with otherness and eliminating sight altogether are not enough to dethrone sight from its pedestal. New alliances among visitors and between the visitors and guides and critical reflections regarding sight as a means of knowledge production take place in the exhibit only in those instances of multisensory experiences and when visitors employ a wide range of sensory information to experience their surroundings and interpret information.

Broadening the meaning of the gaze from the eye to the other senses joins the argument regarding the gaze as a social phenomenon that is not really (just) about looking. Blind women's participation in the staring indicate that the gaze is a social phenomenon that carries cultural meaning about power, dominancy, stigmas, and ideologies. Therefore, members of visual culture (including blind people) can take active part in exercising the gaze (also directing it at each other as Noa described in chapter 6). In addition, when the gaze is not confined solely to looking, but is a set of practices that can serve to dominate or invite communication and a dialogue, it can indeed take place in the dark.

This conceptualization of the gaze challenges the common assumption that blindness is the opposite of sight. This assumption expresses a larger ocularcentric logic that creates binary relations not only between blindness and sight but also between sensation and perception, and between Western and non-Western sensorial contexts: the Western typically associated with sight, articulating vision as objective and detached, and non-Western associated with nonvisual senses, which are understood as subjective and emotional.[1] The broader understanding of the gaze as sensuous and cultural is useful in shaking up such binary distinctions, converging the visual and the sensorial, and objectification and subjectification.

Rethinking such binaries, this section as a whole demonstrated not only the ways vision is linked to the other senses, a topic that will also be central in the next section on blindness and the sensory body, but also the varied mechanisms of power, creativity, embodiment, performance, and resistance that comprise the visual. Blind and sighted people's experiences discussed here reveal that rather than excluding one another, blindness and sight coexist: there are aspects of blindness in seeing, just as there are aspects of the visual experience in blindness. The visual sphere, therefore, consists of varied visual and sensory ways of experiencing seeing and being seen. Blind women's experiences of the gaze and the encounters at the dark exhibit reveal that there is more to vision than the dominant, "chauvinist, Western, colonial, and technified 'gaze'" (Grasseni 2009, 3), and that sight and blindness are multisensorial, consisting of "rapidly changing points of view" (4), and a "community of practices" (5). The visual consists of dialogical, embedded, and creative modes of seeing and being seen, and different ways of resisting visual dominancy.

## Section III

# Blindness and the Sensory Body

———∞∞∞———

In our everyday life, most of us pay little conscious attention to *how* we sense [ . . . ] it is only when routines and habits are interrupted—for example, when we suddenly feel sick, or when a sensation overwhelms us—that our own sensual experience "awakens" our embodied consciousness. (Vannini et al. 2012, 8)

Blindness allows the type of sensory and embodied "awakening" and "interruption of routines and habits" that Vannini, Waskul, and Gottschalk (2012) describe in their discussion of acoustic environments and the performative dimensions of sound. Blindness allows, for example, accentuating the role of the sensory body within gender performance, disrupting the taken-for-grantedness of visual mechanisms as central within gender socialization. In interactions among blind and sighted people, blindness also raises critical questions regarding what a visual skill is and what the relations among the senses are. As Classen (1998) suggests: "By attending to the experience of the blind, we who are sighted can begin to learn what it might be like to apprehend the world as a sound and smellscape, or to appreciate the contours and textures of our environment through touch" (139).

This sensory articulation blindness calls for is investigated in this section through two chapters: the first focusing on the role of the senses in blind women's gender performance, discussing what I call blind women's "sensory capital"; and the second examining the sensory interactions among blind and sighted people within spaces integrating voice, sound, touch, or sight, offering the ethnographic example of a tandem cycling group comprised of blind and sighted participants. Both chapters examine the way blindness accentuates sensory experiences and offers insights into the ways a sensory skill is experienced and expressed. In chapter 8, the sensory body is examined in relation to gender performance and practices of appearance management through narratives of blind women. Chapter 9 considers the sensory body through a social meeting with blindness and in relation to the experiences of both sighted and blind people interacting with each other.

Examined through a sensory prism, in this section I locate blindness within the larger study of the culturally constructed nature of the sensory experience (e.g., Classen 1997; Howes 1991; Seremetakis 1996; Stoller 1989) and alongside the study of other professions and experiences that pay special attention to the senses, including sports, dance, and the arts. Anthropologists of the senses and anthropologists of the body have examined, for example, kinesthetic experiences of dancers, athletes, and performing artists (see Samudra 2008); the experience of sound among musicians (Wilf 2015); of taste among vintners (Shapin 2012); and of smell among chemists (Latour 2004). Downey (2010), for instance, in his research on embodied knowledge in Capoeira, characterized this martial art as "an especially demanding form of embodied knowledge," with "apprenticeship necessitating not simply the acquiring of techniques or skills but a whole body transformation in strength, flexibility, mobility, perhaps even personality" (22).

Borrowing Downey's term, we can think of disability as a "demanding form" of sensory engagement that calls for unique sensory attention (Hull 1992; Macpherson 2009, 1045). Not only blindness, but disability in general, may engender a sensory sensitivity. Belek (2018), for instance, identifies the ways autism offers new distinctions of sensory sensitivities, and Sobchack (2005) discusses the way physical disability challenges the taken-for-granted of everyday tasks such as walking. Describing her own experience of learning to walk again after her leg was amputated, she explains:

> Rather than the transparent capacity for action and intention [ . . . ] my bodily motility no longer absent-mindedly "adjusted it[self] to the objective requirements of the task"—that is, simply, and without a thought, enabled me to walk from here to there. Before the amputation, like most people going about their everyday lives, I just moved in the direction of my intentions without thought of the movement and "without access to the inhuman secret of the bodily mechanism" that got me there. Even if I was relatively graceless, my sense of physical immanence was typically transcended as my attention focused elsewhere—on other things and other thoughts than those. (55)

Sobchack's disability reshaped her sense of physical immanence, offering new experiences of movement, a concrete bodily and spatial presence, and an experience of various rhythms and spaces. Parviainen (2002), in her article on bodily knowledge in dance, also mentions disability as relevant to the study of bodily knowledge, addressing the ways injuries affect a person's relation to the body (19). An injury, she explains, requires the person to (re)learn a new skill, adapting the habits acquired to fit with the new body. When we learn a bodily skill, Parviainen argues, "I am reviving, and reshaping bodily schema—a basic way of doing something, a manner of proceeding, a mode of acting" (19) and develop a "corporeal intellect" (20).

Blindness is another social identity allowing the developing of "sensory intellect," contributing to a line of thought Wilf (2015) calls "sensory self-fashioning" (5). First, researching the everyday experiences of blind women and the encounters between blind and sighted people through a sensory prism allows an ethnographic analysis of the performance of the senses in *everyday life*, which is rare. Second, while previous research typically focused on a single sensory mode, the study of blindness promotes an intersensory analysis by considering sensory and bodily practices located outside the traditional "five-senses model" (Geurts 2002, 178), such as speech, nonverbal communication, and kinesthetic movement. Third, researching the sensory reality of blindness does not focus on a specific bodily practice, such as dance, cycling, or boxing, shared by a closed group of professionals, but rather it examines the everyday life of the sensory body, as shared by sighted, blind, and visually impaired people. Finally, accounting for the ways blindness shapes "sensory self-reflexivity" (Serematakis 1996, 7) uniquely integrates disability into sensory analysis. Interestingly, although disability is highly relevant to sensory studies, neither the fields of anthropology of the senses nor anthropology of performance have tended to focus on disability in the past (an exception is Friedner's and Helmreich's [2012] article on the meeting between sound studies and deaf studies). By asking about the implications of blindness for individuals' "sensory narrations and actions" (Pink 2005, 278) and for their understandings of themselves as able/disabled, sighted/blind, this chapter contributes to what Geurts (2015) identified as a growing "cross-fertilization" (163) between sensory and disability studies. It defamiliarizes the taken-for-grantedness of seeing, documenting a wide range of sensory experiences within the meeting among heterogeneous bodies and promoting a sophisticated awareness of sensory skills across a spectrum rather than as binary oppositions. In addition, looking at how sensory experiences are shaped in relation to blindness, disability, and social otherness allows investigating cultural discourses that imbue sensory experiences and qualities with moral values, addressing not only the ways in which specific values are manifested in and maintained through sensory practices, but also "how these values are challenged or resisted by individuals whose everyday practices go 'against the grain'" (Moore 1994, 82, in Pink 2005, 278). As Schillmeier (2007) argued, focusing on sensory practices in the research of blindness and disability allows us to "outline a concept of (visual) dis/ability" that does not separate social aspects of disability from physiological ones, exploring the ways visual dis/ability is "the outcome of social and non-social, human and non-human configurations" (197).

Addressing blindness from a sensory prism and simultaneously examining the sensorium through the prism of blindness, I do not ask to sketch blindness in a stigmatic way that associates it exclusively with senses other than sight, nor to understand blindness as a sensory consciousness that is essentially different from the way sighted people experience the world. Similar to the way I rejected the stigmatized-romanticized notions of "blind touch" when discussing the role of physical contact within research methods in chapter 2 of this book and my apprehension in describing blind people's sensory abilities as congenital when addressing cultural notions that sexualize blind women in chapter 6, by referring to blindness as a "demanding form" of sensory engagement, I do not dichotomize the sensory-blind-experience of the body versus the allegedly non-sensory-sighted-experience. Rather, by focusing on how blindness allows attending to the sensorium, I argue for the ways blindness evokes a rich, attentive use of the senses that enriches the meanings of both blindness and sight, and connects visual perception to the other senses, enriching the somatic meaning of gender performance, the meeting with social otherness, and visual experience. When blind women interpret, implement, and negotiate visual norms through nonvisual sensory modalities, they bring to the front the variety of sensory experiences that shape everyday gender performance and allow discussion of the role of the sensory body within gender socialization mechanisms and within women's experiences of oppression, discipline, pleasure, and empowerment. When dialogical intersensory meetings with blindness take place in the public sphere, they bring into a mutual conversation fields of meaning that have been seen as separate in the past, including the visual/somatic experience, and invite sighted, blind, and visually impaired people to develop a reflexive awareness regarding their sensory selves and embodied identities.

*Eight*

# Blind Women's Sensory Capital

⎯⎯⎯∞∞∞⎯⎯⎯

There are many ways to see, not only with the eyes; there's touching, smelling, tasting. . . . (Anat, a 34-year-old congenitally blind woman)

Conversations with research participants have shown that feminine performance among blind women accentuates the role of the sensory body, emphasizing haptic, auditory, and olfactory experiences. Blind women described this intensified sensory experience as influential both in their appearance management in everyday life, as well as in social interactions more generally. This sensory attention continues the discussion I offered in chapter 3, referring to the role of hearing and touch within the varied means through which blind women gain awareness of visual knowledge regarding beauty and femininity. In chapter 4, I also mentioned the role of the sensorium within disciplinary mechanisms operating upon blind women's bodies as part of their appearance management. In the following discussion, I continue to explore the role of the senses in gender performance, underscoring a gendered aspect within blind women's "physical capital," foregrounding the embodiment of the sensory body within gender and social relations.

Blind women's narratives regarding the significance of touch, sound, and smell in their bodily practices is not particular to blind women and may be shared with sighted women as well. However, blind women express a unique verbalization of their awareness of sensory experiences within gender performance, an ability to offer "body talk," in Latour's (2004) words, conveying "the many ways in which the body is engaged in accounts about what it does" (206). Relying primarily on senses other than sight, women in this research interpret visual norms through the entire sensorium, highlighting women's embodied sensoriality and the tactile, auditory, and olfactory sensations within both disciplining and empowering practices of gender performance more generally.

## "Sensing Femininity": Sensory Appearance Management and Sensory Pleasure

Women in this research described sensory experiences as inseparable from their use of clothes, jewelry, cosmetics, and hygiene and body products, referring to appearance as greatly affected by choices based on the texture of clothes or the way products smell or feel on the body. Talia, thirty-one years old, blind from age three, identified the sense of touch, for example, as the main reason for her use of nail polish. "When I choose to put it on," she said, "it's because when touching my nails, they feel smoother and shinier. I feel this . . . difference, like between newsprint and colored paper. The colored paper has this special feel in the hand, in the finger." Roni, a twenty-seven-year-old congenitally blind woman, mentioned her sense of touch in relation to her clothes, explaining: "The most important thing is the fabric, its touch, or texture." Liron, a thirty-year-old congenitally blind woman, described the weight, heat, and vibration of the fabric on her body, and said, "I like to wear light clothes, like these jeans, they're fun because they're wide, and I don't like anything tight on my body that you can't breathe and move with [ . . . ] I like shirts with pleasant fabric, so I don't wear wool since it itches." Women also emphasized the cut and shape of clothing. "I [can] feel if the shirt looks nice by its shape," Ora, a twenty-nine-year-old woman who has been blind from age three, said: "When I go shopping [for clothes] I have to touch the clothes, feel how they look, what the cleavage is like, if it's too open or too closed [ . . . ] if it's buttoned or not." "I usually don't buy clothes that have the same shape," Rinat, a forty-four-year-old visually impaired woman, said: "Every item has its nuances. One can have a V cut, and another a boat neckline; they can have the same texture but not the same shape, you understand? Or the same shape but not the same texture." When addressing touch, women also referred to the texture of clothes and even compared it to the visual feedback sighted women rely on when managing their appearance. "First of all, [I notice] the texture," Roni said when I asked her how she chooses her clothes. "The texture of the fabric, its feel. *You* see the color with your eyes; for me, what's important is its feel." Anat also emphasized texture and shape, this time in relation to shoes. "You can feel it," she said,

> With touch—it doesn't have to be with sight. When you see a certain shoe, you feel, I can feel if it's rough or delicate by its shape. If it has

these soft curves, and isn't square, and doesn't have nails and a platform from here till further notice, then I know that it's a more delicate
[shoe].

In addition to touch, women also referred to the role of sound within appearance management, as in the case of high heels, bracelets, or beads. Tzila,
a fifty-nine-year-old congenitally blind woman, explained, "Since I was five,
I've loved dressing up. Why? I don't know, but I liked the sound of high heels;
I was the first in my class to wear high heels. I liked their sound." Women also
described that the smell of clothing (as in the case of shops that use incense
or the smell of a scented laundry powder) affects them, and that smell influences their choices regarding cosmetics as well. Aviva, for instance, twenty-
seven years old, blind from age six, emphasized the importance of buying the
laundry detergent "that makes me feel good and has a pleasant smell."

Sensory richness in blind women's appearance management appeared
deeply and widely embedded in the experiences of research participants and
was expressed by women from nineteen to sixty-six years of age. Yael, Semadar, and Tzila, for instance, emphasized the central role of tactile experiences.
"Beauty is everything that has softness in it," Yael, twenty-six years old said,
"fabrics that are soft, pleasant. Lace is pretty because it's soft and delicate."
"Usually, I prefer tighter clothes," Semadar, thirty-two years old, described,
"and sparkles on pants, so they'll also be interesting to touch, not just to look
at." And Tzila, fifty-nine years old, explained:

> I like silk and sheer fabrics with rich textures, and tints, and embroi-
> deries, and all kinds of interesting textures [ . . . ] I look for soft, flow-
> ing, supple fabrics [ . . . ] I've always looked for dresses and shawls
> with pretty and prominent objects like ribbons, fringes, or trains.

Blind women's emphasis on sensory experiences within gender performance allows embedding the concept of "beauty" with embodied, sensual
meaning, expanding the notion of "aesthetics" from referring to visual forms
of objects associated with harmony, order, and beauty to including multisensory experiences (see Venkatesh et al. 2010, 460). The type of aesthetics
directing blind women's choices regarding appearance emphasizes the haptic
body *as a whole*, expressing the rich, complicated, and diverse experiences
of touch. When describing appearance practices, women mentioned sensations such as heat, weight, and vibration of clothes and jewelry on the body,
which can be "sticky," "clammy," "tight," "flowing," "cumbersome," "warm,"
and more. In addition, the sensory emphasis within blind women's use of

material culture, such as clothing, allows connecting tactility to a personal experience rather than with material objects (Classen 2005, 4) and offers an embodied, sensory standpoint on the subject of women and the use of clothing (see Guy and Banim 2000).

Blind women's descriptions of the richness of touch also included references to inner feelings, such as "pleasant," "comfortable," "sexy," and "modest," capturing what is referred to in sensory ethnography as the "multisensory nature" of experience (Feld 2003; Pink 2009) and pointing out pleasurable sensory experiences in relation to appearance. Karin, a forty-five-year-old visually impaired woman, expressed this as "a kind of . . . desire and need to feel nice and pleasant. . . . Something that's part of me, inside of me." Rinat added in relation to her inner feelings, "I feel what suits me and what doesn't, you understand? You *feel* those things; you learn to sense them." And Aviva explained:

> I know what I like, the way it feels on my body, which type of fabric. It's a lot by sensation. Today, I have clothes that are really *mine*, you understand? They're Aviva's clothes; they make me feel good. If I'm wearing clothes I don't like, let's say, on a morning I get up late, I feel uncomfortable.

This type of sensory attunement and pleasure within gender performance blind women talked about was also described in the writing of Ernestine Amani Patterson (1985), an African-American blind woman. Patterson, who wears her hair braided, emphasizes the sensory stimulation she receives from her hairstyle, a stimulation she emphasizes when hearing remarks such as, "your hair is very pretty. But it's too bad you can't see how nice the style is and how colorful the beads are":

> I always say nowadays: each style has its own shape. And though the beads are a different color, many of them also have their own touch [ . . . ] They are glass, wood, and plastic beads. These are further divided into varying tactile textures. And although I haven't gotten into them yet, you can purchase semi-precious gem beads, and they have their flavor, too. And if I am wearing bells in my hair when these remarks are made, I shake my head a little so they can hear the jingle; hopefully they'll get the message. (240)

"The style of my hair altered the shape of my head within," Patterson concluded. "How many women can say that with satisfaction about any beauty treatment that they try?" (243).

Blind women's narratives about enjoyable sensory experiences, such as feeling satisfaction, fun, comfortable, and pleasant when wearing certain clothes, shoes, and beauty products, emphasize the function of the senses as a stimulus for sensory pleasure, the pleasures received through a heightened awareness of sound, smell, and touch within choices regarding appearance. This type of embodied sensibility exposes the presence of positive experiences within women's appearance management practices, contributing to the feminist debate over women's agency in relation to what Venkatesh et al. (2010) called "aesthetic labor"—a set of embodied capacities and attributes that people (mainly women) use to look "good" and "right," sculpting oneself and one's appearance (460).

Feminist literature is ambivalent regarding the notion of pleasure in relation to appearance practices. Venkatesh et al. (2010), for example, offer that aesthetic labor is typically associated with negative emotions and dissatisfaction with one's looks but can also be linked with liberatory and celebratory notions of fashion; Johnston and Taylor (2008) discuss the different aspects of "feminist consumerism" in relation to women's participation in the capitalist market; Huisman and Hondagneu-Sotelo (2005) address the contradictory ways women are portrayed in relation to dress, victims of consumerism on one hand and empowered by the use of hyperfeminine forms of dress on the other; Guy and Banim (2000) discuss both the restrictive and creative aspects of fashion and clothing use, exploring the boundaries of both the enjoyment and frustration women experience in using their clothes (323); and Tyner and Ogle (2007) argue that "The modern feminist movement has produced two opposing ways of seeing the relationship between women and fashionable dress: fashion as stifling the self and fashion as creating the self" (Wilson 2003 in Tyner and Ogle 2007, 80–81).

Blind women's description of sensory practices that emphasize the realm of pleasure and delight within gender performance can be situated in this feminist debate regarding appearance. Their narratives demonstrate the ambivalent nature of appearance practices. On one hand, as demonstrated in chapter 4, such practices can function as a discipline of women's bodies, with mechanisms relevant specifically to women with disabilities and blind women. On the other hand, blind women's sensory pleasure and awareness within appearance management does not allow interpreting their position as simply that of the docile body, "a body that is controlled and disciplined in accord with prevailing sociocultural discourses of attractiveness" (Tyner and Ogle 2007, 77). While blind women indeed normalize their bodies and appearances into a performance that matches the normalcy standards of a healthy and whole body, they also interpret beauty as affected by inner sensations. Rather than conforming to narrow beauty standards and following an external (male) idea of beauty or surveillance, blind women link beauty with, for example, pleasant fabrics, smooth textures, favorite sounds, and preferable scents, offering sensory versions of beauty that challenge "narrow, male-defined concepts of beauty, value, and power" (Tyner and Ogle 2007, 88). Emphasizing their individual sense of aesthetics rather than those "dictated by a presumably male-dominated fashion industry" (Tyner and Ogle 2007, 94), blind women's bodies become not only a site of control but also a site of personal pleasure derived from sensations, pleasure directed at inner feelings rather than achieved through attracting a romantic/sexual partner or looking aesthetically pleasing to others. Blind women's sensory descriptions regarding appearance also emphasize choice and exploration. And although feminist critique justifiably contextualize such "choices" as already taking place within consumer culture (Bordo 2003), blind women's emphasis on sensory richness and pleasure within appearance management is useful in rethinking women's agentic possibilities in visual and consumer culture. As Butler (1990) advised: "To deconstruct gender ideologies, we must first deconstruct the manner in which the body is associated with power" (in Tyner and Ogle 2007, 78).

Moreover, descriptions of the sensory pleasure in blind women's gender performance express a celebratory approach to blindness, which, while describing its advantages, also criticizes sightedness as flat, lazy, detached, external, and not natural. Yael, for example, who relies on sound also in her profession as a musician and singer, explained the advantages of hearing versus seeing:

> Hearing operates in 360 degrees; however, you can't see what's behind you [ . . . ] I think that when you live with the qualities of sound, in the sphere of hearing and not in sight, there's something else, much deeper. Because when you hear, you can't hear half-heartedly. I can't hear with a glance [ . . . ] I think that in sight, there's something closed; it's about the exterior, like "See how I look."

Talia referred more specifically to the advantages blindness offers in relation to her feminine appearance, arguing that since she is "not dependent on the mirror" but on "inner feelings," she can choose comfortable clothes rather than follow fashion trends. "If I were a sighted person," she elaborated,

> I wouldn't be a person who knows what's natural and what's not, and I would have to comply with social norms that women feel compelled

to follow. And I wouldn't want to be in that place, and I really like the fact that I was spared that. You see? There's something good about blindness.

These critical views of the sense of sight can be read through previous research of sound studies that criticize the eye versus the ear (Bendix 2000, 35, 37), and through the lens of studies in visual culture that have recognized the costs of the increasing visuality of Western culture, identifying the visual as evoking a flat and superficial experience (Renshaw 2009). The Finnish architect Juhani Pallasmaa (2012), for example, who examines visual culture and the senses from an architectural standpoint, argues for the lack of sensory experience in modern Western architecture, pointing to the ways urban landscapes and modern technology alienate and detach individuals both from their surroundings and from their embodied experiences (29). Visuality, in this notion, reflects the distancing of humans from their surroundings, in which the eyes passively receive "icy," "cold" images (Lefebvre 1991, 286). Blind women's experiencing of the senses and their criticism of the qualities of sight produce a novel perspective in this scholarship, as the critique comes from the daily experiences of *blind people*, who have traditionally been located outside the analysis of visual culture.

Blind women's notions of embracing blindness also reflect and contribute to celebratory approaches in disability studies, spawned from research in disability and sexuality, and disability and identity. When speaking about their senses, blind women recognized blindness as allowing a deep and authentic connection with the body, intuition, and femininity. Yael, for example, explained:

> Blindness allows me to feel; it's a freedom to sense your body and to listen to it deeply. Sight makes you occupied with seeing and not sensing; sighted people are obsessed with looking forward, looking around them, and not inside of them. In blindness, there is something very opening and enabling to femininity [ . . . ] It has more attentiveness to the senses . . . to . . . sensation, feminine intuition, you know.

Anat also emphasized the necessity of touch, smell, and taste in her daily life and the kind of intimacy blindness enables:

> When you see, you see it on TV, but as a blind person, you need to touch in order to see. You need to smell, to taste [ . . . ] I think sight is about distance. You see a flower; you can see it from a hundred meters.

I need to go to the flower, to touch it, to smell it, in order to enjoy it. It's a much closer medium, much more intimate, personal, much more pleasant even.

Emphasizing the mediums of sensory experiences blindness call for, blind women's descriptions highlight the realm of disability and delight, and what has been characterized as the "positive disability identity" (Shakespeare 1996, 209) in the context of "disability culture." Somewhat similar to identity politics projects led by members of African American culture, queer culture, or others, "disability culture" is a movement and a collective awareness through which people with disabilities claim their condition as a basis for positive identity politics, developing the notion of a "unique cultural identity" (Peters 2000, 585). This view of disability has been expressed, for example, by Deaf Culture, identifying deafness not as a medical condition in need of a cure but as a social identity having its own sensory practices and community (Padden and Hamphries 2009), even offering the term "Deafhood" (Ladd 2003) to suggest a Deaf sense of being. Blind women's sensory capital enriches this "disability-as-insight" (Brueggemann et al. 2005, 28) approach, emphasizing the ways in which blind women may accept, celebrate, and enjoy their difference.

## Blind Women's "Sensory Capital"

Blind women's acknowledgement of blindness as accentuating the sensory body brings to light an additional aspect within their appearance management, which I identify as "sensory capital"—an essential yet ignored component of Bourdieu's (1986) term "physical/embodied capital" (243–44). Bourdieu's term referred to "aesthetic dispositions" that bear symbolic value and influence practices directed toward the body, such as diet, beauty care, or exercise, as well as styles of walk, talk, and dress (Bourdieu 1984; see also Shilling 2003). The term has been specifically used in theories of late capitalism and consumer culture that discuss individuals' attempts to maintain and control their bodies' shape, size, and weight, as well as gestures, smiles, tonality, and walk, within the capitalist market (Paterson 2006). Physical capital is also relevant to disability studies, which recognizes the importance of a bodily trait hierarchy that "determines the distribution of privilege, status, and power" (Garland-Thomson 1997, 6). Moreover, physical capital is also relevant to disability since it contains a dialectical view of the body both as a biological and social phenomenon and acknowledges the social struggle over "the definition of the legitimate body and legitimate use of the body" (Bourdieu 1978, 827). Blind women's appearance management highlights a sensory component within physical capital, identifying touch, sound, and smell as significant in blind women's various routes to knowledge about appearance. As Aviva related, "I'm very aware of the senses, of their operation; I use them."

Blind women's sensory capital not only emphasizes sensory elements within women's gendered "body schema" but also offers contributions to Bourdieu's (1984) analysis of forms of habitus and class-based social locations. Blind women's meticulous "hyperaware" feminine practices (discussed also in chapter 3) illustrate the ways in which a marginal social group, often affiliated with a lower class and status,[1] performs a careful and attentive use of the body. This challenges the association of the working classes with those who have an instrumental relation to their bodies, who "make a realistic or functionalist use of clothing" (Bourdieu 1984, 200), and "are less aware of the 'market' value of beauty" (206). In contrast, blind women's appearance management is more similar to the petit-bourgeois uneasy experience of the world, the middle class anxiety about appearance, or the bourgeois restrained and measured style. Blind women's hyperaware bodily practices also challenge the "automatic nature" of habitus. Shira, a thirty-three-year-old congenitally blind woman, summed up the role of visual feedback in the construction of her appearance, as well as her active role as a creative agent in choosing the way she looks:

> I really make an effort to look good [ . . . ] I have to receive so much feedback! I constantly have to ask people in order to know how to implement the visual norms. So I take a bit from everything, mix it all together, and from the mixture, create the compound I want.

This kind of effort Shira and many other women described questions the unconscious level of forms of habitus (Bourdieu 1986, 245) and joins other writings on women's awareness of appearance norms and savvy negotiation and implementation of visual standards and material culture, such as dress (Guy and Banim 2000; Tyner and Ogle 2007, 101). More specifically, blind women's appearance work can be seen as an expression of a "situated action," in Shilling's (2004) words, in which "those stigmatized [ . . . ] may reflect on their 'spoiled identity,' having discovered they are more capable than society assumes, and reject this identity in favor of an alternative" (480). Indeed, women described their heightened sensations and rich sensory use of the body as *acquired* skills that are not exclusive or congenital among blind people but rather learned through a deliberate development of sensory awareness.

Blind women's sensory capital also illustrates the fine line between agency and power. On one hand, blind women experience a hyperaware feminine performance that disciplines the body, as described in chapter 3. On the other, their femininity is embedded with sensory pleasure and provokes a rich use of the haptic body. Karin, in our interview, captured this tension, declaring:

> I'm always in some kind of awareness, but this is me, you understand, Gili? This is me! I've accepted this effort; I've embraced it. It raises me; it pushes me forward [ . . . ] I'm attached to its aesthetics, to the movement in it [ . . . ] Do you experience putting on lipstick as an effort? You don't have to answer me. There are days when I feel tired from being careful all the time, and on other days, it's really fun for me, you understand? Am I allowed to say "I feel good in this way?" Will people believe me? I'm not sure they will.

Karin thus emphasizes both the effort required of her in being constantly aware of her appearance, as well as the pleasure she receives from sensory aspects such as aesthetics, movement, and touch.

Karin's and other women's descriptions point out a kind of sensory capital that *simultaneously* expresses resistance, pleasure, obedience, and strife, embedding personal and embodied elements into disciplinary practices. This function of sensory capital is important, considering that women in modern cultures face "ideological dichotomy, ambiguity, and ambivalence of modern feminist discourse on dress and the body" (Tyner and Ogle 2007, 100). In the face of what Tyner and Ogle identified as "incongruous ideologies about fashion and dress" (100), women typically experience a binary construction of dress as either oppressive or liberating, and even as expressing different notions of the self, including, "The woman I want to be," "the woman I fear I could be," and "the woman I am most of the time" (Guy and Banim 2000, 316). Karin and other blind women I talked to do not feel torn between the role of docile bodies and that of free agents, nor between disciplining the body and experiencing sensory pleasure when performing appearance practices. Their sensory capital allows them to be tuned to their embodied preferences, making choices regarding appearance that are somewhat in alliance with their bodily preferences. Appearance practices sill demand high costs from its performers ("I'm always in some kind of awareness," as Karin said) but can also be accompanied by experiences of pleasure, satisfaction, or completion.

This overlap between the body and social expectations calls to mind other instances in which women make decisions about their appearance that resolve the paradoxes of visual, consumer cultures. In their analysis of dress-related meanings in issues of *Ms. Magazine*, Tyner and Ogle (2007), for example, demonstrated how "feminist values and a passion for appearance management need not be mutually exclusive" (93). Citing Guy and Banim's (2000) analysis of the three types of selves women negotiate, Tyner and Ogle (2007) show how specific rhetoric about dress "underscores the possibility that 'the woman I want to be' and 'the woman I am most of the time' need not be mutually exclusive identities but rather can be one and the same" (92). "Women's identity," Guy and Banim (2000) remind us, "is realised through the presentation of many selves" (315).

In addition to serving as a tool to bridge power and agency, blind women's sensory capital affects their social relations and experience of their surroundings more broadly. Participants talked about "sensing an atmosphere" of a place, for example, or having what Michal named "environmental intuition" (*intuizya svivatit*). Neta, a thirty-four-year-old congenitally blind woman who has lived in several countries, explained the ways she senses different locations:

> How do you feel an atmosphere? By different voices, different sounds, you can feel it and not only see it. By . . . the way people walk or talk, by smells, by . . . the air. Italy, for example: very warm people, talk a lot, laugh, good food, good smells, lots of light [ . . . ] Australia: lots of light and it's warm, but something closer, everyone in his own house, people are more restrained. Something's kind of heavy, not flowing [ . . . ] I really like Tel-Aviv. I like the . . . vibrant life, the buzz; it reminds me of New York, everything's accessible 24/7. It's also a bit stressful; it's not always easy, but I like it.

Semadar concentrated more specifically on her impression of different places in Israel, explaining,

> Tel-Aviv, for me, means dust, noise, lots of traffic, boisterous [ . . . ] Jerusalem has something else . . . A heavier feeling. And in the north, well . . . the north is calm, it's . . . these mountainous landscapes and the plants; it has a special smell. The landscape of the north has its

own smell [ . . . ] For me, views are a matter of atmosphere, of smell, of feeling.

Yael also addressed her sensory body in her everyday life, referring to what she described as her "sensitivity to the world." "This sensitivity to the world means to walk into a place and experience its atmosphere," she said, "not to experience sight but literally feeling the atmosphere in its material sense, the air, the changing feelings in the air [ . . . ] This is what blindness enables, this intuition." "As a blind woman," she elaborated,

> I live listening to the world. It's an element I can't do without. It's sensitivity to sound. Much higher sensitivities. Listening! I love, I can spend hours listening to voices from the outside, to noises here at home, this skill of listening is. . . . I think that if lost my hearing I'd go crazy. It would be terrible.

Women's descriptions of their sensory sensitivity and of the centrality of the sensory body in their everyday life expose another aspect of sensory capital—an ability to experience an articulated sensitivity to the world. This sensitivity calls to mind the "quintessential property of the body" Latour (2004) talks about. "Acquiring a body," Latour explains, "is a progressive enterprise that produces at once a sensory medium and a sensitive world" (207). The importance of sensory-embodied awareness was also identified by scholars of movement, arguing for the importance of kinesthetic knowing or feeling, providing "grounding for rich understanding" (McCaughtry and Rovegno 2001, 492) of ourselves and others as embodied selves (see Sanders-Bustle and Oliver 2001, 515). Blind women's sensory capital indeed allows the type of knowledge, feeling, and articulation that makes a sensitive body and world. It allows articulating embodied aspects of gender performance and sensory components of different surroundings. Blind women's sensory capital and the ability to articulate it can be compared to Latour's (2004) discussion of the ways pupils in the perfume industry are trained to distinguish between odors. Before their training, the pupils were "inarticulate"—"they were not able to speak about the odours, and different odours elicited the same behavior" (209). Blind women's sensory capital implies an articulated body, a body that distinguishes between and is affected by different textures, odors, and sounds in everyday life and in relation to gendered embodiment. As Belek (2018) argues, discussing Latour's concepts of articulation in relation to the sensitivity of autistic bodies, "A more sensitive body, therefore, ultimately means a richer world" (2).

An actuation of sensory awareness can be identified not only within blind women's social interactions and gendered practices but also within occasions that emphasize intersensory experiences of blind and sighted people, fostering dialogical encounters with the "Other," as the next section discusses. Sensory capital, therefore, is not confined to blind women but can be developed by critical reflections on the senses that blind and sighted people can share through dialogical experiences.

*Nine*

# Intersensory Experiences and "Dialogical Performances" of Blindness and Sight

—❧—

Dialogical performance is a way of having intimate conversations with other people and cultures. Instead of speaking about them, one speaks to and with them. (Conquergood 1985, 10)

Rich usage of the sensory body can be identified within meetings among people with varied visual skills in the context of events emphasizing intersensory experiences. These occasions, rather than normalizing the blind identity, engender a *social dialogue* among blind and sighted people, challenging distinct binary categories and bodily hierarchies and bringing sighted and blind people into a mutual dialogue. My first encounter with such an "intersensory performance," that is, an event that emphasizes a range of sensory experiences through the meeting with blindness, happened at the beginning of my research, when attending the music concert *Things You Hear from Here* (*devarim sheshomeim mekan*). The concert featured seven blind and visually impaired musicians performing original music and well-known pieces in collaboration with a vocal ensemble and sighted musicians. Around the time of the concert, I was occupied with questions regarding the validity of cultural spaces that seek to inspire dialogue about visual skills. Therefore, when I first saw the headline in the announcement for the concert, asking: "Interested in a unique sensory experience?" I was intrigued, but skeptical. Once in attendance, though, I found that the listening experience the concert created offered some possible answers to my questions regarding the ways that a mutual dialogue between the senses and social identities can take place. What distanced the event from ableist perspectives of blindness and from charitable, telethon-type representations of disability are the elements that characterize intersensory dialogical events in general: the concert was a multisensory experience offering a dialogue among the senses. The program was available in large and standard print, as well as in Braille, and the concert itself featured a variety of sounds, voices, tones, colors and images, plus the sight and smell of special effects such as smoke on the stage. Also integrated into the program were short videos about the lives of the performers, each of which had rich audio and visual content.

The concert initiated a dialogue not only among various senses but also between members of the audience, which included parents, children, youth, and adults; people with musical interests; and blind and visually impaired people and performers with canes and guide dogs—a sight still rare in Israeli theaters. The presence of such a diverse audience allowed unique dialogues to take place during the show. I happened to sit next to Adi, a blind person, which created the opportunity for a conversation: while I offered my interpretation of visual information regarding the number of people on stage, the color and style of the performers' outfits, and the settings of the videos, Adi explained the program and updated me throughout, as he was able to read in Braille in the dark. The performers on stage, like the audience, included people with varied visual skills, but there was no clear division between blind, visually impaired, and sighted musicians, and it was not possible to know only by looking at them who was who. In addition, watching the concert, listening to the music, and absorbing the event, the audience learned of varied ways of grasping, learning, and performing music. Through the videos and performances, the audience received information about the ways a musician is trained and learns music without sight, with Braille notes for example; and through sound, the audience and the musicians themselves, sighted and blind, were exposed to less familiar ways of performing social activity and gaining knowledge in the field of music.

The social dialogue that took place at the concert and in other events I documented can be identified as what Conquergood (1985) called a "dialogical performance"—a performance bringing people into "intimate conversations" with one another. Such occasions, rather than normalizing the blind identity, engender a *social dialogue* among blind and sighted people that challenges distinct binary categories and bodily hierarchies. While Conquergood (1985) and additional anthropologists of performance (see Madison 2006) discussed the term "dialogical performance" in the context of fieldwork and ethnographic work, I apply this notion to discuss the meeting with blindness and to emphasize the role of the senses in dialogical performances.

This particular scrutiny of dialogical performances among blind and sighted people is rare. Previous interpretations of encounters between disabled and nondisabled people in general, and between sighted and blind people in particular, have commonly pointed out the "ableist" interactions demonstrated by the wider society that, projecting the "clinical gaze" (Foucault 1975), defines disability as a medical concern in need of a solution, or attempts to socialize the disabled person into a normative self (Williams and Nind 1999). This normalizing approach has been discussed in relation to numerous subjects, with scholars addressing, for instance, the ways students with disabilities are labeled with medical terminology such as "chronic, degenerative, progressive, profound, and incurable" (Brueggemann and Kleege 2003, 175); the ways the sexuality of women with cognitive disabilities has been commonly suppressed and controlled by society (Williams and Nind 1999); and the ways blindness has been traditionally perceived by modern philosophical, scientific, medical, and pedagogical politics as a state of "epistemological ignorance" (Schillmeier 2006, 471). Scholars have argued that even interactions and spaces that are allegedly inclusive toward disability and blindness, incorporating accessibility and the use of Braille, for example, may deliver negative stereotypes and prejudices, equating blindness with concepts such as "ignorance, prejudice, loss or despair" (Kleege 2006, 209).

In contrast to these normalizing interactions, dialogical performances initiate "conversations" between blind and sighted people and are based on rich sensory experiences in which individuals with varied visual skills meet. In what follows, I focus on an ethnographic example of such a performance: a tandem cycling group pairing blind and sighted cyclists. Focusing on the interactions taking place among people in the group engaging in the somatic experiences of tandem cycling, I demonstrate that a dialogical performance requires the presence of intersensory somatic experiences shared by all participants. The interactions among the group members challenge sensory and cultural boundaries, as blindness serves here as a catalyst for sensory reflections that enrich visual understanding of the sensory self and of the visual field. Therefore, blindness in this context is understood as another form of the human condition rather than as a mysterious and mystifying experience. While avoiding the cliché of associating it with congenital sensory skills, this example allows an understanding of blindness (and disability), in Kleege's (2005) words, as "another way of moving through space, reading, communicating and being in the world" (217).

As opposed to accounts in which blindness can be understood through a hierarchical lens of accommodation, the intersensory performance of tandem cycling, and of dialogical performance of blindness in general, emphasizes the way the meetings between people with different sensory skills can serve as the basis for the development of participants' critical self-reflection, creating new perspectives that challenge the boundaries around the senses (visual/ tactile) and social identities (abled/disabled). In these instances, blindness is understood as a platform *enabling* new ways of approaching the sensory body and bodily knowledge, allowing blind, sighted, and visually impaired people to "reflect back upon themselves" (Turner 1986, 24) while engaging in "sensuous" and "emphatic" (Conquergood 1985, 10) conversations with other people and cultures.

## Dialogical Performance of the Body in the Tandem Cycling Group

In October 2008, I joined a tandem cycling group that pairs sighted and blind riders who go mountain biking in the desert of southern Israel. At the time I joined it, the group was comprised of fifteen to twenty-five members from the ages of fifteen to seventy, including blind and sighted people, and a small number of persons with cognitive and physical disabilities. The number of cyclists varied in each outing (which lasted between one and a half to three hours, 10–20 km), but each usually consisted of at least six tandem bikes, typically with a sighted captain and a blind/visually impaired person as the rear rider, and two handcycles, used by cyclists with physical disabilities such as lower-body injuries.

The tandem cycling group allowed me to study sensory dialogues taking place between "extraordinary" and "normate" bodies, in Garland-Thomson's (1997) terms, where people with varied visual skills participate in a physical, social interaction on a regular basis, outside the context of rehabilitation and education programs for the blind. In contrast to rehabilitation programs that typically ask to regulate "corporeal otherness" (Garland-Thomson 1997, 5) as mentioned earlier, the tandem cycling group initiated a mutual dialogue between people with different bodies and visual skills, challenging binary definitions of "ability/disability" and "blindness/sight." Such dialogues between participants in the group happened quite literally in this activity, and were not only social but also physical, as the paired riders were compelled to share each moment of the ride, coordinating their actions while in close proximity with each other, often for extended periods of time. The presence of blind people in the activity also heightened the required level of awareness and sensitivity to each rider's needs, which engendered a social dialogue between and about blindness and sight, and a dialectical relationship between the cyclist and his/her body, as well as among group members who embody different types of visual skills and sensory awareness. As I described in my fieldwork:

> When the ride is going well, it feels like becoming one with the other person, becoming one rider, coordinating the movements of our legs, hearing only the sound of pedaling in the background. The coordinated movement on the bike is achieved through careful listening. It's a partnership with the other who is with you. Becoming an "us' [ . . . ] a single entity of feeling-seeing-movement (May 2009).

This entity of "feeling-seeing-movement" I described was revealed to me during a year of ethnography conducted while cycling with the group on twenty tandem rides and three two-day cycling trips, while participating in the group's social gatherings and activities, and through formal interviews and informal conversations with group members. Dialogical intersensory performance took place in this activity by means of four main dynamics: (1) the formation of a sense of "togetherness" within the group, shaping the group as a "rolling community" (Furness 2007, 308);[1] (2) the intersensory experiences this activity heightens, offering the opportunity of integrating sight with the other senses for both visually impaired and sighted riders; (3) the re-embodiment of vision as an active and somatic sense, a notion that follows Spinney's (2006) suggestion of "reembodying vision" (721) alongside the other senses; and (4) the promotion of critical self-reflection among group members regarding their bodily identities and sensory experiences, as well as in relation to ability-disability dependency and notions such as "asymmetry" and "mutuality."

## A Sense of "Togetherness"

First, dialogical encounters are formed in the tandem cycling group by the social collaborations it creates based on an interdependency among people with a spectrum of physical functionalities engaged in a social activity that, as Anat, a twenty-eight-year-old congenitally blind woman cyclist put it, "cannot be done alone." Avishay, a visually impaired cyclist in his fifties, similarly stated: "In order to ride with someone on a [tandem] bike, you need to work together." Indeed, tandem cycling requires collaboration and synchronization, creating a "togetherness" engendered by the need to coordinate technicalities such as balance, cadence, and force, as well as to consider the other rider's physical and emotional needs. The togetherness in this particular group results from three main characteristics of the activity: the fact that it is *mountain* biking, which is typically more social than road biking (Hazani 2010); the requirements of *tandem* cycling, obliging trust, collaboration, and synchronization between two riders; and the integration of *blind participants and people with disabilities* into the activity. Riders I interviewed repeatedly emphasized the "tight bonds" among group members, defining tandem cycling as "team work" involving the pair on the bike and the group as a whole. "Listen, it isn't just about riding a bike," Jacky, a blind cyclist in her forties who was born with visual impairment, commented, "it's also about the people you're with." Shira, a blind cyclist in her late forties who had become blind in her twenties, agreed:

> The group is about much more than a sport; it's about friendship and caring for each other. I really enjoy the connection with the members [ . . . ] Listen, very intimate connections are created on these rides. A large part of my social life involves these people, is with these people. They've become really good friends [ . . . ] There's something that goes way beyond a sport in this group. [It] feels like a family, caring for one another [ . . . ]; it's [about] birthdays, and holidays, or offering support when bad things happen. It's everything, really.

This togetherness Shira described, which is achieved over time, is expressed not only through verbal explanations and communication (for example, the front rider, or "captain" informing his/her rear rider of a descent or ascent, or rough terrain), but also through what I call "bodily listening," which doesn't necessarily require words. As Jacky elaborated:

> You get to know the person you're riding with. [You know] how patient or impatient he/she is, if he/she is a sensitive or insensitive person; it's amazing [. . . .] I can tell you that when I get on a bike with someone, I can tell, I can sense, if they're in a good or bad mood, if something happened that day, even without them saying a word. You would think that this is only a bike, not more than a piece of metal, but it's so much more than that.

Jacky emphasized that this level of intimacy does not develop immediately. Once established though, "riding becomes like a conversation." "You don't need to talk," Jacky said, "They [captains] don't need to tell me 'listen, we're going to start' or 'pedal upwards or downwards'; you don't need any of this, you simply hop on, put your feet on the pedals, and start riding."

The engagement in a mutual endeavor by people with different bodily needs within an activity requiring a great degree of synchronization and co-ordination leads, in this case, to a sense of unity between dissimilar bodies, fostering what Bar-On-Cohen (2009) called in her study on the lived body in karate, "homology," which "dissolves the boundaries [among participants] and enables them to encourage and help one another" (622). This sense of to-getherness is fostered not only through the collaborative nature of the activity but is also due to the group's demographic, which calls for a high level of awareness and sensitivity to the other's needs. When one of the riders is blind or visually impaired, the social aspect integral in tandem mountain biking is intensified, as the captain is responsible for verbally signaling any significant feature of the ride, such as obstacles on or above ground, gear changes, a stop, change of speed, or change of direction, and for describing the road and land-scape. Blind riders addressed this responsibility of the captain, who needs to "make sure to tell you, 'we have a descent coming, or an ascent, or cracks, or we're slowing down, or there's *Pudra* [powdery sand] ahead." David, a blind cyclist in his forties who was born with visual impairment, also addressed the ways in which the captain is required to verbally coordinate with him "how to mount the bike, how to start, how to stop, or which leg to take off first when getting off in order to support the bike."

### An Intersensory Experience

The second factor contributing to the dialogues created through tandem cy-cling is a somatic experience of intersensory bodily performance. Jacky, for example, spoke to this when explaining her enjoyment of nature:

> [Feeling] the sun, [smelling] the air, and especially if you're riding with someone who tells you what's going on around you. Hearing the birds; or for example, on the ride we just did to the north [of the country], it was amazing to hear the water, and get into the water, to swim in the Jordan river, to hear the waterfalls on the way [while riding], to sleep in tents.

Visual, sonic, tactile, and olfactory experiences, as well as kinesthetic sensa-tions of movement in space were integral to each ride I documented, incorporating aspects of sound (the bicycle while pedaling and features of the environment, such as birds and water), sight (the landscape and other people), and movement (elements of balance, speed, and vibration). The oral, tactile, sonic, olfactory, and gustatory body is engaged during the physical act of cycling when maintaining balance, changing gears, drinking water, eating snacks, breathing heavily, and speaking; feeling the desert breeze, the protective helmet, the handlebars, and the bicycle seat, as well as burning muscles, an increased heart rate, and rushes of adrenaline.

Both blind and sighted cyclists described these multisensory experiences. When I asked David, for example, if he felt he missed out on some experiences because of his blindness, he explained, "You hear nature through your ears, and the person [riding] with you tries to explain things [ . . . ] and I ask questions; I ask for descriptions, and I use my hearing. I smell things that can be smelled, and touch things that I can feel." When asked about their sensory experiences in our interviews and during ongoing conversations, blind and visually impaired riders paid special attention to sonic sensations they absorbed in nature, as well as to the captain's verbal descriptions of the landscape. Jacky, for example, emphasized her use of hearing while riding, mentioning the "quietness" of the desert when participating in full moon rides. "At night," she explained, "I like hearing my surroundings, the quiet around me." Shira, too, noted the significance of the auditory experience, explaining, "I often ask my captain, checking in with him, if I'm tracking the direction of the ride correctly [ . . . ] [and] when I rode with Oliver [a sighted captain], there wasn't one rock that he didn't describe during that 65-kilometer ride. It was amazing." Alongside hearing, blind and visually impaired riders addressed olfactory experiences, referring, for example, to the smell of flowers and breathing the "fresh air" of nature, as well as rich tactile and haptic experiences, such as sensations of temperature (riding on a hot/cold day, in the sun/the shade), angle and direction (when turning right or left, descending/ ascending), and vibration (of the bike on changing terrain). Some participants described the rush of adrenaline and the "atmosphere" of the group as integral to their cycling experience, while Shira emphasized the sensation of freedom and feeling "high" from being in nature and feeling the open space around her. Anat addressed the feeling of "moving forward" when cycling as a crucial factor contributing to her enjoyment of the activity: "It feels good [ . . . ] there's adrenaline [when riding]; and you're expending energy, and there're hormones released in your brain that make you feel good [ . . . ] and there's the atmosphere [of the group], that's also meaningful."

This intersensoriality of tandem cycling—which also includes the sensations of pain, pleasure, and physical effort, coupled in this case with the heightened sensoriality blindness evokes—initiates a dialectical relationship between the cyclist and his/her body and among group members with different types of visual skills and sensory awareness. In this, group members experience what Sanders-Bustle and Oliver (2001) defined in their article about their shared running experience as "kinesthetic knowing" (514), an embodied means of comprehension that highlights the role of non-cognitive qualities informing knowledge. This awareness offers group members a sophisticated understanding of disability defined not by the absence of senses, movement, or mobility but as a rich existence of sensory inputs and legitimate bodily experiences. Further, as "animalistic" sensations such as muscle tension, fatigue, pain, and hunger surface, and bodily fluids such as sweat, blood, and wastes are exposed, a dialogue based on observations of and conversations about varied and mutual bodily experiences becomes possible. These dialogues challenge the typical nature/culture classification in which disability is associated with the realm of nature (usually connected with illness, sickness, and death), deconstructing the notion of disability as bodily otherness that threatens cultural categories of health and vitality.

## Re-Embodying Sight

The third dynamic initiating the intersensory performance of tandem cycling is the opportunity it provides for re-embodying sight and the visual, acknowledging the visual as an amalgamation of the senses and recognizing it as a source of sensory pleasure. As I described in my journal: "Tandem cycling is something I feel in my body, and with my sight" (May 2009). My conversations with riders and my research observations revealed that visual sensations shaped not only sighted riders' experiences but also those of blind and visually impaired riders, each of whom has a different degree of blindness and many of whom have residual visual skills (e.g., tunnel vision, blurred vision, vision through one eye) and visual memory. Both sighted and visually impaired riders visually immersed themselves in the experience, noticing the changing weather, angle of the sun, flora, terrain, or direction of the road. Both Shira and Avishay, for example, recalled instances when the visual was a significant aspect of their riding experience. In our interview, Avishay recalled a memorable ride in a forest in the north of the country. "We rode on a narrow, winding road, with trees on both sides, so tall they created shade. And so you got to ride on a hot sunny day in the shade. Like in a tunnel. And

I could see and enjoy this view. This is something I remember well." In this description, Avishay, who is going blind, remembered the ride as both visual (the trees and the winding, tunnel-like road) and haptic (the cooling shade on a warm day), revealing the intertwining of the visual with the other senses. While Avishay spoke about a ride in the north of the country, Shira, a blind cyclist in her forties who was sighted until her twenties, recalled the landscape where most of the rides take place—the desert. When asked what she observed when riding and about the sensory inputs she received as a blind cyclist, she explained:

> Unlike people who were born blind, I have a very strong visual memory. So my imagination does a lot of work, my imagination and memory. I fill in the picture using the visual memory I have [ . . . ] I know what a desert is. I know what colors are. You understand? But I also feel. Many times, I ask my captain [ . . . ] I ask and feel [ . . . ] [If] you pass by a mountain, you can feel it. I don't know how to explain it, but you can feel [it]. It can be a shadow, a voice. Remember that in the desert, every sound can really affect you, [every] shadow, rustle of the trees. And my senses work overtime, and you [can] feel those things.

Blind and visually impaired riders' visual skills and memory contribute to and enrich their cycling experience, as in the above example, in which Shira described an intersensory experience of sight: her visual memory interwoven with her riding experience, along with oral/aural communication (with the captain), sonic awareness (of sounds in the desert), and haptic sensations (the feel of a mountain, a shadow).

This integrated embodiment of sight was also described by sighted riders, who re-embodied sight as an "array of senses which the rider uses and experiences" (Spinney 2006, 724). Sighted riders offer close observations of the landscape to provide visual descriptions to one another and to the blind riders, while being simultaneously enriched by the tactile and kinesthetic impressions they receive from the rear rider. Sight also plays a central role during stops; on occasions, for example, when the group stopped at a viewpoint or took a break to enjoy flowers or special landscapes. Accordingly, my pictures from the rides include impressions of nature (hills, caves, and valleys), objects (flowers, rocks, a herd of goats, a group of camels), and landscapes (open spaces, sunsets). On such occasions, group members asked each other about the ways people of different visual skills perceive what they see, deconstructing the neutrality of sight and acknowledging varied ways of seeing. For example, on one ride I participated in, taking the role of a rear rider, I documented the communication between the front and rear riders on the bike next to me. At one point, the captain asked his partner what she could see, feel, and hear, and following her response, offered visual descriptions of the fields we were riding through and named the kinds of crops growing in them. As a rear rider myself, I too needed visual descriptions and cautions from my captain, as my location on the bike limited my ability to see the terrain ahead of me. It did, however, allow me to look outward at the landscape and exchange visual information with the captain, offering details he might have missed when focusing on the road ahead.

This type of active seeing echoes what Grasseni (2004) called "skilled vision"—"a capacity to look in a certain way as a result of training" (41). Yet, in contrast to the type of professional vision Grasseni addressed, the embodied vision of the riders I encountered was based on both the intersensory characteristics of the activity they participated in, as well as on the mutual dialogue developed among people with different visual skills. Such experiences offer an opportunity to understand the visual as simultaneously *felt and seen*, and as a significant component of our relationship to our bodies, to one another, and to our environment. As such, they encourage exploring "the activity of seeing" (Hockey and Collinson 2006, 70) as an intersensory performance, both integrated with other senses and shaped by cultural contexts (Classen 1993; Howes 2003). Sighted and blind riders' descriptions of the visual, as well as my own field notes, point out sight as a varied skill and bodily sensation changing from one moment to the other (depending on the rider's role on the bike, his/her visual memory), rendering the visual as a spectrum of variation in terms of awareness and skill. Sight, in these instances, depends on the rider's place on the bike, as well as on a complicated web of practices and awareness consisting of a rider's particular mood; knowledge (of crops, types of rocks, landscapes); haptic capacities (being able to sense a mountain); and ways of interpretation, communication, and observation. This embodied sight is also useful in recognizing the full body sensorium, and in challenging visual dominancy. In this activity, participants do not have to close their eyes, experience darkness, or try to simulate being blind in order to enrich their visual experience, but do so instead through intimate conversations with people with varied visual skills and through developing awareness of their own changing vision. The re-embodiment of sight in integrated tandem cycling challenges visual dominancy through a practice I identify as *challenging sight within sight*. Offering additional ways of seeing that emphasize sight as a whole somatic experience, inclusive tandem cycling allows a complicated

deconstruction of visual primacy and the everyday of seeing through an embodied experience that engenders a heightened sensitivity to the spectrum of
bodily actions and sensory experiences of all participants. Challenging sight
within sight is experienced not only by those who are blind and visually impaired but also by sighted people through engagements with blindness that
enrich their visual knowledge and the ways they perceive the social world.

## Critical Self-Reflections

Finally, the social and bodily dialogues in tandem cycling are also fostered
by awareness among group members of the spectrum of sensory experiences
this activity calls for, broadening the meanings attached to the acts of cycling,
sensing, and moving, as well as those attached to more ordinary aspects of everyday life, such as cooking, parenting, and reading. All of these experiences,
participants come to realize, can be achieved and are experienced through
multiple modalities. This critical awareness and the encounter with a wide
variety of bodily skills provokes transformation and change among group
members, generating questions regarding perceptions of and attitudes toward
the "Other" on both sides of the ability-disability spectrum. For example,
on one occasion, during a car ride back to the city after a ride in the desert,
several members began to discuss their experiences with the group, and the
sighted members all agreed that their interactions with the group had erased
their initial fear of blindness and disability. One of them, a woman in her
twenties, admitted that before joining the group, blindness was in fact her
greatest fear. Accordingly, a blind participant described his feeling of being
accepted by the group. "It's because of the warm relationships [in the group],
and the mutual appreciation, [of me] as a friend, a member (*haver*), and not
as handicapped (*mugbal*)," he told me.

Perspectives toward disability and blindness also changed among blind
and visually impaired members. Avishay indicated the value of being exposed
to different kinds of disabilities after meeting people with cognitive disabilities and amputees who ride handcycles. And Shira, though blind herself, described the ways the group changed her own stigmas of blind people. Since
she had never participated in an integrated activity with other blind people
before joining the group, it was important for her to meet other "people like
me." As she explained:

I never hung out with blind people [before]; I had some sort of aver-
sion to making friends with them [ . . . ] I always had this stigma

about blind people that they're very bitter and stayed closed inside the house. And my exposure to this group really showed me a completely different side [of blindness], of people who love life, and laugh, even at their own disability, at their limitations; it made me aware of this whole side that I didn't even think existed [ . . . ] And all of the sudden, I saw that there're more people like that. It was a very powerful experience, discovering people who enjoy themselves, and have fun, and laugh, and who use dark humor [ . . . ] This was the most surprising thing for me, meeting people who're like me, breaking my stigmas about blindness. My entire worldview about blind people changed. Today, I'm much more open; I became a much more accepting person. And it also made me accept myself more easily, accept my disability.

Encountering blindness and disability also complicates members' perceptions of notions such as dependency, mutuality, equality, and asymmetry and their role within the meeting with the other, encouraging riders to debate over the proper way to offer help (with respect versus denigration), the extent to which blind riders are dependent on sighted ones, and how to constitute equal relations within a setting in which bodily differences require accommodation. Anat, whom I asked about the relationships in the group and the nature of the meeting between a sighted and a blind person, responded, "It's a complicated question. I would have liked to say that they [the relationships] are [equal]; but it's not a true equality." "Almost every meeting between two people who are different [from one another] is not equal," she reflected.

Indeed, alongside the unity created between the riders in tandem cycling, the activity contains aspects of social dependency and asymmetrical relations between blind and sighted members of the group, in which blind participants are, to some extent, dependent on sighted members. These elements are engendered by the captain's necessarily greater degree of control over the bike, the trust a rear rider must place in his/her captain, and the context of this activity, as blind riders are dependent on the presence of sighted participants in order to go cycling at all. It is an accepted fact among group members that if there isn't a sufficient number of sighted people on a given day, blind members may not be able to ride. On the other hand, if a sighted participant is left without a partner, he/she can ride on a "single" [traditional] bike and join the group on his/her own. Blind riders acknowledged these realities, also mentioning that they are required to adjust their time and training schedule to that of the group, since riding by themselves is not an option. Elements of dependency and asymmetrical social relations also arise when blind participants get off the bike. As the group's sighted guide explained: "I think blindness becomes an issue . . . [for example] when you need to take someone to the bathroom. To physically lead him, taking him by the hand." These elements of dependency and asymmetry within social relations in tandem cycling are complex and cannot be framed within a simple blind/sighted/ able/disabled hierarchy. For instance, blind and visually impaired cyclists addressed the different meanings of the terms "dependency" and "help" they experience, recognizing different ways of offering and receiving help, from "patronizing" to an "equal" exchange. Moreover, Avishay, David, and Jacky emphasized their active role as rear riders, understanding the value of their presence and their ability to request the front rider's awareness and consideration of their needs. Therefore, somewhat similar to the "dialectical" asymmetries Kisch (2008, 239) recognized between deaf and hearing members of a Bedouin community, the relationships between blind, sighted, and visually impaired people in the group are based on mutual exchange; an exchange inspired by both the coordination and collaboration needed in this activity, as well as by the participants' varied social affiliations and differences based on age, gender, profession, sensory skills, attitudes toward nature, and physical strength. This variety allows interpreting the dependency in the group as "situational" (Kisch 2008, 296), controlled by particular settings (for example, when getting off the bike or navigating an unfamiliar area) and containing agency and choice on the part of the blind rider (e.g., choosing who to ride with, the amount of force used in pedaling, the speed of the bike). Furthermore, in these accounts, dependency is not only a factor of disability; for example, when a strong blind rider is paired with a less physically strong or experienced sighted one, the question of dependency and help is revised, and the sighted one benefits from the help of the blind rider. On one of my first rides, for instance, while just learning the intricate skills of tandem mountain biking, I paired with Avishay, an experienced visually impaired rider. As my rear rider, he used the ride to provide me with detailed explanations about the bike, its gears, and how to coordinate our pedaling and balance. Without his explanations and help, I would have been lost.

The critical awareness of the other created in tandem cycling and the fine line between dependency and interdependency participants navigate is achieved by the fact that differences in the group are not erased, but openly acknowledged, allowing cyclists to learn from their differences as members of a shared community, fostering relations of intimacy and trust while initiating critical self-reflexive knowledge and an awareness of a spectrum of bodily experiences and social identities. Rather than addressing disability as an "anomaly" (Douglas 1966), which as such must be "settled" into the normative social order by eliminating it, segregating it, or allowing it a temporary liminal existence (Turner 1969, 1990), the meeting with disability in an embodied, intersensory context promotes self-reflection, agency, and new kinesthetic possibilities that acknowledge difference. Intersensory performance, then, generates the great paradox of the dialogical performance, by which "the deeply different become deeply known without becoming any less different" (Conquergood 1985, 10), promoting a more pluralistic approach to bodily ways of being in the world that can also be applied in pedagogical contexts of meeting with the other.

As a whole, the intersensory dialogues between blindness and sight taking place in the cycling group initiate collaborations across ability/disability social affiliations. The meetings taking place within the tandem cycling group are valuable for discussing the nature of social dialogue and human encounters, indicating that relations based on mutual discussion, acknowledgment of the differences and richness among human beings with varied bodily functionality and intersensory experiences, empower numerous aspects of social relations. Moreover, this type of social performance may even encourage social change, a phenomenon expressed, for example, by sighted riders looking for opportunities in other social arenas and contexts to engage with blind people, and by the blind riders whose own perceptions of blindness and disability were altered by the opportunity to position their bodies and identity in an equal and non-exoticizing location, outside the normalizing ideology. These dialogues also reveal the important role the sensory, lived body plays in mutual exchanges within a multisensory environment, giving rise to an acknowledgment of a wide variety of physical embodiments and forms of being in the world (Merleau-Ponty 1964). The sensory prism is crucial, therefore, for understanding social events that not only defamiliarize taken-for-granted sensory and bodily skills such as seeing but also promote a sophisticated awareness of sensory skills across a spectrum rather than in binary oppositions, reminding us that "down to and into our bones, we are all bodies [ . . . ] sensing, moving creatures" (Sheets-Johnstone 1992, 1). The mutuality and intimacy within the tandem cycling group, as well as the multiple senses actively operated in this activity, create proximity among social actors, fostering relationships that challenge the processes that turn the blind/disabled into an exotic other, producing a space of democracy and difference, where, "fellow travellers are deeply and meaningfully interacting with one another in highly performative ways as they cross borders and travel across territories" (Madison 2006, 323). As Shira summarized in our interview: "You want the bottom line of this whole conversation? It [the cycling group] changed my life. Really! The exposure to this group changed my life. [It] truly caused a revolution in the way I think."

# Conclusion

## *Blindness as Broadening the Sensory Self*

The sensory awareness discussed in this section reveals the ways blindness heightens attention to sound, touch, movement, and sight, and evokes a rich use of the senses. Blind women's sensory capital, and the intersensory performances taking place in the meeting between blind and sighted people, carry trifold implications: they indicate the central role of the senses within socialization processes and social interactions; they articulate the senses as a *spectrum* of physical and cultural experiences both sighted *and* blind people share; and they recognize the role of intersensory events in promoting dialogical encounters with blindness and bodily difference. Riding tandem bikes in the open desert landscape and experiencing femininity through the multiple senses demonstrate the ways blindness allows developing what Banes and Lepecki (2007), in their anthology *The Senses in Performance*, identified as "a descriptive language for taste, textures, aromas, and sounds [ . . . ] that is as rich and detailed as that for sight and musical or verbal sounds" (2).

Blind women's sensory practices expand the realm of gender performance and femininity to one of multiple senses and sensory pleasure, contributing to our understanding of the ways social categories such as gender and femininity are embedded with sensory experiences and awareness. This conscious attention to the senses is also present within intersensory events bringing together blind and sighted people, such as the tandem cycling group. Such occasions indicate the ways intersensory experiences and dialogical meetings with blindness are intertwined. Research within the fields of the anthropology of performance and disability performance have indeed indicated the ways a dialogue between individuals different from one another may result in new understandings of social identities (Conquergood 1985; Garland-

Thomson 2009; Schechner 1985; Turner 1986) and cultural norms about the body (Kuppers 2004; Quinlan and Bates 2008). Madison (2006), for example, in her article, *The Dialogic Performative in Critical Ethnography*, called for a "reinvigoration of our thinking about the Other through a theory of the dialogical performative" (321). The tandem cycling group offers an example of how such a dialogue can be achieved, emphasizing the role of intersensory experiences in challenging the ways blindness and disability are perceived. It reveals that dialogical encounters with blindness are encouraged by the presence of multiple senses, identities, and bodily skills, indicating that when individuals who are different from one another critically reflect upon their sensory practices, dialogical performances have the potential to fulfill the goal of redirecting social behaviors toward mutuality and multiplicity, acknowledging both blindness and sight as rich, bodily experiences that inform each other.

Blind women's sensory capital, as well as the intersensory performances within the tandem cycling group, are useful in exposing larger theoretical contributions offered by *the crossroads of blindness and the senses*. The ways blind women speak of their sensory practices, and the critical reflections on the senses participants in intersensory performances share, emphasize active and conscious aspects of embodied skills, continuing scholarly works challenging traditional theorization of bodily learning and the habitus (Csordas 1993; Harris and van Drie 2015; Rice 2013; Samudra 2008) as silent and practical, "unconscious and purely mimetic" (Bourdieu in Downey 2010, 25). Blind women's descriptions of appearance practices, as well as blind and sighted people's reflections on their sensations, open the path for considering the conscious and active aspects of embodied knowledge and of sensory modalities other than sight (Hammer 2017). Moreover, these narratives provide a unique perspective on the questions of embodiment and language. A central question occupying researchers of embodied learning is the problem of language: the difficulty of verbalizing and making explicit sensory embodied knowledge (Hinojosa 2002; Rose 1999; Sieler 2014). Blind women's descriptions of sensory capital and embodied narratives of participants in intersensory performances allow developing a language with which to describe bodily actions and sensations, including bodily processes, visual knowledge, and kinesthetic experiences. Such sensory conciseness is important in order to enrich everyday experience and understanding of the self.

The sensory experiences discussed here reveal that blindness is crucial for the research of the sensorium, allowing not only defamiliarizing taken-for-granted sensory and bodily skills such as seeing but also documenting a wide range of sensory experiences among people with and without disabilities. Researching the senses while paying a nuanced attention to bodily difference, therefore, is valuable for understanding disability as a fluid state and that many of our sensory and bodily identities are not static. This line of thought offers a possible answer to the question of, "How one might [ . . . ] take steps toward an ecology of the senses, their linkages to cognition, their collaboration in providing us with aesthetic pleasure?" (Bendix 2000, 40). One possible answer is: by listening to the "alternative sensory and intellectual territory" (Classen 1998, 160) blindness evokes.

*Ten*

# Conclusion

*Blindness as a Critical Consciousness*

⸺∞⸺

In the conclusion of his book, Michalko (1998) wrote: "The extraordinary story of blindness reveals itself in the realm of the ordinary" (159). Indeed, the conclusion of the story of blindness and sight I offered in my book can be reflected in an ordinary event. In May 2007, while leafing through a local newspaper, a review of an art exhibit at the Sommer Contemporary Art gallery in Tel-Aviv, Israel, caught my eye. Titled *The Invisible Snake Show* (Helfman et al. 2007), the exhibit was inspired by an infamous Coney Island attraction of the same name. Housed in a dark pavilion, the Coney Island "show" consisted of a large snake terrarium, which, when closely inspected by paying customers, appeared to be empty. The snake, as promised, was invisible. In Tel-Aviv, the attraction's contemporary reincarnation was designed to raise questions about visible and hidden elements in art and life and about notions of presence and absence, challenging visitors to "see the invisible, and then again not to see it, since it's not there" (Sheffi 2007).

As I read about *The Invisible Snake Show* and its playful approach to visibility and invisibility, its invitation to question the meaning of these concepts in art and life while inserting a symbolic blindness into a space typically governed by sight, I recognized my own goals in exploring blindness. Through this book, my intention was to blur the lines between blindness and sight, to challenge the taken-for-grantedness of sight, and to provoke reflection upon the wealth of meaning within seeing and being seen, and if I return to the metaphor of dance, to ask about the dance between seeing and being seen as it intersects with blindness. While in the exhibit in Tel Aviv blindness was used to rethink concepts such as absence and presence, in this book, I regarded blindness as potentially evoking a critical awareness of the way we perceive ourselves and others, and as an opportunity that may challenge binaries such as agency/power systems, ability/disability, blindness/ sight, and me/other. In chapter 1, I introduced this theoretical understanding of blindness as insight. And in the different chapters, I discussed the numerous ways in which blindness may allow revealing hidden elements within the construction of gender, visual culture, and the senses, with the overarching argument that blindness can be chosen as a "critical consciousness," evoking what Geertz (1973) coined as "thick description"—an interpretation that "enlarges the universe of human discourse" (14). This critical awareness is not essentialist for blindness. Rather, as one of the readers of this book emphasized, it must be chosen. The type of defamiliarization with everyday visual gendered norms, with the concept of the gaze, and with sensory realities blindness can lead to, is a matter of a critical consciousness that does not just happen automatically when blindness is around. It can be socially and culturally developed by blind women who choose to pay attention to the way visual culture works, to interpret it, and to negotiate it, as well as by sighted people coming into contact with blindness in a way that shakes up taken-for-granted concepts of others and themselves. In the epilogue of this book, I discuss the ways I cultivated such a consciousness through my work with blind women. When I use the term "critical consciousness," what I mean is an approach of delayed judgment, a critical thought process that purposely engages in inquiry about concepts we otherwise think of as natural or automatic, or perhaps do not consider at all. For instance, what is a gaze? What are the nonvisual components staring is made of? How have we come to treat a certain appearance as "normal" or "feminine"? And how are sight and the other senses cultivated in our everyday gendered choices and social interactions? These are the questions that, when confronted with blindness, are transformed into opportunities for new insights.

The critical awareness blindness may evoke was examined in relation to three topics: gender, visual culture, and the senses. Within the realms of *gender performance* and the development of gender identity, I argue for the ways blind women's narratives reveal: (1) the multisensorial characteristics of gender performance and socialization; (2) the idea of gender performance as pleasure-inducing, as well as disciplinary, on a sensorial level; and (3) women's subversive use of the gaze as a tool of communication and agency. Blind women's narratives explored here indicate the ways they strategically employ normative gender performance as a tool of stigma resistance and negotiation of stereotypes of gender, blindness, and disability, claiming their identity as a "feminine-blind-person." In addition, while scholars have identified the ways feminist theory typically emphasizes gender socialization as a process compelling rigorous discipline of the body in an effort to comply with visual norms, blind women's descriptions of appearance management narrate the ways these practices function as a complicated vehicle for the expression and reception of sensory pleasure and social empowerment, while also as a project of docility. Finally, blind women's keen awareness of stares and gazes, as well as their varied means of "staring back" and negotiating staring and the gaze through humor, irony, and self-reflection, demonstrates similarities and differences between gender and disability systems, thereby distinguishing between the terms "gaze" and "staring," as well as complicating the passive meaning of the "gaze" and the passivity typically associated with individuals subjected to visual power (whether these subjects are women, women with disabilities, or blind women).

The second topic within which I have examined the critical awareness blindness may evoke is *visual culture*, employing blindness to offer insights into the ways the experiences of seeing and being seen are performed, socialized, and embodied by both blind and sighted individuals. Blind women's narratives, and the meetings between people with varied visual skills, allow conceptualizing the visual experience as: (1) a spectrum rather than an ability people either do or do not have; (2) a performative, active, somatic skill both sighted and blind individuals employ, conducted in conjunction with the other senses and tangled with nonvisual mechanisms such as linguistic performance and body language; and (3) a complex web of awareness and means of communication. Blind women's awareness and usage of visual norms acknowledge blind people's active position within visual culture as inside agents who make active and rational choices regarding appearance and social relations. This is demonstrated through the numerous ways blind women negotiate visual norms, revealing the processes through which blind women are socialized into and develop an awareness of feminine appearance—in other words, blind women's ways of "doing sight" (Michalko 1998, 112). In addition, social dynamics between blind and sighted people disclose the richness of visual experience, offering a broader definition of the term "visual skill" as not merely physical but fashioned also by visual knowledge and sensory awareness that can be shared by sighted and blind people. Sight (and blindness) is not homogenous but rather an experience of changing colors, light, and shadows, shaped by attentiveness, knowledge, and a set of skills a person has and develops. Encounters with blindness also reveal the ways the visual experience is enriched among *sighted* members of society, who, when coming in contact with blind people in non-ableist contexts, are encouraged to critically reflect upon their own sensory identities and bodily functionalities through an intersensory performance. As part of this process, sighted people are offered an opportunity to "re-embody sight" as a somatic sense and to develop awareness of their tactile and sonic body. My discussion of sight as a somatic, multisensory experience implies two additional arguments: First, that the (male) gaze is not the sole sense employed in gendered and social power relations. Rather, socialization, objectification, and Othering processes may take place through senses other than sight. Second, that for blind women, the visual may serve as the basis for communication, agency, and critical reflection rather than merely a disciplinary mechanism.

The third topic blindness allows to be critically examined is *the sensory body*, raising questions about the role of the senses within socialization processes. Blindness lends itself to not only identify the various roles of the senses within social encounters but also the sensory aspects of both Othering and de-Othering processes. On one hand, the senses may serve to normalize blind women's looks and behavior and to ensure the sighted person's "normative" social position. Senses such as sound and touch may serve to assimilate blind individuals into the visual gender norms of sighted society, through, for example, teaching blind women to avoid "blind mannerisms" and to use cosmetics in a beauty care class; and the senses can also serve to classify blindness as otherness when sighted people direct an orientalist gaze at blindness in spaces such as the dark museum exhibit. On the other hand, sensory experiences may also be used to de-Other Otherness, enriching the ways women experience gender and femininity, as well as deepening sighted and blind people's understandings of themselves through dialogical and intersensory events. The heightened awareness of the senses blindness evokes is also important in shaping research methodology, pointing out the visual framework of the production of knowledge and promoting the method of sensory knowledge in the field, revealing the ways the researcher's somatic experiences inform her collection, understanding, and analysis of research materials.

---

In addition to framing blindness as a possible choice of critical consciousness, this book reveals the social phenomenon of blindness as a realm of contradictions. For a long time, my main goal within this research was to arrange the materials into neat analytical categories, to create an organized scholarly picture of the many ideas and stories I encountered in the field. However, I was faced again and again with the dualities contained both within blind women's narratives and within the performance of blindness in the public sphere.

Such dualities were expressed by research participants, who addressed their complicated position between visual culture and blindness and the fine line they navigate between visual norms and their own feelings. As Talia, thirty-one years old, blind from age three, who has become a central interlocutor and a close friend, said:

> I think about the difference between me and a sighted woman—someone who's surrounded by norms and things that show her what's right and what's not, what's fashionable and what's a "no-no" in fashion. On the one hand, we're supposed to be free from these norms, because there's no constant visual feedback on a daily basis; while on the other, we're caged inside these norms, because someone sighted will dictate to me what needs to be done.

Conversations with Talia revealed the dualities of her position and that navigating the visual is not simple. On one hand, she described her blindness as a blessing, an "inner mirror," she calls it, which may set her free from visual norms, as I also mentioned in chapter 8. On the other hand, Talia acknowledges that there are in fact "social conventions and norms of visual aesthetics" she consciously conforms to. "I live among sighted people, and I don't want to make them feel uncomfortable. And it gives me a better feeling when my appearance is pleasant for a sighted person to look at."

Such contradictions in blind women's experiences were also expressed by Ayelet, a thirty-three-year-old congenitally blind woman, whose narrative informed the analysis in this book, specifically in her critical assessment of gender norms, as well as of her position as a research participant. My last question for Ayelet in our interview (which was my routine question with which I concluded my interviews) was, "Is there anything you might have done differently if you were sighted?" In other words, I wanted to get to the crux of it—how the fact that Ayelet is blind has specifically directed her life course and social behavior. In response, Ayelet reflected on the ways her blindness differentiated her from her peers, fostering hardships but also offering advantages. As a woman who grew up in what she called a "difficult neighborhood," now working in media, she talked about how her blindness exposed her to the radio. "If I were sighted," she said, "for sure, I would do many things differently, [but] there's something good about my blindness. I'm glad that I'm blind, considering where I grew up." "Because if I had been sighted," she said,

I would have been like all the other girls, a stupid little bimbo. And if I had been sighted, I would have missed the great pleasure of my life: radio, and media in general. My blindness actually exposed me to what brings me joy. There are many radio people I admire, and considering the place I grew up in, I would have never been exposed to them.

"But maybe I would give this joy up," Ayelet wondered, "if I could grow up in another place, of course, be sighted and mobile, and many other things." "If I could change [something]," Ayelet concluded, "I can't be sure what I would change: the place I grew up in or the blindness."

Additional women from marginal social groups mentioned blindness as a tool that broadened their spectrum of choices, expressing the subversive potential embedded in blindness, which challenges cultural expectations and social conventions. Such incongruities influenced other subjects as well. Blind women's appearance management practices, for instance, and their dating experiences, reveal that on one hand, blindness functions as a disciplinary mechanism operated upon women's bodies. Fostering a meticulous and conscious use of the body, blindness restricts blind women to the world of the sighted, disciplining the body in accordance with the visual norms of sighted society and heightening blind women's visibility as the object of staring. On the other hand, women's experiences reveal the ways blindness disrupts the panoptic ocular logic. Allowing agentic negotiations of visual norms and traditional gender and social expectations, blindness emphasizes experiences other than sight within gender performance, giving voice to active ways of negotiating the gaze, thus broadening blind women's range of choices within social and romantic relations.

The dualities blindness evokes also accompanied my discussion of research observations in spaces where blind and sighted people meet. On one hand, in these instances blindness operates as a symbol of social otherness that reinforces cultural classifications between "us" and "them," fostering stigmatic attitudes toward blind people. This was evident in the dark museum exhibit, where through the orientalist gaze blindness is treated as Otherness. On the other hand, encounters with blindness may provoke a reflexive subjectivity among society members that raises questions regarding the ways sight, blindness, and the other senses operate. This was evident in the tandem cycling group, where people come to know blindness and sightedness as intertwined experiences.

It took me some time to realize that instead of resisting the dualities blindness evokes, I should work *with* them, locating the contradictions at the heart of my work when interpreting blind women's gender performance and the cultural representations of blindness and sight.

⸺⸺

The contradictions inherent in blindness, and its function as a critical consciousness, are where I end this journey. These ideas were beautifully expressed in the words of Noa, a twenty-five-year-old congenitally blind research participant, whose narrative was central in chapter 6 when discussing blind women's negotiation of the gaze. Talking about the difficulties of her blindness, which can cause her to be slow and unsure in some tasks and situations, she used trains and water as metaphors to explain her situation. "The train eventually arrives at the station," she said,

> It goes slowly but eventually arrives. You know, in the countryside, water penetrates the soil directly but gets to the very same place as water that penetrates the ground in the city. Only in the city, it gets there slower, because there's asphalt and all kinds of things that are blocking its way. But eventually, it will get to the same place.

In response, trying to elicit a more positive notion of blindness than a "slow train," I asked, "But maybe your train has better cars than others?" In her answer, Noa returned to water, and explained:

> Many times, I imagine blindness as a springboard: a place to jump from. It's like I'm swimming in shallow water but don't dare to stand, for fear it might be too deep; and only after I double check or wait for a very long time, I discover that this thing I was so afraid of, and thought of as so dangerous, I suddenly discover that all I needed to do was stretch my legs out, and I'd be able to stand.

Noa's answer stayed with me for a long time and taught me a valuable lesson about giving up control and trusting myself. I could practically feel Noa's metaphor in my body: the fear of drowning, struggling in the water, and then discovering that all along I could have just stretched out my legs, and I would have been able to stand and touch the ground. Embracing this advice, I end this book with an invitation to create further research of blindness and disability that establishes stable ground and yet embraces the fluidity and change water brings, calling for additional work that takes bodily variety, the senses, and the lived body into consideration and examines their influences on each other.

This idea has also guided the research project I embarked on after concluding my work on blindness, as I am now examining the meaning of movement and kinaesthetic experiences among people with varied bodies dancing together. Exploring the meeting between people with diverse physicality negotiating concepts such as rhythm, use of space, partnering, and pacing, I once again turn to disability as a site of diversity that allows us to contemplate our daily bodily and sensory experiences, provoking considerations about the creativity taking place when different moving bodies are creating together. While I turned to blindness to also learn about sight, in the project on integrated dance, I focus on physical disability to learn about movement.

My work with blind women taught me that research into the lives of individuals who challenge the ability-disability binary resembles in many ways what we may experience in the pool of water. While it can surround us in uncertainty and fluidity, threaten boundaries, and blur visual expectations and norms, if we look into it closely and carefully, it can also reflect who we are.

# Epilogue

A book's epilogue is a liminal section, not part of the official analysis but in close contact with it. Given that freedom, I would like to embrace this space as an opportunity to turn the mirror back toward myself, on my own biography, and offer some afterthoughts about the research from a now ten-year distance in time. Building on the knowledge this book provided me, I ask to better understand my own experiences and the ways I examine them. To this end, I ask, what are some of the counterpoints between my interviewees' narratives of the visual and my own as the ethnographer? And in which ways has this research influenced and shaped my current work that emerged from this study?

In contextualizing my analysis of blind women within my own story, I embrace an autoethnographic sensitivity that has long directed ethnographic writing and autoethnographic works focused on disability such as those of Murphy (1990) and Zola (1982).[1] Autoethnography is shaped by the researcher's reflexive awareness of her positionality and the ways it informs her analysis. As Wasserfall (1993) explained in her article on reflexivity within feminist methodology:

> Reflexivity is the process by which an anthropologist understands how her social background influences and shapes her beliefs and how this self awareness pertains to what and how she observes, attributes meanings, interprets action and dialogues with her informants. (25)

A somewhat similar reflexive awareness was offered by Kleege (1999), who noted that while writing her book made her blind, it also made her recognize "how sighted I am" (1). In recognizing the role of her writing in shaping her understanding of her own identity as a blind woman and her involvement in the visual world, Kleege's reflexive awareness informed her analysis of the cultural image of blindness and the characteristics of visual culture.

Such an autoethnographic awareness was also important in my journey into blind women's gender identity and the cultural construction of blindness and sight. The research and my exposure to the experiences of research participants made me rethink and more fully experience my sightedness, as well as my blind spots, offering the impetus to reflect on my personal experiences of visibility and invisibility that drew me to this study and to recognize the tools I have as a woman to negotiate the gaze. This reflexive awareness led me to broader questions about what it meant for me to live with a constant awareness of my visual exposure and of how a visual consciousness and the experience of serving as a spectacle affect the ways we inhabit the world and interact with others. When listening to the tension blind women described experiencing between visibility and invisibility in their lives, I tried to identify the components and context most crucial for each woman's story. Here, I would like to briefly exercise the same analytical tool on my story as well. In my case, my experience of the visual was shaped mainly by the physical setting where I grew up, feeling highly visible and yet also invisible.

---

Twenty-one stairs, and 70 feet. That's the door-to-door distance between my parents' and grandparents' houses in Nahalal, the place where I grew up—a small cooperative farming village located in the Jezreel Valley in the north of Israel. In addition to being Israel's first Moshav, Nahalal is known for its unique physical layout, its homes—my home—nestled in the nucleus of ever-widening circles of barnyards, gardens, and fields. The path leading to my grandparents' runs from my parents' two-story white house, and crossing the small alley between us and the neighbors, passes my great-aunt's house, then under the lemon tree and into her well-kept garden. The stairs begin just in front of my great-aunt's curtain-covered screen door, then midway turn sharply right onto a walkway leading to an old wooden door, the door to the small guest room, once my great-grandmother's room. At the top of the stairs is my grandparents' front door, rarely locked, as is the custom in the village, and next to it, a rectangular window displaying the scenario inside: family members sitting at the round kitchen table, often with guests, sharing a meal. From the time I can remember, my grandfather, Bam (Avraham), has sat at his fixed place at the head of the table (only in Nahalal can a round table have a head), every year moving the table an inch further away to make room for himself and his belly to fit in. So many family meals, dinners, and holiday feasts have been served at this table; so many card games have been played around it; and every day but Saturday, ever since my parents left Tel-Aviv and returned to the Jezreel valley when I was six, my father, the son who took over the farm, has had his four o'clock coffee at this table, discussing with his parents the Moshav's latest news, what the grandchildren are up to, or the amount of rainfall this year, based, of course, on my grandfather's own measuring from his improvised weather station.

Those twenty-one stairs and that 70-foot path encircled in the nucleus of Nahalal were the landscape of my childhood. And even though I wasn't born in Nahalal and, therefore, unlike my youngest sister for instance, I am not a true native *Nahalalit*, as the first grandchild and fourth generation of the Hammer family in Nahalal, I became aware at an early age that I had a lot to prove. I grew up sensing the heavy heritage on my narrow shoulders; the heritage of a lineage of strong women, beginning with my great-grandmother, Savta Miriam, who ran the place with an iron fist after her husband's early death left her with two babies to raise and a farm to manage; the heritage of the masculine and heroic *Sabra* figure embedded in the history of Nahalal as a symbol of Hebrew culture;[2] and the heritage of people intimately connected to their land—the land on which my grandfather was born when his mother gave birth in a shed on the farm—the land on which my grandfather has insisted he will die. This heritage and these intimate and compact spaces—the family farm, with my grandparents' upstairs house and its balcony overlooking the alley; my great-aunt's "downstairs" house; and my parents' large-windowed house—formed the framework of my Panopticon, where I began my negotiation with visibility and the visual, the stage where my experiences as a young girl and woman were displayed.

As a shy and quiet girl who preferred spending her time reading books and watching documentaries set in faraway places, preferably about travelers in Antarctica, mountaineers who conquered Mount Everest, or religious saints in India, I didn't exactly fit the Israeli farm-girl image: the barefoot *Moshavnikit* in shorts, running outside with the neighborhood kids. Adding to that my skinny body and skeletal physicality, I always felt like a misfit, watched by disappointed, disapproving eyes. This feeling was one of the things that drew my anthropological curiosity toward silenced and marginal voices and eventually raised my interest in blind women, as I imagined them to be at odds with the visual world, feeling invisible and unfit—feelings I could empathize with.

My feeling that I was being disapprovingly observed is not unique but was indeed gender-related, an experience passed down through the generations. My grandmother, who arrived in Nahalal at the age of twelve as a student in the famous girl's school for agriculture, tells a pivotal story of herself as a twenty-two-year-old woman and a mother of three, a story that eventually leads to her hiding, terrified, under her bed. During one of her visits to the local grocery store, she found herself without enough money and promised to return with the missing two liras (an old Israeli currency). However, upon returning home, occupied with the many responsibilities of the household, she forgot about her debt, until she heard the sound of footsteps accompanied by the shouting of her name. First looking for her in her sister in-law's house downstairs, acting as though he was looking for a thief, and then climbing up the twenty-one stairs, making enough noise for the entire neighborhood to hear, the storekeeper searched for her. Terrified, and feeling overwhelmed with fear and shame, my grandmother ran to the back room and crawled under the bed, hiding there until it was dark. Her fear of public condemnation, of what people might think of her, of what they *already* thought of her, and of her in-laws' judging eyes, was just that strong.

My mother, who was originally a city girl, met my father during their military service. Arriving at the Moshav at the age of thirty-three with three kids, she struggled with the transition from city life to the life of the isolated valley, and with the difficulties of living next to her in-laws. Our first year there was not easy: my mother was trying to rebuild her career after leaving her university job, my three-year-old sister cried incessantly, my brother contracted both chicken pox and mumps, and I spent most of the year in bed. I had suffered from pneumonia early on, which left my already tiny body bony and shrunken. I was so skinny as an infant that one time my mother called in Dr. Virt, the family pediatrician, because there was something sticking out of my chest, only to have him explain that this protrusion was simply my heart. That first year in Nahalal I suffered from sicknesses again and my body rejected the antibiotics, leaving no choice but to confine me to my bed for weeks, to recuperate on my own. At one point, noticing that we kids missed a lot of school and hearing my little sister's crying, a neighbor offered my mother his advice. Standing in front of her with his tall, stout farmer's body, he told her that maybe if she did less "running around," and was "at home more," her children would be healthier. My mother was shocked and offended by his interpretation of her work outside the limits of the Moshav as "running around" and by his suggestion that she was to blame for our sicknesses. She was also disturbed by how nonchalantly he offered his advice, providing her a clear understanding that she was being watched and judged as a woman and a mother by the people surrounding her. Needless to say, this advice was never given to my father. He was a native. He was a hard-working farmer. He wasn't "running around."

My own memories from this first year are a blur, but what I do remember is how difficult it was to draw my blood, as I had no visible veins left in my body and therefore had to be pricked by the needle again and again during the many visits to the nurse, leaving me with blue tracks along my arms. Obviously, spending my days in bed didn't make me the most popular girl at my new school, and even though the marks on my arms were kind of cool, they were much more scary than attractive. I finally began to recover in the springtime, approaching Holocaust Memorial Day, and I remember being aware of the way people looked at me when I ran around outside the house, playing with my brother and enjoying the freedom of being out of bed and trusting my body again. I had lost so much weight that year (and was skinny to begin with) that, at times, people gasped at the sight of me. My body reminded them of the *Muselmann*, the skeleton-like Holocaust survivors, spurring comments that made me horrifically ashamed of the way I looked. That year's sickness kept me eerily skinny until I reached nineteen, so that during my adolescent years I often felt compelled to prove that no, I did not have an eating disorder, and, yes, I did like eating, even chocolate and snacks. For my bat mitzvah, the Jewish coming of age ceremony, I was the only one among my classmates who didn't wear a fancy puffy dress, instead insisting on simple jeans and a white shirt. I wish I could say I did it out of some feminist instinct, but the truth is that I was desperately trying to hide my stick legs, painfully fearful of them being publicly displayed. This attempt to hide, to cover the shape of my body, continued as I secretly wore layers of clothing, even in the hot, unair-conditioned summer of the Jezreel valley. Yet, people continued to stare at me, and I, for my part, felt highly visible, but also highly invisible, without the voice, the skills, or the ability to talk back or to divert the gaze of the eyes surrounding me.

Against the background of my upbringing and considering the conservative family I come from, blind women's open conversations with the visual and their active negotiations with the gaze were novel and intriguing to me. I saw this, for instance, through my time spent with Talia, a blind research participant who became a key informant and a good friend. Talia discusses openly not only her blindness but also her femininity and sexuality, addressing her blindness as a sort of "blessing" that frees her from the obsessions and complexes sighted women suffer from. When Talia described to me her open conversations with her parents, whose Polish accent she mimics with great talent and humor, and when I later witnessed their interactions myself, I was astonished and even envious. I could not comprehend the straightforwardness of it, and the ways Talia's romantic relations were so openly discussed. In rigid, puritan Nahalal, and in my family, open conversations about our personal lives are unimaginable, and these issues are typically addressed indirectly, perhaps by mentioning offhandedly during dinner, "The neighbor's daughter got married, you know? Is she your age or your sister's?" "The other girl from your class is having her second child now. Their house is so noisy with children that we can hear the screams when passing by there when we 'walk in the circle' [of Nahalal]." Hearing these remarks, I have found myself shrinking in my chair and lowering my head, simply replying, "oh, yeah?" interpreting the words as an indication of my family's disappointment over my choice to pursue a doctorate before pursuing a child.

Blind women's stories amazed me not only because of the openness of the discussion about the ways they are seen but also because of their capacities of staring back. Their narratives about the ways they reclaim their bodies and looks offered me new resources with which to understand my own engagement with the visual world, not only from the prism of subordination but also from the standpoint of subversion. Before my obligatory military service, and right after it, I chose to work as a nature guide, leading kids, youth, and families on hikes in the Judean desert and the Galilee. During my research, I began to reflect on this choice and came to understand the ways it had allowed me to take some control over my visuality by putting myself on display in a position of authority. I was the one holding the knowledge and leading the way, and somewhat serving as the eyes of the people in my group, directing their sight toward the landscape, flora, animals, and history I made visible to them.

Another engagement with the visual has been my preoccupation with painting, which, from high school and into adulthood, has been one of my favorite hobbies. It was even something I was doing while also writing the draft of this book, having enrolled in an adult painting class at The Israel Museum in Jerusalem. Once a week, I ended a long day of writing and sitting in front of the computer with three hours immersed in colors, shapes, and textures instead of words. One of the paintings I was working on was Camille Pissarro's "Woman and Child at the Well" (1882), colorfully depicting an exchange of looks between a young but tired-looking woman leaning against a well and the younger girl whom she is facing. Each of them is looking at the other or, more likely, at what they were or are about to become. It was not until a year after finishing working on this painting, when listening again to the recordings of my 2008–2009 interviews, that I came to appreciate the connection between this painting and my research, reading it as telling a story about an exchange of looks between women and of a woman's inner dialogue with how she is seen. Looking at the postcard of this painting hanging in my University of Michigan basement office while contemplating the gaze and women's visuality during my post-doctoral appointment, I realized an additional layer of interpretation my research offers me and the role of painting in my life.

In our last interview, Talia addressed the tension she is struggling with between staying true to herself and the visual standards she encounters, and her fear of not being able to follow the visual norms because of her blindness. "It's so confusing," she said, "this place, the uncertainty of it . . . the . . . notion that I will always have question marks and moments of doubt." "And all I have left," she concluded,

> Really, all I have left, is to find the solution in my own head, and there'll always be these questions, like . . . I don't know, there will always be these fears, these moments of doubt, question marks, in so many things in life [ . . . ] am I defective? Am I missing something? I'm a very positive person, but here and there, I have these moments when I suddenly find myself *stop*. And . . . find myself in a very difficult place.

I wanted to tell Talia, "of course you're not defective." But all I could think about while listening to her were my own blind spots as a girl and a woman; the compromises I was ready to make in my own life, and my own ongoing dialogue with the visual and with the double-edged sword of women's visibility and invisibility. Nevertheless, listening to her and to other blind women inspired me to take more control over my life, and to change some of the things I was taught to ignore or not to see. Having shared these deeply personal experiences, we finished the interview, turned off the tape, and went shopping for clothes.

My encounters with blind women have affected not only the way I understand my personal story but also my scholarly thinking. Almost a decade after beginning this study, I can identify three main insights that resulted from it and that continue to direct my current research as well.

First, researching blindness made me aware of the complex intersection of *disability and performance*. When talking about their gender performance in their everyday lives, blind women described the sense of serving as performers, being stared at, and serving as a spectacle even when simply walking down the street. The idea of being in a position in which you are forced to negotiate your visibility, taking the role of a performer, continued to fascinate me after ending this research, making me curious also about theatrical and institutionalized performances of disability, of instances that are consciously created and directed toward an audience. Why, I wondered, would a person with a disability, who already serves as a kind of performer in his or her daily life, choose to go on stage? And how is the gaze negotiated in this setting in comparison to the dynamics in blind women's everyday lives? These questions directed me to focus my current work on the field of "disability culture," working with performance groups of people with disabilities. As a result, I am currently focusing on integrated dance programs in which people with sensory impairments, such as deafness or blindness, or performers using wheelchairs, crutches, or prosthetics, collaborate with able-bodied individuals to create public art performances, asking questions about the intersection of performance and disability and about the choices performers employ on stage.

The second aspect I took from my study with blind women, which became central in my current work, is the *sensory body*. Studying blindness made me realize not only the varied roles of the senses within our social life but also the importance of disability and bodily difference in exposing the ways our sensory selves are socialized and embodied. While in my work with blind women I employed blindness to focus mainly on the senses of sight, hearing, and touch, in my current study on disability culture, I investigate the ways disability performance art exposes the taken-for-grantedness of our sense of movement. When working with dance programs, for instance, I focus mainly on the *kinesthetic body* and the senses involved in movement, asking about the ways concepts such as rhythm, use of space, partnering, and pacing are shaped in the dance studio by people with and without disabilities. I once again, therefore, turn to disability as a site of diversity that allows challenging our daily sensory experiences.

The third analytical anchor I discovered in my research on blindness is the importance of a *dialogue* between people who are different from one another. The role of intersensory dialogues among blind and sighted individuals in fostering critical self-reflection directed my current study's focus on *integrated* projects, examining the sensory body and disability embodiment within the *meeting* between people with a wide variety of bodily skills who dance and perform together. My research on blindness taught me that this meeting is important for exposing the creativity taking place when people with diverse physicality are engaged in activities that require shared understanding and implementation of bodily notions, notions that are learned and expressed through multiple modes and bodily functionalities. These dialogical encounters are of substantial anthropological significance, as they engender a critical understanding of what a body can do and what disability is.

Since beginning the study this book is based on, some changes have taken place in my field. When beginning this work, disability studies virtually did not exist in Israel. For this reason, I spent one year of my doctorate at UC Berkeley, in one of the leading disability studies programs in the United States. I used that year as an opportunity to take as many courses as I could in disability studies and came back home with a suitcase full of books and articles. That year changed the way I conceptualized blindness and disability, informing my writing to include the social model of disability on one hand and discussions of the bodily aspects of disability on the other, and making me aware of the complex relations disability and other social affiliations share. Although in its infancy in Israel when I left to study in the United States in 2010, the field of disability studies has changed since then.[3] More and more disability studies-related programs have opened in the country;[4] more courses are given in departments of education, social work, and sociology; and disability rights debates now commonly find their way into the media. When teaching a course about disability and bodily difference in 2015, for example, I could bring to class daily examples of disability rights debates from the news. In addition, the first disability studies reader in Hebrew appeared in 2016 (Mor et al.).

Unfortunately, I cannot say that much has changed for blind women in the country, in terms of social attitudes, since blindness is still on the margins of public awareness and scholarly research. Stigmatic attitudes toward blindness were present, for example, in a survey (mentioned in chapter 2) that The Center for the Blind in Israel published in March 2016. Asking nondisabled women about their attitudes toward blind women, the survey revealed that one in five sighted women believe a blind woman cannot successfully fulfill the role of wife and mother, and that two-thirds of the sighted women polled think a "typical mother" would try to prevent her son from marrying a blind woman. This survey is one example that not only reflects ongoing stereotypes about blindness and gender but also policymakers' tendency to learn about blindness from the perspectives of sighted people. Instead of using the survey as an opportunity to understand better the reality of a blind woman in Israel of 2016, it focused on sighted women's standpoints. It also did not address the ways these attitudes can be changed. These are the kinds of methods I wanted to avoid in this book, instead passing the ball to blind women and sighted people involved in the field and critically examining dynamics that engender or delay change.

Garland-Thomson (1996) noted that the extraordinary body is "fundamental to the narratives by which we make sense of ourselves and our world [ . . . ] fir[ing] rich, if anxious, narratives and practices that probe the contours and boundaries of what we take to be human" (1). This research has not only raised my awareness of the importance of the extraordinary body to scholarly narratives but also of the unexpected elements within *all* our bodies and sensory experiences, allowing me to rethink my own biography as well as the means through which I interpret the sociocultural world.

# Notes

----- ∝∝∝ -----

### Introduction

1. Sociological and philosophical theorists have argued that the modern Western era is a visual one (e.g., Bull and Back 2003; Classen 1998; Howes 2003; Kleege 1999; Pallasmaa 2012), recognizing the "society of the spectacle" (Debord 1994) as our cultural context, understanding femininity as a "way of being seen" (Berger 1973), and embracing Foucault's Panopticon (1977) as the central metaphor for modern power relations, a structure through which society exercises the disciplinary "gaze" while producing docile bodies in schools, prisons, and the workplace.

2. The study of blind people in Israel has been rarely addressed in the past and has occurred mainly within the fields of psychology, public policy, or education (e.g., Almog 2011; Hess 2010; Noishtat 2007). An exception is the pioneering anthropological work of Deshen (1992), which, nevertheless, did not refer in detail to the issue of gender and feminine identity or specifically to the lives of blind women, rather establishing a "disability anthropology" (190) as a whole.

3. Dundes (1980), for example, wrote about the ways academic language in general, and anthropological research in particular, is visual-oriented, emphasizing "participant observation" and the search for new "insights."

4. Kleege (2005) referred to the subject of blind writers using visual language, such as Helen Keller's *The World I Live In*, in which "Keller makes good use of her Radcliffe education to show that the more one knows about language, the harder it is to find vocabulary which does not have some root in sighted or hearing experience. But, she argues, to deny her the use of seeing-hearing vocabulary would be to deny her the ability to communicate at all" (185).

5. For an account of blindness and gender focusing on masculinity in the context of negotiating the stare, refer to Kuppers 2009.

6. For an analysis of the ways blindness has served as central within philosophical debates, religious traditions, cultural mythologies, literary representations, and folklore around the world, refer to the studies of Barasch (2001), Kleege (1999, 2005), Klobas (1988), Schor (1999), Rodas (2009), Sentumbwe (1995), Wagner-Lampl and Oliver (1994), Deshen (1992), Schillmeier (2006, 2008), Bolt (2014), and Wheatley (2010).

7. One example of a cultural archetype of blindness is the story of Tiresias, the blind prophet of Thebes found in the Greek mythologies of Antigone, Oedipus, and The Bacchae, mirroring common depictions of blindness as a cruel punishment cast upon villains and sinners, or as a mysterious condition initiating prophetic abilities, musical talent, and objective judgment. Petra Kuppers (2008), in her article *Tiresian Journeys*, offers a beautiful reading of this figure, describing the ways Tiresias challenges boundaries of the cultural order and nature-culture distinctions, living both as a man and a woman, sighted and blind, disabled and nondisabled, and prophesying based on multisensorial inputs.

8. On the association of sight with knowledge, subjectivity, and perception, and of blindness with darkness, ignorance, and castration, refer to Bolt (2005, 2014), Kleege (1999), and Michalko (1998).

9. Recent books on blindness include: *The Metanarrative of Blindness: A Re-reading of Twentieth-Century Anglophone Writing* (Bolt 2014), *Blind to Sameness: Sexpectations and the Social Construction of Male and Female Bodies* (Friedman 2013), *Borderlands of Blindness* (Omansky 2011), *Blinded by Sight: Seeing Race through the Eyes of the Blind* (Obasogie 2013), and *Stumbling Blocks before the Blind: Medieval Constructions of a Disability* (Wheatley 2010).

10. Anthropological studies, mainly in the field of medical anthropology, have also addressed blindness, focusing on the subjects of socialization, rehabilitation, and education (Keating and Hadder 2010; Sentumbwe 1995); blind people's body image (Kaplan-Myrth 2000); public health policy (Kaplan-Myrth 2001); and bio-medical advocacy (Goldin 1990). In the different chapters of this book, I engage with these lines of thought, discussing their impact on theories of gender, visual culture, and the sensory body.

11. On the gaze operated on women's bodies, refer to Bordo 2003; Fraser 1997; King 2004; Odette 1994; Wolf 1992; Young 1980.

## Chapter 2

1. Critiques on ableist approaches within the research of blindness and disability have been made by disability studies scholars such as Barton 2005; Battles and Manderson 2008; Colligan 2001; Davis 2000; Deegan and Willett 2001; Frank 2000; Oliver 1996; Shakespeare 1996; Shuttleworth and Kasnitz 2004; Stone and Priestley 1996; Whyte and Ingstad 1995.

2. Methodological sensitivity within the "reflexive turn" in anthropology has resulted in greater attention to the subjects of power relations and the researcher's gaze—addressing, for example, "micro-relations between informants and ethnographers" (Rabinow 1985), the interrelationship between observer and observed (Krieger 1985), power relations between researcher and researched (Murphy and Dingwall 2001), and a "confrontation" between the ethnographer and "his informants" (Crapanzano 1997).

3. Classen and Howes (1996) address anthropology as a discipline that has tended to "experience and interpret societies visually, rather than sensually" (93). Accordingly, Keating and Hadder (2010) referred to the "visual-centrism" of the

anthropological endeavor. Also on this matter, refer to: Dundes 1980; Fabian 1983; Kaplan-Myrth 2000; Stoller 1984.

4. For a discussion of representations of blind women in literature and cinema, refer to: Kleege (1999); Asch and Sacks (1983); Elder (1983).

5. Kurssiya and Gleitman 2009; Gleitman, Kurssiya, and Marom 2008.

6. Ronit Roccas, "Light at the End of the Darkness," *Haaretz*, January 6, 2009 [Hebrew]; Edward Rothstein, "Darkness Visible, and Palpable," *New York Times*, August 18, 2011; Pam Block, "To Turn on the Camera, and See for the First Time, *Haaretz*, October 11, 2009 [Hebrew]; Ricki Rat, "On Blindness," *Makor Rishon*, May 1, 2009 [Hebrew]; Rutty Sinai, "Law Requires Accessible Transportation, Many Blind People Stay at the Station," *Haaretz*, April 27, 2007 [Hebrew].

7. "Is Academia Accessible and for Whom?" The Hebrew University of Jerusalem, November 22, 2011; "Rethinking Disability: The State, the Community and the Individual," International Disability Studies Conference, Tel Aviv University, December 30–31, 2010.

8. Talia Sarnetzky, *The Blind Optimist*, http://www.theblindoptimist.com/; Daniel Aronoff, *The Real Blind Taste Test*, http://www.blindtastetest.net/author/blindblogny

9. Studies have addressed the category of race within Jewish studies outside the Israeli context. On the interplay of race and religion among Jews in the American context, refer, for example, to Brodkin 1998. Falk (2017) also addressed race in the context of Judaism, addressing race and the Zionist movement.

10. For a discussion addressing teaching about and with a disability and the ways it challenges normalized classroom dynamics, refer to: Brueggemann et al. 2005.

11. For ethnographic examples of research on the body based on participant observations, refer to: Bar-On Cohen 2006; Browning 1995; Spinney 2006; Wacquant 2004; Wade 2011. For studies focusing on a specific group or bodily practice, such as dance, cycling, boxing, or martial arts shared by a closed group of tourists, fans, or professionals, refer to: Bar-On Cohen 2006; Browning 1995; Kohavi 2007; Buckingham and Degen 2012; Lund 2005; Spinney 2006; Wacquant 2004.

12. On the stigmatized notion of blind touch, refer to Kleege 2006, 213.

13. I visited the center along with a colleague, Nitsan Almog, a PhD student at Bar Ilan University at the time. Almog (2011) briefly addresses this experience in her dissertation, referring to it as "making observations with eyes closed" (49).

14. An elaborated discussion of the term "legal blindness" and the variety of visual skills it actually consists of appears in chapter 4 of this book.

15. For additional discussion of the notion of "forced intimacy" people with disabilities experience, refer to Mingus 2017.

## Introduction to Section I

1. The vast majority of the literature on women's bodies and gender identity has expressed an ocularcentric focus, concentrating on visual interaction and the ways in which women see and are seen in the media (Beller 2006; Geraghty 1991), by the beauty industry (Bordo 2003; Wolf 1992), in cinema and art (Berger 1973; Mulvey

1975), and by the law (Kamir 2007). To some extent, while criticizing the objectifying gaze, the feminist critique has adopted a "panoptic" terminology that sketches modern patriarchal power relations as consisting of women who are subjected to the dominant masculine gaze, requiring them to present a calculated feminine appearance that will be perceived as neither overly provocative nor neglected (Bartky 1997; King 2004; Wolf 1992). Furthermore, even studies that have focused on senses other than sight, such as sense of motion (see Young 1980) or touch (Irigaray 1985), have yet emphasized the gaze and identified the visual as sites of rationality and masculinity, taking sight for granted.

2. On the central and influential role of appearance in women's lives, refer to: Bartky 1997; Bordo 2003; Dellinger and Williams 1997; Fraser 1997; King 2004; Webster and Driskell 1983; Weitz 2001; Wolf 1992; Zones 1997.

## Chapter 5

1. Since the majority of the participants in this study identified themselves as heterosexual (refer to chapter 2 of this book), when talking about "partners," they usually refer to male partners.

2. It is important to note that the social reality in which heroic disability is associated exclusively with men has been changing in Israel in recent years, as Israeli government policies (from 1998 and 2011) now offer people who are casualties of terror attacks the same benefits and status military veterans receive. As a result, institutions that once took care of only military veterans (mainly men), may now offer services also to women and blind people. However, this relatively new aspect of Israeli militarism has not yet been studied in relation to gender and disability and did not come up in my interviews with blind women.

3. While the topic of motherhood is outside the scope of this book, it is worthy of further research. Blind women such as Anna and Dvora indeed fought for the right to make their own decisions about their private spaces and their bodies, and whether or not they would become mothers, confronting the stigmatic attitudes of family members, partners, and authorities. For additional analysis of the experiences of mothers with disabilities, see Frederick 2017.

## Introduction to Section II

1. Disability studies scholar Brenda Brueggemann (Brueggemann et al. 2005) called this experience of people staring at her when she walks with a person with a visible disability the "disability by association dynamic" (23). "This [ . . . ] kind of dynamic happens when I walk on campus or around town with Georgina [a blind scholar]," Brueggemann describes. "They do this looong stare—from Georgina's cane in front of her, up her arm, then way way up to her head [ . . . ] They do this looong look up, and then they go back to the cane and then their gaze stops for just a moment, absorbing it all. And then they look over at me, and this strange thing has always come over their face when they look at me, and finally [ . . . ] I've identi-

fied it. It's a little halo they put over me [ . . . ] I certainly don't get that look from people when I'm just out walking by myself" (23).

2. For additional discussion of the ways blindness and disability shed light on visual processes and ways of seeing, refer to: Benin and Cartwright 2006; Crow 2014; Davis and Smith 2006; Garland-Thomson 2006, 2009; Grigely 2006; Kleege 2005, 2006; Kudlick 2005, 2011; Rodas 2009; Michalko 1998.

3. On the matter of disability as serving as spectacle, refer to: Davis 1995; Davis and Smith 2006; Garland-Thomson 2005a, 2009; Phillips 1990.

4. There is a debate concerning whether ocularcentrism is unique to modernity or a feature of human and visual culture in general. Mitchell (2002), for example, refuses to consider what he calls the "visual turn," or hegemony of the visible, as a feature of modern culture. As he explains: "Vision has played the role of the sovereign sense since God looked at his own creation and saw that it was good, or perhaps even earlier when he began the act of creation with the division of the light from the darkness" (174).

5. Sparkes (2009) similarly cautioned scholars against adopting an "anti-visualist agenda," which, "Would lead to just another form of sensory supremacy in research whereby ethnographers ignored vision [ . . . ] and then elevated one of these [other] senses over all others" (31). Instead, echoing Howes' (2003) approach, he suggests understanding culture in a multisensory context. Grasseni (2009) also identified an "anti-ocularcentric" approach to sight as leading to a "sweeping condemnation of vision, taken *as a whole* as a dominant gaze" (2). Grasseni opposes such notions, arguing that acts of vision are "multisensory practices, where look is coordinated with skilled movement, with rapidly changing points of view, or with other senses such as touch" (4).

6. An anthropology of vision consists of works set to explore the meaning of seeing and the visual based on ethnographic analysis of the visual experience, such as Ewart's (2008) analysis of seeing, hearing, and speaking among the Panara in Central Brazil, Grasseni's (2004) studies of skilled vision among dairy breeders in the Italian Alps, Ingold's (2000, 2012) research of the perception of landscape and environment, Hockey's and Collinson's (2006) examination of the visual within the body in sport, and Willerslev's (2009) analysis of "double perspective" among Yukaghir hunters.

## Chapter 6

1. In this quote, Garland-Thomson refers to Jacob Lawrence's 1938 painting "Blind Beggars," which appears on the cover of her book *Staring: How We Look* (2009). The painting depicts a blind couple walking arm in arm along a city sidewalk, canes in hand, the man carrying a cup for coins, while around them children are happily playing, some staring at them. Garland-Thomson employs this canonical image of the blind beggar as a platform for her argument about staring relations, describing them as a "visual dance."

2. Here, I do not make a comparative argument regarding blind women's expe-

rience of staring versus the staring blind men or sighted women cope with. I do, however, offer insights into the complicated position of blind women as subject of the gaze and the unique contradictions they experience. For an account of blindness and gender focusing on masculinity in the context of negotiating the stare, refer to Kuppers 2009.

3. On how society considers women with disabilities as asexual, refer to: Heumann 1982 in Asch and Fine 1988; Howland and Rintala 2001; Kef and Bos 2006; Limaye 2003; Lonsdale 1990; Mazor 2015; Moin, Duvdevany, and Mazor 2009.

4. In Talia's case, her sexualization is related to an exoticization of her sense of touch. Blind women may be eroticized also because of their inability to return the gaze. As Kleege (1999) explains: "Blind girls in some cultures, have been sold into prostitution. Presumably they were expected to service men even other professionals would find repulsive to look at. Or else they could serve the Peeping Tom trade. Customers could enjoy the particular titillation of watching a woman who couldn't look back" (24).

5. For additional examples and discussion of the ways blind women are aware of feminine visual standards and criticize them, refer to chapters 3 and 4 of this book.

6. For further writings about the figure of the blind beggar as a constitutive image of blindness, refer to Kleege 1999 and Rodas 2009.

## Chapter 7

1. The exhibits differ slightly from country to country but typically express similar principles, structures, and design, usually including a park, a ride in or on a form of transportation, a music room, a market, and a bar, culminating in a conversation (still in darkness) between the group and the guide. While the analysis is based on an ethnography conducted at the exhibit in Israel, it is not focused on the treatment of blindness and disability within Israeli society or the history of museums in this country but rather on the construction of categories whose "cultural scripting" (Garland-Thomson 2009, 42) is tightly connected to general human relations, such as ability/disability and blindness/sight.

2. On the dominancy of the gaze within museum design, refer to: Alpers 1991; Cain 2010; Classen 2007; Classen and Howes 2006; Edwards et al. 2006; Handler 1993; Howes 2014. On the historical development of the museum as a space dominated by sight during the nineteenth century, refer to: Classen and Howes 2006; Classen 2007.

3. I borrow the terms "sensory immersion" and "distance viewing" from Losch's (2006) analysis of the role of the senses within the Margaret Mead Hall of Pacific Peoples at the American Museum of Natural History. Losch identifies these dynamics as operating simultaneously in the exhibit, expressing a duality in which the visitor experiences a sensory immersion in a "sensescape, a particular imaginary sensorium" (224), while also a "rationalized visual system" (227), locating him/her in the role of a distanced viewer exercising the gaze as a kind of power.

## Conclusion to Section II

1. The association of the sense of sight with a "Western worldview" (Rice 2008, 295) and of modern discourse with vision (Edwards et al. 2006, 7) have been discussed by scholars of the senses and visual culture, examining the association of vision and the gaze with Western science and rationalism and of non-Western contexts with senses other than sight (Howes 2003; Geurts 2003; Grasseni 2009; Wilf 2015). This association of vision with Western science has also affected anthropological research of the senses, which, as Wilf (2015) described, is more likely to focus on the role of the (nonvisual) senses in non-Western cultural contexts (5).

## Chapter 8

1. While this chapter does not focus on disability and class, scholars have recognized the relationships between these categories, reporting that "those living below the poverty line are twice as likely to report that they have children with a disability" (Scott 2010, 673). Scholars have also identified the connection between gender, class, and disability, reporting that women with disabilities are employed far less than are either nondisabled women or disabled men and are more likely than disabled men to live in poverty and to rely on government income support (Asch and Fine 1988, 11–12).

## Chapter 9

1. Furness (2007) used the notion of a "rolling community" in a different context, relating to Critical Mass' monthly event in which bicyclists briefly take over city streets, emphasizing the urban aspect of cycling in the city, during which "people can talk to each other and experience safety in numbers" (308).

## Epilogue

1. Some of the autoethnographic works that have most influenced my reflexive awareness I build on here are Myerhoff's (1978) work on aging in an elderly Jewish community in Florida, Abu-Lughod's (1995) writings on reproductive practices and fertility among Bedouin women in Egypt, Behar's (1996) writing on the role of personal witnessing within the anthropological craft, and El-Or's (2010) discussion of her ethnic and religious identity in her studies. My autoethnographic account delivered here was initially developed in Ruth Behar's course, Ethnographic Writing, at the University of Michigan in the fall of 2013.

2. *Nahalal* occupies a central place in the history of the Zionist movement and in Hebrew culture and has been the focus of poems and prose, informing, for example, the books of the writer Meir Shalev (1991), with *The Blue Mountain* (in Hebrew, Roman Russi), originally published in 1988.

3. For an updated summary of the development of disability rights and advocacy and disability studies in Israel, refer to Ziv et al. 2016.

4. For instance, an interdisciplinary Centre for Disability Studies is about to open in the fall of 2016 in the School for Social Work at The Hebrew University of Jerusalem, and an MA program focused on disability is offered at the Department of Community Mental Health at Haifa University. In addition, the Alin Beit Noam organization runs a knowledge center and research group on disability studies, and the Israel Sociological Society includes a disability studies community.

# Bibliography

Abu-Lughod, Lila. "Fieldwork of a Dutiful Daughter." In *Arab Women in the Field: Studying Your Own Society*, edited by Soraya Altorki and Camillia Fawzi El-Solh, 139–61. Syracuse: Syracuse University Press, 1988.

Abu-Lughod, Lila. "A Tale of Two Pregnancies." In *Women Writing Culture*, edited by Ruth Behar and Debora A. Gordon, 339–49. Berkeley: University of California Press, 1995.

Adams, Rachel. "Casting Light on Disability." *American Quarterly* 64, no. 4 (2012): 851–60.

Almog, Nitsan. "Academic and Social Adjustment of University Students with Visual Impairment." PhD diss., Bar-Ilan University, 2011.

Alpers, Svetlana. "The Museum as a Way of Seeing." In *Exhibiting Cultures: The Poetics and Politics of Museum Display*, edited by Ivan Karp and Steven D. Lavine, 25–32. Washington, DC: Smithsonian Institution Press, 1991.

Ameeriar, Lalaie. "The Sanitized Sensorium." *American Anthropologist* 114, no. 3 (2012): 509–20.

Asch, Adrienne, and Michelle Fine, eds. *Women with Disabilities: Essays in Psychology, Culture, and Politics*. Philadelphia: Temple University Press, 1988.

Asch, Adrienne, and Lawrence H. Sacks. "Lives without, Lives within: Autobiographies of Blind Women and Men." *Journal of Visual Impairment and Blindness* 77, no. 6 (1983): 242–47.

Banes, Sally, and André Lepecki, eds. *The Senses in Performance*. New York: Routledge, 2007.

Bar-On Cohen, Einat. "Kibadachi in Karate: Pain and Crossing Boundaries within the 'Lived Body' and within Sociality." *Journal of the Royal Anthropological Institute* 15, no. 3 (2009): 610–29.

Bar-On Cohen, Einat. "Kime and the Moving Body: Somatic Codes in Japanese Martial Arts." *Body and Society* 12, no. 4 (2006): 73–93.

Barasch, Moshe. *Blindness: The History of a Mental Image in Western Thought*. New York and London: Routledge, 2001.

Bartky, Sandra Lee. "Foucault, Femininity, and the Modernization of Patriarchal Power." In *Writing on the Body: Female Embodiment and Feminist Theory*, edited by Katie Conboy, Nadia Medina, and Sarah Stanbury, 93–111. New York: Columbia University Press, 1997.

Barton, Len. "Emancipatory Research and Disabled People: Some Observations and Questions." *Educational Review* 57, no. 3 (2005): 317–27.

Battles, Heather T., and Lenore Manderson. "The Ashley Treatment: Furthering the Anthropology of/on Disability." *Medical Anthropology: Cross-Cultural Studies in Health and Illness* 27, no. 3 (2008): 219–26.

Behar, Ruth. *The Vulnerable Observer: Anthropology that Breaks Your Heart.* Boston: Beacon Press, 1996.

Belek, Ben. "Articulating Sensory Sensitivity: From Bodies with Autism to Autistic Bodies." *Medical Anthropology: Cross Cultural Studies in Health and Illness* (2018): 1–14: http://doi.org/10.1080/01459740.2018.1460750

Beller, Jonathan. *The Cinematic Mode of Production: Attention Economy and the Society of the Spectacle.* Hanover, NH: Dartmouth College Press, 2006.

Bendix, Regina. "The Pleasure of the Ear: Toward an Ethnography of Listening." *Cultural Analysis* 1 (2000): 33–52.

Benin, David, and Lisa Cartwright. "Shame, Empathy and Looking Practices: Lessons from a Disability Studies Classroom." *Journal of Visual Culture* 5, no. 2 (2006): 155–71.

Berger, John. *Ways of Seeing.* London: British Broadcasting Corporation; New York: Penguin Books, 1973.

Berkovitch, Nitza. "Motherhood as a National Mission: The Construction of Womanhood in the Legal Discourse in Israel." *Women's Studies International Forum* 20, no. 5–6 (1997): 605–19.

Block, Pam. "To Turn on the Camera, and See for the First Time." *Haaretz*, October 11, 2009 (Hebrew).

Bolt, David. "From Blindness to Visual Impairment: Terminological Typology and the Social Model of Disability." *Disability and Society* 20, no. 5 (2005): 539–52.

Bolt, David. *The Metanarrative of Blindness: A Re-Reading of Twentieth-Century Anglophone Writing.* Ann Arbor: University of Michigan Press, 2014.

Bordo, Susan. *Unbearable Weight: Feminism, Western Culture, and the Body.* Berkeley: University of California Press, 2003.

Borges, Jorge Luis. *Seven Nights.* New York: New Directions Publishing, 1984.

Bourdieu, Pierre. *Distinction: A Social Critique of the Judgment of Taste.* Translated by Richard Nice. Cambridge: Harvard University Press, 1984.

Bourdieu, Pierre. "The Forms of Capital." In *Handbook of Theory of Research for the Sociology of Education*, edited by J. Richardson, 241–58. New York: Greenwood, 1986.

Bourdieu, Pierre. "Sport and Social Class." *Theory and Method* 17, no. 6 (1978): 819–40.

Brodkin, Karen. *How Jews Became White Folks and What That Says about Race in America.* New Brunswick, NJ: Rutgers University Press, 1998.

Browning, Barbara. *Samba: Resistance in Motion.* Bloomington: Indiana University Press, 1995.

Brueggemann, Brenda J., Rosemarie Garland-Thomson, and Georgina Kleege.

"What Her Body Taught (or Teaching about and with a Disability): A Conversation." *Feminist Studies* 31, no. 1 (2005): 13–33.

Brueggemann, Brenda J., and Georgina Kleege. "Gently Down the Stream: Reflections on Mainstreaming." *Rhetoric Review* 22, no. 2 (2003): 174–84.

Brune, Jeffrey A., and Daniel J. Wilson, eds. *Disability and Passing: Blurring the Lines of Identity*. Philadelphia: Temple University Press, 2013.

Buckingham, Susan, and Monica Degen. "Sensing Our Way: Using Yoga as a Research Method." *The Senses and Society* 7, no. 3 (2012): 329–44.

Bull, Michael, and Les Back, eds. *The Auditory Culture Reader*. Oxford and New York: Berg, 2003.

Burgstahler, Sheryl, and Tanis Doe. "Disability-Related Simulations: If, When, and How to Use Them in Professional Development." *Review of Disability Studies: An International Journal* 1, no. 2 (2004): 8–18. http://rdsjournal.org/index.php/journal/article/view/385

Butler, Judith. *Gender Trouble: Feminism and the Subversive of Identity*. New York: Routledge, 1990.

Cain, Victoria E. M. "'The Direct Medium of the Vision': Visual Education, Virtual Witnessing and the Prehistoric Past at the American Museum of Natural History, 1890–1923." *Journal of Visual Culture* 9, no. 3 (2010): 284–303.

Carmeli, Yoram S., and Kalman Applbaum, eds. *Consumption and Market Society in Israel*. Oxford: Berg, 2004.

Charmaz, Kathy. *Constructing Grounded Theory: A Practical Guide through Qualitative Analysis*. London: Sage, 2006.

Classen, Constance. *The Book of Touch*. Oxford and New York: Berg, 2005.

Classen, Constance. *The Colors of Angels: Cosmology, Gender, and the Aesthetic Imagination*. London and New York: Routledge, 1998.

Classen, Constance. "Foundations for an Anthropology of the Senses." *International Social Science Journal* 49, no. 153 (1997): 401–12.

Classen, Constance. "Museum Manners: The Sensory Life of the Early Museum." *Journal of Social History* 40, no. 4 (2007): 895–914.

Classen, Constance. "Odor of the Other: Olfactory Symbolism and Cultural Categories." *Ethos* 20, no. 2 (1992): 133–66.

Classen, Constance. *Worlds of Senses: Exploring the Senses in History and across Cultures*. London; New York: Routledge, 1993.

Classen, Constance, and David Howes. "Making Sense of Culture: Anthropology as a Sensual Experience." *Etnofoor* 9, no. 2 (1996): 86–96.

Classen, Constance, and David Howes. "The Museum as Sensescape." In *Sensible Objects: Colonialism, Museums and Material Culture*, edited by Elizabeth Edwards, Chris Gosden, and Ruth B. Phillips, 199–267. Oxford: Berg, 2006.

Cohen, Asher, and Bernard Susser. "Jews and Others: Non-Jewish Jews in Israel." *Israel Affairs* 15, no. 1 (2009): 52–65.

Colligan, Sumi. "The Ethnographer's Body as Text and Context: Revisiting and Revisioning the Body through Anthropology and Disability Studies." *Disability Studies Quarterly* 21, no. 3 (2001): 113–24.

Conquergood, Dwight. "Performing as a Moral Act: Ethical Dimensions of the Ethnography of Performance." *Literature in Performance* 5, no. 2 (1985): 1–13.

Crapanzano, Vincent. "On the Writing of Ethnography." *Dialectical Anthropology* 2, no. 1 (1977): 69–73.

Crockett, David. "Paths to Respectability: Consumption and Stigma Management in the Contemporary Black Middle Class." *Journal of Consumer Research* 44, no. 3 (2017): 554–81.

Crow, Liz. "Scroungers and Superhumans: Images of Disability from the Summer of 2012: A Visual Inquiry." *Journal of Visual Culture* 13, no. 2 (2014): 168–81.

Csordas, Thomas J. "Somatic Modes of Attention." *Cultural Anthropology* 8, no. 2 (1993): 135–56.

Curry, Marry Ann, Dena Hassouneh-Phillips, and Anne Johnston-Silverberg. "Abuse of Women with Disabilities: An Ecological Model and Review." *Violence against Women* 7, no. 1 (2001): 69–79.

Davis, John M. "Disability Studies as Ethnographic Research and Text: Research Strategies and Roles for Promoting Social Change?" *Disability and Society* 15, no. 2 (2000): 191–206.

Davis, Lennard J. *Enforcing Normalcy: Disability, Deafness, and the Body*. London: Verso, 1995.

Davis, Lennard J., and Marquard Smith. "Editorial: Disability-Visuality." *Journal of Visual Culture* 5, no. 2 (2006): 131–36.

De-Certeau, Michel. *The Practices of Everyday Life*. Berkeley, Los Angeles, and London: University of California Press, 1984.

Debord, Guy. *The Society of the Spectacle*. Translated by Donald Nicholson-Smith. New York: Zone Books, 1994.

Deegan, Mary Jo, and Jeffrey Willett. "Liminality and Disability: Rites of Passage and Community in Hypermodern Society." *Disability Studies Quarterly* 21, no. 3 (2001): 137–52.

Dellinger, Kirsten, and Christine L. Williams. "Makeup at Work: Negotiating Appearance Rules in the Workplace." *Gender and Society* 11, no. 2 (1997): 151–77.

Deshen, Shlomo. *Blind People: The Private and Public Life of Sightless Israelis*. Albany: State University of New York Press, 1992.

Douglas, Mary. *Purity and Danger: An Analysis of Concepts of Pollution and Taboo*. New York: Praege, 1966.

Downey, Greg. "'Practice without Theory': A Neuroanthropological Perspective on Embodied Learning." *Journal of the Royal Anthropological Institute* 16, no. s1 (2010): 22–40.

Dundes, Alan. *Interpreting Folklore*. Bloomington: Indiana University Press, 1980.

Edwards, Elizabeth, Chris Gosden, and Ruth Phillips. "Introduction." In *Sensible Objects: Colonialism, Museums and Material Culture*, edited by Elizabeth Edwards, Chris Gosden and Ruth Phillips, 1–34. Oxford: Berg, 2006.

Eisenhauer, Jennifer. "Just Looking and Staring Back: Challenging Ableism Through Disability Performance Art." *Studies in Art Education* 49, no. 1 (2007): 7–22.

El-Or, Tamar. *Reserved Seats: Religion, Gender, and Ethnicity in Contemporary Is-*

*rael.* Translated by Haim Watzman. Detroit, MI: Wayne State University Press, 2010.

Elder, Billie P. "Rehabilitation: The Double Blind for Blind Women." *Journal of Visual Impairment and Blindness* 77, no. 6 (1983): 298–300.

Elkins, James. *The Object Stares Back: On the Nature of Seeing.* San Diego: Harcourt Brace, 1997.

Ewart, Elizabeth. "Seeing, Hearing and Speaking: Morality and Sense among the Panara in Central Brazil." *Ethnos* 73, no. 4 (2008): 505–22.

Fabian, Johannes. *Time and the Other: How Anthropology Makes Its Object.* New York: Columbia University Press, 1983.

Falk, Raphael. *Zionism and the Biology of Jews.* Berlin: Springer, 2017.

Featherstone, Mike. "The Body in Consumer Culture." In *The Consumption Reader*, edited by David B. Clarke, Marcus A. Doel and Kate M. L. Housiaux, 163–68. London: Routledge, 2003.

Feld, Steven. "A Rainforest Acoustemology." In *The Auditory Culture Reader*, edited by Michael Bull and Les Back, 223–39. Oxford; New York: Berg, 2003.

Feldman, Allen. "Violence and Vision: The Prosthetics and Aesthetics of Terror." *Public Culture* 10, no. 1 (1997): 24–60.

Feldman, Dina, and Shaul Yahalom. "Corrective Discrimination for People with Disabilities in Israel." In *Corrective Discrimination and Advocacy Assurance in Israel*, edited by Anat Ma'or, 399–426. Tel Aviv: Ramot, 2004 (Hebrew).

Forsey, Martin Gerard. "Ethnography as Participant Listening." *Ethnography* 11, no. 4 (2010): 558–72.

Foucault, Michel. *The Birth of the Clinic: An Archaeology of Medical Perception.* Translated by A. M. Sheridan Smith. New York: Random House, 1975.

Foucault, Michel. *Discipline and Punish: The Birth of Prison.* Translated by Alan Sheridan. New York: Pantheon Books, 1977.

Frame, Melissa J. *Blind Spots: The Communicative Performance of Visual Impairment in Relationships and Social Interaction.* Springfield: Charles C Thomas Publisher, 2004.

Frank, Gelya. *Venus on Wheels: Two Decades of Dialogue on Disability, Being Female in America.* Berkeley: University of California Press, 2000.

Fraser, Laura. *Losing It: America's Obsession with Weight and the Industry That Feeds on It.* New York: Dutton, 1997.

Frederick, Angela. "Visibility, Respectability, and Disengagement: The Everyday Resistance of Mothers with Disabilities." *Social Science and Medicine* 181 (2017): 131–38.

French, Sally. "Simulation Exercises in Disability Awareness Training: A Critique." *Disability, Handicap and Society* 7, no. 3 (1992): 257–66.

French, Sally. "The Wind Gets in My Way." In *Disability Discourse*, edited by Marian Croker and Sally French, 21–27. Buckingham and Philadelphia: Open University Press, 1999.

Friedman, Asia. *Blind to Sameness: Sexpectations and the Social Construction of Male and Female Bodies.* Chicago and London: University of Chicago Press, 2013.

Friedner, Michele, and Stefan Helmreich. "Sound Studies Meets Deaf Studies." *The Senses and Society* 7, no. 1 (2012): 72–86.

Frith, Hannah, and Kate Gleeson. "Clothing and Embodiment: Men Managing Body Image and Appearance." *Psychology of Men and Masculinit* 5, no. 1 (2004): 40–48.

Furness, Zack. "Critical Mass, Urban Space and Vélomobility." *Mobilities* 2, no. 2 (2007): 299–319.

Garland-Thomson, Rosemarie. "Dares to Stares: Disabled Women Performance Artists and the Dynamics of Staring." In *Bodies in Commotion: Disability and Performance*, edited by Carrie Sandahl and Philip Auslander, 30–55. Ann Arbor: University of Michigan Press, 2005a.

Garland-Thomson, Rosemarie. *Extraordinary Bodies: Figuring Physical Disability in American Culture and Literature*. New York: Columbia University Press, 1997.

Garland-Thomson, Rosemarie. "Feminist Disability Studies." *Signs* 30, no. 2 (2005b): 1557–87.

Garland-Thomson, Rosemarie. "Integrating Disability, Transforming Feminist Theory." *NWSA Journal* 14, no. 3 (2002): 1–32.

Garland-Thomson, Rosemarie. "Introduction: From Wonder to Error—A Genealogy of Freak Discourse in Modernity." In *Freakery: Cultural Spectacles of the Extraordinary Body*, edited by Rosemarie Garland-Thomson, 1–22. New York and London: New York University Press, 1996.

Garland-Thomson, Rosemarie. *Staring: How We Look*. Oxford, England: Oxford University Press, 2009.

Garland-Thomson, Rosemarie. "Ways of Staring." *Journal of Visual Culture* 5, no. 2 (2006): 173–92.

Geertz, Clifford. *The Interpretation of Cultures: Selected Essays by Clifford Geertz*. New York: Basic Books, 1973.

Geraghty, Christine. *Women and Soap Opera: A Study of Prime Time Soaps*. Cambridge, UK: Polity, 1991.

Geurts, Kathryn Linn. "On Embodied Consciousness in Anlo-Ewe Worlds: A Cultural Phenomenology of the Fetal Position." *Ethnography* 4, no. 3 (2003): 363–95.

Geurts, Kathryn Linn. "On Rocks, Walks, and Talks in West Africa: Cultural Categories and an Anthropology of the Senses." *Ethos* 30, no. 3 (2002): 178–98.

Geurts, Kathryn Linn. "Senses." In *Keywords for Disability Studies*, edited by Rachel Adams, Benjamin Reiss, and David Serlin, 161–63. New York: New York University Press, 2015.

Gill, Carol J. "Divided Understanding: The Social Experience of Disability." In *Handbook of Disability Studies*, edited by Gary L. Albrecht, Katherine D. Seelman, and Michael Bury, 351–72. Thousand Oaks, London, and New Delhi: Sage Publications, 2001.

Gleitman, Ilana, Yossi Kurssiya, and Orna Marom. *A Blind Person, a Better Masseur: A Decade of the Training Program for Blind and Visually Impaired Medical Massage Masseurs in the Wingate Institute*. State of Israel: Ministry of Social Affairs and Social Services, Service for the Blind, 2008 (Hebrew).

Goffman, Erving. *Notes on the Management of Spoiled Identity*. Englewood Cliffs, NJ: Prentice Hall, 1963.

Goffman, Erving. *Relations in Public: Microstudies of the Public Order.* Middlesex and Victoria: Penguin Books, 1972.

Goldin, Carol S. "Stigma, Biomedical Efficacy, and Institutional Control." *Social Science and Medicine* 30, no. 8 (1990): 895–900.

Gooldin, Sigal. "Anorexia in Israel or Israeli Anorexia? Some Remarks on a Culture-Bound-Syndrome in a Global Context." *Israeli Sociology* 4, no. 1 (2002): 105–41, (Hebrew).

Grasseni, Cristina. "Introduction." In *Skilled Visions: Between Apprenticeship and Standards,* edited by Cristina Grasseni, 1–22. New York and Oxford: Berghahn Books, 2009.

Grasseni, Cristina. "Learning to See: World-Views, Skilled Visions, Skilled Practice." In *Knowing How to Know: Fieldwork and the Ethnographic Present,* edited by Narmala Halstead, Eric Hirsch, and Judith Okely, 151–72. New York and Oxford: Berghahn Books, 2008.

Grasseni, Cristina. "Skilled Vision: An Apprenticeship in Breeding Aesthetics." *Social Anthropology* 12, no. 1 (2004): 41–55.

Grigely, Joseph. "Blindness and Deafness as Metaphors: An Anthological Essay." *Journal of Visual Culture* 5, no. 2 (2006): 227–41.

Guy, Alison, and Maura Banim. "Personal Collections: Women's Clothing Use and Identity." *Journal of Gender Studies* 9, no. 3 (2000): 313–27.

Haldrup, Michael, Lasse Koefoed, and Kirsten Simonsen. "Practical Orientalism—Bodies, Everyday Life and the Construction of Otherness." *Geografiska Annaler, Series B: Human Geography* 88, no. 2 (2006): 173–84.

Hammer, Gili. *"Insights from the Glass Cage": Blind Women and Gendered Identities.* PhD diss., The Hebrew University of Jerusalem, Israel, 2013.

Hammer, Gili. "You Can Learn Merely by Listening to the Way a Patient Walks through the Door": The Transmission of Sensory Medical Knowledge." *Medical Anthropology Quarterly* 32, no. 1 (2017): 138–54.

Handler, Richard. "An Anthropological Definition of the Museum and Its Purpose." *Museum Anthropology* 17, no. 1 (1993): 33–36.

Harris, Anna, and Melissa Van Drie. "Sharing Sound: Teaching, Learning, and Researching Sonic Skills." *Sound Studies* 1, no.1 (2015): 98–117.

Hazani, Asaf. *"To Catch a Wheel": Shaping the Space of Road Cyclists in Israel.* Ph.D. diss., The Hebrew University of Jerusalem, Jerusalem, Israel, 2010 (Hebrew).

Helfman, Michal, Yitzhak Livneh, and Sharon Ya'ari. *The Invisible Snake Show.* Sommer Contemporary Art Gallery, Tel-Aviv. May 3–June 15, 2007.

Herzfeld, Michael. *Anthropology through the Looking-glass: Critical Ethnography in the Margins of Europe.* Cambridge: Cambridge University Press, 1987.

Hess, Itay. "Visually Impaired Pupils in Mainstream Schools in Israel: Quality of Life and other Associated Factors." *British Journal of Visual Impairments and Blindness* 28, no. 1 (2010): 19–33.

Hever, Hannan, Yehouda Shenhav, and Pnina Motzafi-Haller. *Mizrahim in Israel: A Critical Observation into Israel's Ethnicity.* Tel-Aviv: Van Leer Institute Press/ Hakibbutz Hameuchad Publishing House, 2002 (Hebrew).

Hine, Robert. *Second Sight*. Berkeley, Los Angeles, and London: University of California Press, 1997.

Hinojosa, Servando Z. "'The Hands Know': Bodily Engagement and Medical Impasse in Highland Maya Bonesetting." *Medical Anthropology Quarterly* 16, no. 1 (2002): 22–40.

Hockey, John, and Jacquelyn Allen Collinson. "Seeing the Way: Visual Sociology and the Distance Runner's Perspective." *Visual Studies* 21, no. 1 (2006): 70–81.

Howes, David. "Introduction to Sensory Museology." *The Senses and Society* 9, no. 3 (2014): 259–67.

Howes, David. *Sensual Relations: Engaging the Senses in Culture and Social Theory*. Ann Arbor: University of Michigan Press, 2003.

Howes, David. *The Varieties of Sensory Experience: A Sourcebook in the Anthropology of the Senses*. Toronto, Buffalo and London: University of Toronto Press, 1991.

Howland, Carol A., and Diana H. Rintala. "Dating Behaviors of Women with Physical Disabilities." *Sexuality and Disability* 19, no. 1 (2001): 41–70.

Huisman, Kimberly, and Pierrette Hondagneu-Sotelo. "Dress Matters: Change and Continuity in the Dress Practices of Bosnian Muslim Refugee Women." *Gender and Society* 19, no. 1 (2005): 44–65.

Hull, John M. *Touching the Rock: An Experience of Blindness*. New York: Pantheon Books, 1992.

Hutson, David J. "Standing OUT/Fitting IN: Identity, Appearance, and Authenticity in Gay and Lesbian Communities." *Symbolic Interaction* 33, no. 2 (2010): 213–33.

Hyndman, David. "Dominant Discourses of Power Relations and the Melanesian Other: Interpreting the Eroticized, Effeminizing Gaze in National Geographic." *Cultural Analysis* 1 (2000): 15–32.

Ingold, Tim. *Imagining Landscapes: Past, Present and Future*. Farnham: Ashgate Publishing, 2012.

Ingold, Tim. *The Perception of the Environment: Essays on Livelihood, Dwelling, and Skill*. London: Routledge, 2000.

Irigaray, Luce. *This Sex which Is Not One*. Translated by Catherine Porter and Carolyn Burke. Day Hall: Cornell University Press, 1985.

Jay, Martin. *Downcast Eyes: The Denigration of Vision in Twentieth-Century French Thought*. Berkeley, Los Angeles, and London: University of California Press, 1993.

Jay, Martin. "Introduction: Genres of Blur." *Common Knowledge* 18, no. 2 (2012): 220–28.

Johnston, Josée, and Judith Taylor. "Feminist Consumerism and Fat Activists: A Comparative Study of Grassroots Activism and the Dove Real Beauty Campaign." *Signs: Journal of Women in Culture and Society* 33, no. 4 (2008): 941–66.

Kafer, Alison. "Compulsory Bodies: Reflections on Heterosexuality and Ablebodiedness." *Journal of Women's History* 15, no. 3 (2003): 77–89.

Kamir, Orit. *Human Dignity, Feminism in Israel: A Socio-Legal Analysis*. Haifa: Carmel Publishing House, 2007 (Hebrew).

Kapchan, Deborah. "The Promise of Sonic Translation: Performing the Festive Sacred in Morocco." *American Anthropologist* 110, no. 4 (2008): 467–83.

Kaplan-Myrth, Nili. "Alice without a Looking Glass: Blind People and Body Image." *Anthropology and Medicine* 7, no. 3 (2000): 277–99.

Kaplan-Myrth, Nili. "Blindness Prevention in Mali: Are Improvements in Sight?" *Disability Studies Quarterly* 21, no. 3 (2001): 91–103.

Kaya, Laura Pearl. "The Criterion of Consistency: Women's Self-Presentation at Yarmouk University, Jordan." *American Ethnologist* 37 no. 3 (2010): 526–38.

Keating, Elizabeth, and Neill R. Hadder. "Sensory Impairment." *Annual Review of Anthropology* 39 (2010): 115–29.

Kef, Sabina, and Henny Bos. "Is Love Blind? Sexual Behavior and Psychological Adjustment of Adolescents with Blindness." *Sexuality and Disability* 24, no. 2 (2006): 89–100.

Kent, Deborah. "Beyond Expectations: Being Blind and Becoming a Mother." *Sexuality and Disability* 20, no. 1 (2002): 81–88.

Kent, Deborah. "In Search of Liberation." In *With Wings: An Anthology of Literature by and about Women with Disabilities*, edited by Marsha Saxton, 82–83. New York: The Feminist Press, 1987.

Khazzoom, Aziza. *Shifting Ethnic Boundaries and Inequality in Israel: Or How the Polish Peddler Became a German Intellectual.* Stanford: Stanford University Press, 2008.

King, Angela. "The Prisoner of Foucault and the Discipline of the Female Body." *Journal of International Women's Studies* 5, no. 2 (2004): 29–40.

Kisch, Shifra. "'Deaf Discourse': The Social Construction of Deafness in a Bedouin Community." *Medical Anthropology* 27, no. 3 (2008): 283–313.

Kleege, Georgina. "Beauty and the Blind." *The Courier UNESCO*, July/August (2001): 47–48.

Kleege, Georgina. "Blindness and Visual Culture: An Eyewitness Account." *Journal of Visual Culture* 4, no. 2 (2005): 179–90.

Kleege, Georgina. *Sight Unseen.* New Haven and London: Yale University Press, 1999.

Kleege, Georgina. "Visible Braille/Invisible Blindness." *Journal of Visual Culture* 5, no. 2 (2006): 209–18.

Klobas, Lauri E. *Disability Drama in Television and Film.* Jefferson, NC: McFarland, 1988.

Kohavi, Tal. *Between Dance and Anthropology.* PhD diss., The Hebrew University of Jerusalem, Israel, 2007 (Hebrew).

Kravel-Tovi, Michal. "'National Mission': Biopolitics, Non-Jewish Immigration and Jewish Conversion Policy in Contemporary Israel." *Ethnic and Racial Studies* 35, no. 4 (2012): 737–56.

Krieger, Susan. "Beyond 'Subjectivity': The Use of the Self in Social Science." *Qualitative Sociology* 8, no. 4 (1985): 309–24.

Krumer-Nevo, Michal. *Women in Poverty, Life Stories: Gender, Pain, Resistance.* Tel-Aviv: Hakibbutz Hameuchad Publishing House, 2006 (Hebrew).

Kudlick, Catherine J. "Black Bike, White Cane: Nonstandard Deviations of a Special Self." *Disability Studies Quarterly* 31, no. 1 (2011): http://dsq-sds.org/article/view/1373/1537

Kudlick, Catherine J. "The Blind Man's Harley: White Canes and Gender Identity in America." *Signs* 30, no. 2 (2005): 1589–606.

Kuppers, Petra. *Disability and Contemporary Performance: Bodies on Edge.* New York and London: Routledge, 2004.

Kuppers, Petra. "Tiresian Journeys." *TDR/The Drama Review* 52, no. 4 (2008): 174–82.

Kuppers, Petra. "Toward a Rhizomatic Model of Disability: Poetry, Performance, and Touch." *Journal of Literary and Cultural Disability Studies* 3, no. 3 (2009): 221–40.

Kurssiya, Yossi, and Ilana Gleitman. "Entitlement for a Blind Card in Israel, Final Report for 2008." *The Service for the Blind, Ministry of Social Affairs and Social Services,* the State of Israel, 2009 (Hebrew).

Kuusisto, Stephen. *Planet of the Blind: A Memoir.* New York: Dial, 1998.

Ladd, Paddy. *Understanding Deaf Culture: In Search of Deafhood.* Clevedon: Multilingual Matters, 2003.

Latour, Bruno. "How to Talk about the Body? The Normative Dimension of Science Studies." *Body and Society* 10, no. 2–3 (2004): 205–29.

Lefebvre, Henri. *The Production of Space.* Oxford: Blackwell, 1991.

Limaye, Sandhya. "Sexuality and Women with Sensory Disability." In *Women, Disability and Identity,* edited by Asha Hans and Annie Patri, 89–100. New Delhi, India: Sage, 2003.

Linton, Simi. *Claiming Disability: Knowledge and Identity.* New York and London: New York University Press, 1998.

Linton, Simi. "Reassigning Meaning." In *The Disability Studies Reader,* edited by Lennard J. Davis, 161–72. New York and London: Routledge, 2006.

Lomsky-Feder, Edna, and Tamar Rapoport. "Homecoming, Immigration, and the National Ethos: Russian-Jewish Homecomers Reading Zionism." *Anthropological Quarterly* 74, no. 1 (2001): 1–14.

Lonsdale, Susan. *Women and Disability: The Experience of Physical Disability among Women.* London: Macmillan Education, 1990.

Losch, Diane. "The Fate of the Senses in Ethnographic Modernity: The Margaret Mead Hall of Pacific Peoples at the American Museum of Natural History." In *Sensible Objects: Colonialism, Museums and Material Culture,* edited by Elizabeth Edwards, Chris Gosden, and Ruth Phillips, 223–44. Oxford: Berg, 2006.

Luhrmann, Tanya M. *When God Talks Back: Understanding the American Evangelical Relationship with God.* New York: Alfred A. Knopf, 2012.

Lund, Katrin. "Seeing in Motion and the Touching Eye: Walking over Scotland's Mountains." *Etnofoor* 18, no. 1 (2005): 27–42.

Macpherson, Hanna. "Articulating Blind Touch: Thinking through the Feet." *The Senses and Society* 4, no. 2 (2009): 179–94.

Madison, Soyini D. "The Dialogic Performative in Critical Ethnography." *Text and Performance Quarterly* 26, no. 4 (2006): 320–24.

Mathur, Saloni. "Living Ethnological Exhibits: The Case of 1886." *Cultural Anthropology* 15, no. 4 (2001): 492–524.

Mazor, Daniela. "The Social Construction of Sexuality in Women with Physical and Sensorial Disabilities Compared with Non-Disabled Women." PhD diss., University of Haifa, 2015.

McCaughtry, Nate, and Inez Rovegno. "Meaning and Movement: Exploring the Deep Connections to Education." *Studies in Philosophy and Education* 20, no. 6 (2001): 489–505.

McRuer, Robert. "As Good as It Gets: Queer Theory and Critical Disability." *GLQ: A Journal of Lesbian and Gay Studies* 9, no. 1–2 (2003): 79–105.

McRuer, Robert. "Compulsory Ablebodiedness and Queer/Disabled Existence." In *The Disability Studies Reader*, 3rd ed., edited by Lennard J. Davis, 383–92. London: Routledge, 2010.

Merleau-Ponty, Maurice. "The Primacy of Perception and Its Philosophical Consequences." In *The Primacy of Perception: And Other Essays on Phenomenological Psychology, the Philosophy of Art, History and Politics*, edited by James M. Edie, 12–42. Translated by James M. Edie. Evanston, IL: Northwestern University Press, 1964.

Merleau-Ponty, Maurice. *The Visible and the Invisible*. Translated by Alphonso Lingis. Evanston, IL: Northwestern University Press, 1968.

Michalko, Rod. *The Mystery of the Eye and the Shadow of Blindness*. Toronto, Buffalo, and London: University of Toronto Press, 1998.

Mingus, Mia. "Forced Intimacy: An Ableist Norm." *Leaving Evidence*, August 6, 2017. https://leavingevidence.wordpress.com/2017/08/06/forced-intimacy-an-ableist-norm/

Mitchell, William J. T. "Showing Seeing: A Critique of Visual Culture." *Journal of Visual Culture* 1, no. 2 (2002): 165–81.

Mitchell, William J. T. "Seeing Disability." *Public Culture* 13, no. 3 (2001): 391–98.

Moin, Victor, Ilana Duvdevany, and Daniela Mazor. "Sexual Identity, Body Image and Life Satisfaction among Women with and without Physical Disability." *Sexuality and Disability* 27, no. 2 (2009): 83–95.

Mollow, Anna. "Disability Studies Gets Fat." *Hypatia* 30, no. 1 (2015): 199–216.

Mor, Sagit. "Between Charity, Welfare, and Warfare: A Disability Legal Studies Analysis of Privilege and Neglect in Israeli Disability Policy." *Yale Journal of Law and the Humanities* 18 (2006): 63–136.

Mor, Sagit, Neta Ziv, Arlene Kanter, Adva Eichengreen, and Nissim Mizrachi, eds. *Disability Studies: A Reader*. Tel-Aviv: Van Leer Institute Press/Hakibbutz Hameuchad Publishing House, 2016 (Hebrew).

Morris, Jenny. *Pride against Prejudice*. Philadelphia: New Society, 1991.

Mulvey, Laura. "Visual Pleasure and Narrative Cinema." *Screen* 16, no. 3 (1975): 6–18.

Murphy, Elizabeth, and Robert Dingwall. "The Ethics of Ethnography." In *Handbook of Ethnography*, edited by Paul Atkinson, Amanda Coffey, Sara Delamont, John Lofland, and Lyn Lofland, 339–51. London: Sage Publications, 2001.

Murphy, Robert F. *The Body Silent*. New York: Norton, 1990.

Myerhoff, Barbara. *Number Our Days*. New York: Simon and Schuster, 1978.

Noishtat, Nurit. "Accessibility's Principles for Persons with Visually Impairment." In *The Accessibility of the Israeli Society for Persons with Disabilities on the Threshold of the 21st Century*, edited by Dina Feldman, Yael Danieli-Lahav, and Shmuel Haimovitz, 525–46. Ministry of Justice: The State of Israel, 2007 (Hebrew).

Noland, Carrie. *Agency and Embodiment: Performing Gesture/Producing Culture*. Cambridge: Harvard University Press, 2009.

Obasogie, Osagie. *Blinded by Sight: Seeing Race through the Eyes of the Blind*. Stanford: Stanford University Press, 2013.

Odette, Francine. "Body Beautiful/Body Perfect: Challenging the Status Quo—Where Do Women with Disabilities Fit In?" *Canadian Women Studies* 14, no. 3 (1994): 41–43.

Oliver, Mike. "Changing the Social Relations of Research Production." *Disability, Handicap and Society* 7, no. 2 (1992): 101–14.

Oliver, Mike. "A Sociology of Disability or a Disablist Sociology?" In *Disability and Society: Emerging Issues and Insights*, edited by Len Barton, 18–42. New York: Longman Publishing, 1996.

Omansky, Beth. *Borderlands of Blindness*. Boulder: Lynne Rienner Publishers, 2011.

Omansky, Beth. "Researching the Social Construction of Blindness." *Review of Disability Studies: An International Journal* 1, no. 1 (2004): 128–32.

Ophir, Hodel. "The Signature of the Moving Body: Agency and Embodied Education Ideologies of Dance Teachers." *Anthropology and Education Quarterly* 47, no. 2 (2016): 186–202.

Padden, Carol, and Tom Humphries. *Inside Deaf Culture*. Cambridge: Harvard University Press, 2009.

Pallasmaa, Juhani. *The Eyes of the Skin: Architecture and the Senses*. Chichester: Wiley-Academic and Hoben, 2012.

Parviainen, Jaana. "Bodily Knowledge: Epistemological Reflections on Dance." *Dance Research Journal* 34, no. 1 (2002): 11–26.

Paterson, Mark. *Consumption and Everyday Life*. London and New York: Routledge, 2006.

Paterson, Mark. "Re-Mediating Touch." *Senses and Society* 4, no. 2 (2009): 129–40.

Patterson, Ernestine Amani. "Glimpse into Transformation." In *With the Power of Each Breath: A Disabled Women's Anthology*, edited by Susan E. Browne, Debra Connors, and Nanci Stern, 240–43. Pittsburgh: Cleis Press, 1985.

Peiss, Kathy. "Making Up, Making Over: Cosmetics, Consumer Culture, and Women's Identity." In *The Sex of Things: Gender and Consumption in Historical Perspective*, edited by Victoria De Grazia and Ellen Furlough, 311–36. Berkeley: University of California Press, 1996.

Peters, Susan. "Is There a Disability Culture? A Syncretisation of Three Possible World Views." *Disability and Society* 15, no. 4 (2000): 583–601.

Petersen, Amy J. "Research with Individuals Labeled 'Other': Reflections on the Research Process." *Disability and Society* 26, no. 3 (2011): 293–305.

Phillips, Marilynn J. "Damaged Goods: Oral Narratives of the Experience of Disability in American Culture." *Social Science and Medicine* 30, no. 8 (1990): 849–57.

Pink, Sarah. "Dirty Laundry. Everyday Practice, Sensory Engagement and the Constitution of Identity." *Social Anthropology* 13, no. 3 (2005): 275–90.

Pink, Sarah. *Doing Sensory Ethnography*. London: Sage, 2009.

Pink, Sarah. "An Urban Tour: The Sensory Sociality of Ethnographic Place-Making." *Ethnography* 9, no. 2 (2008): 175–96.

Pinquart, Martin, and Jens P. Pfeiffer. "What Is Essential Is Invisible to the Eye: Intimate Relationships of Adolescents with Visual Impairment." *Sexuality and Disability* 30, no. 2 (2012): 139–47.

Quinlan, Margaret M., and Benjamin R. Bates. "Dances and Discourses of (Dis)Ability: Heather Mills's Embodiment of Disability on *Dancing with the Stars*." *Text and Performance Quarterly* 28, no. 1–2 (2008): 64–80.

Rabinow, Paul. "Discourse and Power: On the Limits of Ethnographic Texts." *Dialectical Anthropology* 10, no. 1–2 (1985): 1–13.

Rapoport, Tamar, and Tamar El-Or. "Cultures of Womanhood in Israel: Social Agencies and Gender Production." *Women's Studies International Forum* 20, no. 5–6 (1997): 573–80.

Rat, Ricki. "On Blindness." *Makor Rishon*, May 1, 2009 (Hebrew).

Renshaw, Sarah. "Designing the Sensorium." *The Senses and Society* 4, no. 2 (2009): 247–51.

Rice, Tom. "'Beautiful Murmurs': Stethoscopic Listening and Acoustic Objectification." *The Senses and Society* 3, no. 3 (2008): 293–306.

Rice, Tom. *Hearing and the Hospital: Sound, Listening, Knowledge and Experience*. Herefordshire: Sean Kingston Publishing, 2013.

Rimon-Greenspan, Hila. "Disability Politics In Israel: Civil Society, Advocacy, and Contentious Politics." *Disability Studies Quarterly* 27, no. 4 (2007).

Roccas, Ronit. "Light at the End of the Darkness." *Haaretz*, January 6, 2009 (Hebrew).

Rodas, Julia M. "A Blind Man Goes into a Whorehouse . . . Blindness, Representation, Hypersexualization." Paper presented at the Holman Society, Berkeley, CA, January 14, 2011.

Rodas, Julia M. "On Blindness." *Journal of Literary and Cultural Disability Studies* 3, no. 2 (2009): 115–30.

Roginsky, Dina. "Performing Israeliness: Nationalism, Ethnicity and Israeli 'Folk and Ethnic' Dance." PhD diss., Tel Aviv University, 2004 (Hebrew).

Rose, Mike. "'Our Hands Will Know': The Development of Tactile Diagnostic Skill-Teaching, Learning, and Situated Cognition in a Physical Therapy Program." *Anthropology and Education Quarterly* 30 (1999): 133–60.

Rothstein, Edward. "Darkness Visible, and Palpable." *New York Times*, August 18, 2011.

Rudd, Nancy A., and Sharron J. Lennon. "Body Image and Appearance-Management Behaviors in College Women." *Clothing and Textiles Research Journal* 18, no. 3 (2000): 152–62.

Saerberg, Siegfried. "The Dining in the Dark Phenomenon." *Disability Studies Quarterly* 27, no. 3 (2007).

Said, Edward W. *Orientalism*. New York: Pantheon Books, 1978.

Samudra, Jaida Kim. "Memory in Our Body: Thick Participation and the Translation of Kinesthetic Experience." *American Ethnologist* 35, no. 4 (2008): 665–81.

Samuels, Ellen Jean. "Critical Divides: Judith Butler's Body Theory and the Question of Disability." NWSA Journal 14, no. 3 (2002): 58–76.

Sandahl, Carrie. "Ahhhh Freak Out! Metaphors of Disability and Femaleness in Performance." *Theatre Topics* 9, no. 1 (1999): 11–30.

Sanders-Bustle, Lynn, and Kimberly L. Oliver. "The Role of Physical Activity in the Lives of Researchers: A Body-Narrative." *Studies in Philosophy and Education* 20, no. 6 (2001): 507–20.

Sartre, Jean-Paul. *Being and Nothingness: An Essay on Phenomenological Ontology*. New York: Washington Square Press, 1966.

Sasson-Levy, Orna. "Contradictory Consequences of Mandatory Conscription: The Case of Women Secretaries in the Israeli Military." *Gender and Society* 21, no. 4 (2007): 481–507.

Saxton, Marsha. *With Wings: An Anthology of Literature by and about Women with Disabilities*. New York: The Feminist Press, 1987.

Schechner, Richard. *Between Theatre and Anthropology*. Philadelphia: University of Pennsylvania Press, 1985.

Schillmeier, Michael. "Dis/abling Spaces of Calculation: Blindness and Money in Everyday Life." *Environment and Planning D: Society and Space* 25, no. 4 (2007): 594–609.

Schillmeier, Michael. "Othering Blindness—on Modern Epistemological Politics." *Disability and Society* 21, no. 5 (2006): 471–84.

Schillmeier, Michael. "(Visual) Disability—from Exclusive Perspective to Inclusive Differences." *Disability and Society* 23, no. 6 (2008): 611–23.

Schor, Naomi. "Blindness as Metaphor." *Differences: A Journal of Feminist Cultural Studies* 11, no. 2 (1999): 76–105.

Scott, Ellen K. "'I Feel as if I Am the One Who Is Disabled': The Emotional Impact of Changed Employment Trajectories of Mothers Caring for Children with Disabilities." *Gender and Society* 24, no. 5 (2010): 672–96.

Scott, Robert A. *The Making of Blind Men: A Study of Adult Socialization*. New York: Russell Sage Foundation, 1969.

Sentumbwe, Nayinda. "Sighted Lovers and Blind Husbands: Experiences of Blind Women in Uganda." In *Disability and Culture*, edited by Benedicte Istgad and Susan Reynolds Whyte, 159–73. Berkeley, Los Angeles, and London: University of California Press, 1995.

Sered, Susan. *What Makes Women Sick? Maternity, Modesty, and Militarism in Israeli Society*. Hanover: Brandeis University Press, 2000.

Seremetakis, Nadia C., ed. *The Senses Still: Perception and Memory as Material Culture in Modernity*. Chicago: University of Chicago Press, 1996.

Shakespeare, Tom. "Power and Prejudice: Issues of Gender, Sexuality, and Disability." In *Disability and Society: Emerging Issues and Insights*, edited by Len Barton, 191–214. New York: Longman, 1996.

Shalev, Meir. *The Blue Mountain*. Translated by Hillel Halkin. New York: Harper Collins, 1991.

Shapin, Steven. "The Tastes of Wine: Towards a Cultural History." *Rivista di Estetica* 51 (2012): 49–94.

Sheets-Johnstone, Maxine, ed. *Giving the Body Its Due.* Albany: State University of New York Press, 1992.

Sheffi, Smadar. "Seeing the Invisible." *Haaretz,* May 17, 2007 (Hebrew).

Shilling, Chris. *The Body and Social Theory.* 2nd ed. London: Sage, 2003.

Shilling, Chris. "Physical Capital and Situated Action: A New Direction for Corporeal Sociology." *British Journal of Sociology of Education* 25, no. 4 (2004): 473–87.

Shuttleworth, Russell. "Exploring Multiple Roles and Allegiances in Ethnographic Process in Disability Culture." *Disability Studies Quarterly* 21, no. 3 (2001): 103–13.

Shuttleworth, Russell P., and Devva Kasnitz. "Stigma, Community, Ethnography: Joan Ablon's Contribution to the Anthropology of Impairment-Disability." *Medical Anthropology Quarterly* 18, no. 2 (2004): 139–61.

Siebers, Tobin. "Disability as Masquerade." *Literature and Medicine* 23, no. 1 (2004): 1–22.

Siebers, Tobin. *Disability Theory.* Ann Arbor: University of Michigan Press, 2008.

Sieler, Roman. "Patient Agency Revisited: 'Healing the Hidden' in South India." *Medical Anthropology Quarterly* 28, no. 3 (2014): 323–41.

Sinai, Rutty. "Law Requires Accessible Transportation, Many Blind People Stay at the Station." *Haaretz,* April 27, 2007 (Hebrew).

Slevin, Kathleen F. "'If I Had Lots of Money . . . I'd Have a Body Makeover:' Managing the Aging Body." *Social Forces* 88, no. 3 (2010): 1003–20.

Smooha, Sammy. "Ethnic Democracy: Israel as an Archetype." *Israel Studies* 2, no. 2 (1997): 198–241.

Sobchack, Vivian. "'Choreography for One, Two, and Three Legs' (A Phenomenological Meditation in Movements)." *Topoi* 24, no. 1 (2005): 55–66.

Sparkes, Andrew C. "Ethnography and the Senses: Challenges and Possibilities." *Qualitative Research in Sport and Exercise* 1, no. 1 (2009): 21–35.

Sparkes, Andrew C., and Brett Smith. "Sport, Spinal Cord Injury, Embodied Masculinities, and the Dilemmas of Narrative Identity." *Men and Masculinities* 4, no. 3 (2002): 258–85.

Spinney, Justin. "A Place of Sense: A Kinaesthetic Ethnography of Cyclists on Mont Ventoux." *Environment and Planning D: Society and Space* 24, no. 5 (2006): 709–32.

Stasch, Rupert. "Introduction: Double Signs and Intrasocietal Heterogeneity in Primitivist Tourism Encounters." *Ethnos* 80, no. 4 (2015): 433–47.

Stoller, Paul. "Eye, Mind and Word in Anthropology." *L'Homme* 24, no. 3–4 (1984): 91–114.

Stoller, Paul. *The Taste of Ethnographic Things: The Senses in Anthropology.* Philadelphia: University of Pennsylvania Press, 1989.

Stone, Emma, and Mark Priestley. "Parasites, Pawns and Partners: Disability Research and the Role of Non-Disabled Researchers." *British Journal of Sociology* 47, no. 4 (1996): 699–716.

Strauss, Anselm, and Juliet Corbin. *Basics of Qualitative Research: Grounded Theory Procedures and Techniques.* Newbury Park, CA: Sage, 1990.

Tabib-Calif, Yosepha, and Edna Lomsky-Feder. "Symbolic Boundary Work in Schools: Demarcating and Denying Ethnic Boundaries." *Anthropology and Education Quarterly* 45, no. 1 (2014): 22–38.

Terry, David P. "Once Blind, Now Seeing: Problematics of Confessional Performance." *Text and Performance Quarterly* 26, no. 3 (2006): 209–28.

Thomas, Carol. "The 'Disabled' Body." In *Real Bodies: A Sociological Introduction*, edited by Mary Evans and Ellie Lee, 64–78. New York: Palgrave, 2002.

Turner, Victor. *The Anthropology of Performance*. New York: PAJ Publications, 1986.

Turner, Victor. *Dramas, Fields, and Metaphors: Symbolic Action in Human Society*. London: Cornell University Press, 1974.

Turner, Victor. "Liminality and Community." In *Culture and Society: Contemporary Debates*, edited by Jeffery Alexander and Steven Seidman, 147–54. Cambridge: Cambridge University Press, 1990.

Turner, Victor. *The Ritual Process: Structure and Anti-Structure*. New York: Aldine De Gruyter, 1969.

Tyner, Kelia, and Jennifer Paff Ogle. "Feminist Perspectives on Dress and the Body: An Analysis of *Ms.* Magazine, 1972 to 2002." *Clothing and Textiles Research Journal* 25, no. 1 (2007): 74–105.

Tyler, Stephen A. "The Vision Quest in the West, or What the Mind's Eye Sees." *Journal of Anthropological Research* 40, no. 1 (1984): 23–40.

Vannini, Phillip, Dennis Waskul, and Simon Gottschalk. *The Senses in Self, Society, and Culture: A Sociology of the Senses*. New York: Routledge, 2012.

Vannini, Phillip, Dennis Waskul, Simon Gottschalk, and Carol Rambo. "Sound Acts: Elocution, Somatic Work, and the Performance of Sonic Alignment." *Journal of Contemporary Ethnography* 39, no. 3 (2010): 328–53.

Venkatesh, Alladi, Annamma Joy, John F. Sherry, and Jonathan Deschenes. "The Aesthetics of Luxury Fashion, Body and Identify Formation." *Journal of Consumer Psychology* 20, no. 4 (2010): 459–70.

Wacquant, Loïc. *Body and Soul: Ethnographic Notebooks of an Apprentice-Boxer*. New York and Oxford: Oxford University Press, 2004.

Wacquant, Loïc. "Carnal Connections: On Embodiment, Apprenticeship, and Membership." *Qualitative Sociology* 28, no. 4 (2005): 445–74.

Wade, Lisa. "The Emancipatory Promise of the Habitus: Lindy Hop, the Body, and Social Change." *Ethnography* 12, no. 2 (2011): 224–46.

Wagner-Lampl, Annie, and George W. Oliver. "Folklore of Blindness." *Journal of Visual Impairment and Blindness* 88, no. 3 (1994): 267–67.

Wasserfall, Rahel. "Reflexivity, Feminism and Difference." *Qualitative Sociology* 16, no. 1 (1993): 23–41.

Webster, Murray, and James E. Driskell. "Beauty as Status." *American Journal of Sociology* 89, no. 1 (1983): 140–65.

Weiss, Meira. *The Chosen Body: The Politics of the Body in Israeli Society*. Stanford: Stanford University Press, 2002.

Weitz, Rose. "Women and Their Hair: Seeking Power through Resistance and Accommodation." *Gender and Society* 15, no. 5 (2001): 667–86.

Wendell, Susan. *The Rejected Body; Feminist Philosophical Reflections on Disability*. New York: Routledge, 1996.

West, Candance, and Don H. Zimmerman. "Doing Gender." *Gender and Society* 1, no. 2 (1987): 125–51.

Wheatley, Edward. *Stumbling Blocks Before the Blind: Medieval Constructions of a Disability*. Ann Arbor: University of Michigan Press, 2010.

White, Patrick. "Sex Education or How the Blind Became Heterosexual." *GLQ: A Journal of Lesbian and Gay Studies* 9, no. 1–2 (2003): 133–47.

Whyte, Susan Reynolds, and Benedicte Ingstad. *Disability and Culture*. Berkeley: University of California Press, 1995.

Wilf, Eitan. "Modernity, Cultural Anesthesia, and Sensory Agency: Technologies of the Listening Self in a US Collegiate Jazz Music Program." *Ethnos: Journal of Anthropology* 80, no. 1 (2015): 1–22.

Willerslev, Rane. "'To Have the World at a Distance': Reconsidering the Significance of Vision for Social Anthropology." In *Skilled Visions: Between Apprenticeship and Standards*, edited by Cristina Grasseni, 23–46. New York and Oxford: Berghahn Books, 2009.

Williams, Lindsey, and Melanie Nind. "Insiders or Outsiders: Normalization and Women with Learning Difficulties." *Disability and Society* 14, no. 5 (1999): 659–72.

Wolf, Naomi. *The Beauty Myth*. New York: Harper Perennial, 1992.

Wulff, Helena. "To Know the Dancer: Formations of Fieldwork in the Ballet World." In *Knowing How to Know: Fieldwork and the Ethnographic Present*, edited by Narmala Halstead, Eric Hirsch, and Judith Okely, 75–91. New York and Oxford: Berghahn Books, 2008.

Young, Iris M. "Throwing Like a Girl: A Phenomenology of Feminine Body Comportment Motility and Spatiality." *Human Studies* 3, no. 1 (1980): 137–56.

Ziv, Neta, Sagit Mor, and Adva Eichengreen. "Introduction: Disability Studies in Hebrew—An Emerging Academic Field." In *Disability Studies: A Reader*, edited by Sagit Mor, Neta Ziv, Arlene Kanter, Adva Eichengreen, and Nissim Mizrachi, 11–54. Tel-Aviv: Van Leer Institute Press/Hakibbutz Hameuchad Publishing House, 2016 (Hebrew).

Zola, Irving. *Missing Pieces: A Chronicle of Living with a Disability*. Philadelphia: Temple University Press, 1982.

Zones, Jane Sprague. "Beauty Myths and Realities and Their Impact on Women's Health." In *Women's Health: Complexities and Differences*, edited by Sheryl Burt Ruzek, Virginia L. Olesen, and Adele E. Clarke, 249–75. Columbus: Ohio State University Press, 1997.

# Index

White, Patrick, 16, 38, 61, 72, 78, 92
Whyte, Susan Reynolds, 24, 55
Wilf, Eitan, 118, 119
Williams, Lindsey, 57, 136
Wilson, Daniel J., 57, 125
women: attitudes toward disability,
  67–69. *See also* femininity; gender

Wulff, Helena, 18

Yahalom, Shaul, 70

Zola, Irving, 161